About this Book

What is Africa really like today? For all the ordinary townsmen, villagers, and particularly mothers, breadwinners and children who live there? Cutting through the Western media's stereotype picture of a continent wracked only by civil conflict and AIDS, Torild Skard has written an engrossing introduction to a continent in change. Based on her extensive travels through the length and breadth of the region when she served as UNICEF's Director in West and Central Africa in the 1990s, this experienced writer combines eyewitness accounts, lively description and deeply informed insight to portray the human reality of Africa to-day. With honesty, cultural sensitivity and a commitment especially to women, she frankly describes the social, health and other problems experienced by its people, but also the sources of hope for the future represented by courageous individuals, innovative community-level projects and sensible programmes being implemented in the region by the international agency whose work she coordinated.

This highly readable account ranges over the social, economic and political realities of modern-day Africa, as well as introducing the reader to its history and complex cultures. It also raises well founded questions relating to Western aid and thereby increases our understanding of how to combat poverty and misery.

It is ideal for the general reader, sixth form students and particularly aid workers, agency staff and volunteers who are about to travel or work in the Continent.

About the Author

Torild Skard is a well known public figure who has built a significant reputation as a writer, researcher and politician in her own country, Norway, as well as internationally. An educationist who taught children as well as training teachers, she became a member of parliament in 1973 and first woman president of the Norwegian Upper House. Her work in the field of international development has included several years as a senior official in the Norwegian Ministry of Development Cooperation; she subsequently became deputy secretary general for international development in the Ministry of Foreign Affairs. She has also worked for UNESCO as a director with special responsibility for women's affairs. In 1994, UNICEF persuaded her to start a four year job as their regional director for West and Central Africa and it was out of this intense experience getting to know some two dozen African countries that she gathered the material on which this book is based.

CONTINENT OF MOTHERS, CONTINENT OF HOPE

Understanding and promoting development in Africa today

Torild Skard

Zed Books Ltd

LONDON · NEW YORK

Continent of Mothers, Continent of Hope: Understanding and Promoting Development in Africa Today was first published in English by Zed Books Ltd, 7 Cynthia Street, London N1 9JF, UK and Room 400, 175 Fifth Avenue, New York, NY 10010, USA in 2003.

Originally published in Norway as *Mødrenes kontinent* by Pax, 2001.

The publishers gratefully acknowledge the financial support for the translation of this work, which was provided by MUNIN, the Marketing Unit for Norwegian International Non-Fiction.

Cover picture of doll from Collection Florence Carité, courtesy of UNICEF

Cover designed by Lee Robinson, Ad Lib Design, London,
lee@adlib-design.com
Set in Monotype Baskerville and Univers Black by Ewan Smith, London
Printed and bound in Malaysia

Distributed in the USA exclusively by Palgrave, a division of St Martin's Press, LLC, 175 Fifth Avenue, New York, NY 10010, USA

A catalogue record for this book is available from the British Library
Library of Congress Cataloging-in-Publication Data: available

ISBN 1 84277 106 X cased
ISBN 1 84277 107 8 limp

Contents

Glossary

Aid – official and private grants and loans to countries and peoples in the South to promote development. Includes technical cooperation

Alphabetization – teaching illiterate people to read, write and do maths

Animism – the belief that spirits live in natural objects, such as trees, rivers and stones. Animists perform ceremonies to placate the spirits

Balafon – African musical instrument, xylophone-like, with small gourds hanging on the underside that give it a hollow sound

Bassia butter – a plant fat used for medical purposes or cosmetics

Batik – a method of dyeing cotton fabric after some parts have been covered by wax

Bilateral aid – aid collaboration between two parties, usually two states

Bogolan – a textile from Mali

Boubou – a traditional wide coat used in sub-Saharan Africa

Bride-price – money paid to the bride or her family before marriage, usually by the husband's family

Calabash – fruit similar to a gourd. The hard shell is used as a vessel

Cash crops – production of agricultural products to obtain cash income

Cassava – a plant with a tuber that is used for food

CFA franc – a monetary unit from the African financial union (Communauté Financière Africaine), which is tied to the French franc

Circumcision, genital mutilation or cutting – ceremonial removal of a part of male or female genital organs as a rite of initiation into adulthood

Clan – a subgroup of people within a tribe, family, lineage, descent line

Climate fever – a common name for diseases like malaria, dysentery, yellow fever and Guinea worm

Communauté – a union of former French colonies, departments and territories created by France in 1958

Couscous – North African food made of semolina with meat and vegetables in a sauce

Debt crisis – the economic situation of a number of developing countries as a result of large-scale foreign borrowing, after they got into difficulties servicing the loans. The crisis became serious in the early 1980s, as a result of heavy borrowing in the previous decade

Development bank – a bank created to promote development, such as the

World Bank and the regional development banks. These banks provide aid in the form of soft (cheap) loans to developing countries

Dibia – traditional healer

Fancy – colour prints produced with rotating cylinders

Fetish – object or animal with magical qualities that are positive for the owner

Fistula – pathological opening between two internal organs, here between the vagina and the intestine and/or urinary tract

Foufou – traditional dish consisting of mashed bananas, cassava and/or yam with a tasty sauce

Grigri – amulet or magic object that protects the bearer against evil influences

Griot – traditional skald (bard), singer and storyteller in Africa

Gross domestic product (GDP) – total production of goods and services in a country in one year, less the goods used in production

Gross national income (GNI) (previously gross national product) – total value added from domestic and foreign sources of the residents of a country in the course of a year

Imam – Muslim religious leader

Ivorian – person from the Ivory Coast

Iyalode – Yoruba queen

Karité butter – a plant fat used for medical purposes or cosmetics

Kente or *kita* cloth – traditional cloth woven by Akan people in the Ivory Coast and Ghana

Kola nut – a nut containing stimulating substances. Used symbolically, on solemn occasions and in certain rituals

Kora – African musical instrument, a harp-lute with 21 strings, supported on a long neck of wood which pierces a large hemispherical gourd

Least-developed countries (LDC) – group established by the United Nations. Includes developing countries that fall below established thresholds for income, economic diversification and social development. In 2002, this category comprised 79 countries

Low-income country (LIC) – developing country with a low GNI per capita. In 2001, this was US$745 or less

Lukasa – memory board of the Luba, a flat, hand-held wooden board studded with beads and pins or covered with incised or carved ideograms used to assist memory

Machete – large knife with a short handle, used both as a tool and a weapon

Magic – sorcery, witchcraft or rituals aimed at influencing the course of events or counteracting the negative effects of hostile sorcery and witchcraft

Malachite – attractive green stone that can be carved and polished for jewels and decorative objects

Marabout – holy man in Islam

Mask – object used to cover the face to hide behind, adorn or protect oneself, or to express a belief, wish or fear. Also applies to the person carrying a mask

Matriarchy – social, political and legal system in which women have a decisive influence; a social organization in which descent and inheritance are traced through the female line

Middle-income country (MIC) – developing country with a mid-level GNI per capita. This range in 2001 was between US$746 to US$9,205

Millefiori – a thousand flowers, a special type of cylindrical or round Venetian glass beads with a mosaic of tiny, coloured flowers. Produced between the fifteenth and twentieth centuries

Miwa – my child, in the language of the Ivory Coast

Moors – Berbers living in the western Sahara

Multilateral aid – aid provided by an international organization with many member states, predominantly the UN system and international financial institutions such as the IMF and the World Bank

Mwadi – female incarnation of a Luba King

Nafa – useful, advantageous (Guinea)

Nana – matron, respectful African title for a woman. A *nanette* is the daughter of a *nana*

Négritude – the spiritual and cultural values of the black people

Net primary school enrolment – the number of children enrolled in primary school who belong to the age group that officially corresponds to primary schooling

Oba – a Yoruba chief with the task of executing political decisions

Obi – head of the community in Igbo society

Omu – female head or mother of the Igbo community

Palaver tree – centrally placed tree in African villages where meetings and deliberations are held

Papaya – fruit of the papaya tree, similar to a melon

Patriarchy – social, political and legal system in which men have a decisive influence; social organization in which descent and inheritance are traced through the male line

Peul – language spoken from Senegal to Cameroon and people speaking the language

Pirogue – traditional light boat similar to a canoe, and propelled by a sail or paddle

Purdah – a curtain separating the women's part of the house from the rest; a social system involving the seclusion of women

Reproductive health – health related to sexuality and reproduction, forms part of primary health care and includes fertility and family planning, maternal health, mother/child health, sexually transmitted diseases and harmful traditional practices like female genital mutilation

Savanna – a relatively homogeneous grassland with scattered trees in areas with a precipitation of about two to 60 inches per year. There are forest, tree, grass, bush and scrub savannas

Sorghum – a grass cultivated for its grain, which is used for food and fodder

Structural adjustment programme – economic reform programme agreed with the IMF or World Bank to adjust the economy of a country in crisis and lay the foundations for more sustainable economic development

Tissu pagne or *pagne* – loincloth; cloth for a long skirt for women

Tontine – traditional savings arrangement for groups of depositors

Tostan – 'breakthrough' in Wolof language of Senegal

Totem – animal or plant considered to be a mythological ancestor or distant relative of a group of people, often a tribe

Tsetse fly – African fly that carries sleeping sickness. Spread all over Africa, but avoids the driest areas. Makes settling difficult and prevents the farming of livestock such as horses and cattle in more than one-third of Africa

Vidomégon – child maids in Benin

Yam – a climbing plant with a tuber used for food

Abbreviations

AWCY	Association of Working Children and Youth
CDC	Centers for Disease Control and Prevention, USA
CEDAW	Convention on the Elimination of All Forms of Discrimination Against Women
DRC	Democratic Republic of Congo
ECA	United Nations Economic Commission for Africa
ECOMOG	Economic Community Monitoring Group (West African military force)
ECOWAS	Economic Community of West African States
ENDA	Environmental Development (NGO)
FAWE	Forum for African Women Educationalists
GAVI	Global Alliance for Vaccines and Immunization
ILO	International Labour Oranization
IMF	International Monetary Fund
NGO	non-governmental organization
OAU	Organization of African Unity
OCCGE	Organization to Combat the Great Endemic Diseases
OECD	Organization for Economic Co-operation and Development
ORT	oral rehydration therapy: a solution of water, salts and sugar to prevent diarrhoeal dehydration
UN	United Nations
UNAIDS	Joint United Nations Programme on AIDS
UNDP	United Nations Development Programme
UNESCO	United Nations Educational, Scientific and Cultural Organization
UNFPA	United Nations Population Fund
USAID	US Agency for International Development
WHO	World Health Organization
WID	Women in Development: strategy to include the needs and interests of women in the development processes of a country and in development aid
UNHCR	United Nations High Commissioner for Refugees
UNICEF	United Nations Children's Fund

To Africa's women and children
and their friends

ONE

'Bereavement – What Do We Mean by Bereavement?'

It's only a roof of straw on four poles, but it protects against sun and rain. Fifty young boys and a handful of girls sit tightly packed on the rough-hewn wooden benches. The teacher by the blackboard asks: 'Bereavement – what do we mean by bereavement?' Everyone has experienced it personally. They have lost parents, sisters and brothers, uncles, aunts and grandparents, neighbours and friends – and were often forced to watch while these people were shot or tortured to death. Many of the boys have committed such acts themselves. The boy with the big round eyes, toothy smile and spindly four-foot frame looks more like a mischievous schoolboy than a cold-blooded killer. But – at the age of 16 – this is exactly what Liberia's warring adults have turned him into.

Tommy was ten and in primary school when fighters occupied his town and threatened to kill Tommy's father if he did not let the boy go. Once recruited as a soldier and separated from his family, Tommy was easy prey. He had to do what he was told. The military forced him to slither along in the dust and crawl over creeks while being fired on. They gave him a gun and showed him how to use it. When he refused to shoot, his commander placed him in front of a line of captured civilians. He said he would kill them one by one until Tommy complied. After the fourth execution, Tommy submitted. But he was not 'brave' enough to do his own killing unaided. Cigarettes, amphetamines and cocaine gave him extra courage before going into battle – and he took sleeping pills to calm down at night. 'I felt so badly for my people. From the time they took me away, I was only thinking about my people,' Tommy says. 'They killed my uncle. It is bad because we were small, small, and they made us fight. So they are bad.'

Sandra is silent. Hiding close to a girlfriend, she clenches her hands in her lap. Every now and again her eyes fill with tears. She is not yet 14, small and skinny. But she has already given birth to a child, which died at a few weeks old. When she was eleven, her family was shot trying to escape. She was kidnapped by the soldiers, tortured and declared the 'wife' of one of the leaders. She was given drugs, abused sexually and forced to cook, wash clothes and fetch water. She was not quite 13 when she became pregnant. Her body was immature, and there was no assistance far out in the bush. She scarcely survived. Since then she has had stomach pains and bleedings.

Thousands of children – perhaps as many as 15,000 – were drawn into Liberia's war machine. Mainly boys, but also some girls. With a devilish logic the children were used as soldiers, unskilled labourers and sex slaves, because they were more obedient and easier to manipulate than adults. Stripped of all loving care, tortured, abused and drugged, forced to commit the most bestial acts, the child soldiers became the most ferocious in attacks and terrorist actions.

Usually, it is reckoned that the civil war in Liberia lasted from 1989 to 1997. But its roots go further back, as far as 1847 when Liberia was founded by freed American slaves. The republic was controlled by the new settlers, Americo-Liberians as they are called, for 133 years. All power was in the hands of the ruling class. The indigenous population – who outnumbered their colonists by 20 to one – was oppressed and exploited. As a result, most people became impoverished and alienated, while the elites prospered.

There were rebellions and opposition. In 1980, a military coup brought Samuel Doe from the Krahn tribal people to power. This was welcomed by many Liberians. But the new regime soon turned out to be as oppressive as the old. Violence and mismanagement were the order of the day. Ethnic tensions grew, and the economy fell apart. In 1989, Charles Taylor, an Americo-Liberian, attempted a counter-coup. It failed, and the Doe regime took revenge with extreme brutality. Taylor's supporters retaliated. A protracted civil war followed, with one rival ethnic-based group after another being formed and fighting the others to gain power and resources. Villages were captured and recaptured. The population was subjected to terror and killings, arrests and forced labour, rape and looting. Regional organizations, together with the UN, tried to stop the warfare. After 14 failed peace agreements, the 1996–97 one seemed to last. By then, tens of thousands of people had been killed, most of them civilians. Half the population of around 2.4 million was internally displaced or driven out of the country.

When peace was agreed, more than four thousand child soldiers and 'wartime women' (as they call themselves) were demobilized. Tommy and Sandra were among them. But they could not be reunited with their families straight away. First they had to be detoxified and kept off a serious drug habit. Then they had to be allowed to behave like children again – as far as this was possible. The boys had to learn how to manage without a gun. As the drugs wore off, reactions were strong: anxiety, guilt and anger. Some had nightmares, wet themselves and hid under the bed. They withdrew and refused to speak. Others threw temper tantrums and attacked furniture and people. The facilitator explained:

> Talking about what they have gone through is painful for them as well as for me, but we have to do it. They have to get over the past. Otherwise they cannot go on. The child soldiers must accept that they have done wrong, and that they must live in a different way. Otherwise we will not have peace in Liberia. Many find comfort and support in religion – they confess their guilt and ask God for forgiveness. This helps them start a new life.

The authorities, in collaboration with local organizations and churches, the United Nations Children's Fund (UNICEF) and other donors set to work on the 'WAY-project' for War-affected Youth. Using simple means, efforts are made to bring the ex-combatants and wartime women back to society. They learn to read, write and do maths. They are taught agriculture and trades, such as poultry farming, carpentry, tinsmithing and sewing. They do sports, sing and play. And they are encouraged to talk about their experiences.

TWO
Out in the Unknown with UNICEF

I did not know much about West and Central Africa when I became regional director of the UN Children's Fund (UNICEF) with responsibility for the work of the organization in the region. Although Africa is the continent closest to Europe, the mental leap across the Mediterranean and the Sahara desert is long. Media in a country like Norway pay little attention to the countries south of the Sahara. From the mid-1980s, I worked with development aid in the government administration in Oslo. Enthusiasts and government authorities have established an extensive collaboration with parts of Eastern and Southern Africa, but West and Central? Here contacts were only sporadic.

I knew that West and Central Africa had the lowest living standards in the world, the highest mother and child mortality and the most widespread illiteracy. Images of starving children with stick legs and stomachs like balloons, and worn-out women with despondent faces were burnt into my retina. I was to see much poverty and distress. But the problems turned out to be different from what I expected. They came from contexts that were new and unknown. Besides, they were just part of reality. The region has some of the most diverse and vigorous societies on earth, and admirable efforts were often being made to improve living conditions.

'Children First!'

It was UNICEF's leader at the time, Jim Grant, who recruited me as regional director. Grant was an outstanding person, with a commitment to women and children that could convince the most sceptical. After he became executive director in 1980, he mobilized people from all sectors and groups of society: politicians and religious leaders, artists and sporting stars, professionals and volunteers. The organization grew rapidly. Its income more than tripled in 15 years and impressive results were achieved. I worked closely with Grant while I was chairperson of the UNICEF executive board late in the 1980s. Grant insisted on 'children first' and used every opportunity to urge people to combat the 'silent emergency' – the tragedy experienced by millions of children caught in the vicious circle of poverty, population growth and environmental degradation. And he had visions of a better life. He often quoted the British writer, George Bernard Shaw, who said: 'You see how things are and you ask "why?", but I dream about things that have never existed and say "why not?"'

Grant was a person who could make visions come true. He was American, but had grown up as the child of a missionary in China and had acquired a deep respect for other cultures. He used this understanding to seek practical solutions to people's problems. 'We have to find do-able strategies – simple and cheap,' he would say. He always had a packet of oral rehydration salts or iodized salt in his pocket, which he would pull out to show heads of state or rural women how easily diarrhoea or goitre could be combated. Everyone remembers the packets when they speak of Grant. In his time, UNICEF contributed to a dramatic reduction in the prices of vaccines and essential drugs, water pumps and health services. Many children owe their lives to Grant. At the same time, the emphasis on technologically simple measures and rapid results led to a limitation of UNICEF's perspective. More complicated and long-term development interventions were given less attention.

Grant also gave women active support. During his leadership, UNICEF became one of the UN organizations with the highest number of women staff, and they were also in management positions. In all, women amounted to 40 per cent of the professional staff. To achieve this, Grant decided during a two-year period that there had to be special reasons *not* to recruit women to vacant posts. His impulsiveness and unlimited demands for action, combined with his lack of order and system, could give his closest collaborators grey hair. We had several confrontations, when I felt that decisions were being taken over lock, stock and barrel. The discussions were tough. He must be relieved to get rid of an irritating nuisance, I thought, when my appointment as chairman ended. Then, a few years later, he was suddenly on the phone asking me to become regional director.

I Spoke French

I had one reservation: 'I don't know much about West and Central Africa. Wouldn't it be better to place me in Eastern and Southern Africa?' Grant wouldn't listen. He needed me in Abidjan. It didn't matter if I lacked knowledge about the region – I spoke French. Besides, I had many other qualifications. So Grant got what he wanted.

Eighty-five per cent of the UNICEF staff are engaged in fieldwork.

Country offices are established all over the world. As regional director, I was supposed to operate in the region to support the activities at country level. In West and Central Africa, the regional office is in the Ivory Coast. It covers an area twice the size of Europe, from Mauritania in the west to Chad and the Democratic Republic of Congo (previously Zaire) in the east. The region includes more than 300 million people living on dry savannas on the border of the Sahara, in tropical rainforests along the Gulf of Guinea and in modern cities with skyscrapers and slums. There are 23 countries in all, from the giant of Africa, Nigeria, to mini-states like Equatorial Guinea and Cape Verde. Nearly all are very poor developing countries, and most have French as their national language.

UNICEF's executive board and secretariat are in New York. The board establishes policies, reviews programmes and approves budgets for the organization. UNICEF promotes the interests of children all over the world, but programmes of assistance are only implemented in developing countries. In every country the UNICEF representative and the government design a programme of activities. It includes services for women and children in primary health care, nutrition, basic education, safe water and sanitation. It may also include support to particularly exposed groups, such as children in armed conflict, street children, children being exploited as labour or being sexually abused. Usually the national authorities, private organizations and local communities implement the activities. UNICEF recommends priorities and strategies, gives technical advice and financial assistance and purchases goods and equipment.

With activities spread over 160 countries and territories, it is not easy to choose strategies and areas of intervention. As regional director, I was supposed to contribute. Grant and I had long discussions about the work in West and Central Africa. He was a true friend of Africa. The last time I saw him, a few months before he died in January 1995, we talked only about Africa. He was suffering from terminal cancer and was obviously weak, but he would not quit as executive director. When I visited him in the hospital, the nurse said: 'Not more than 20 minutes.' But Grant was so eager. His eyes were glowing: 'What shall we do for the children of Africa? What will have the greatest impact? Who can we mobilize for support?' He was persuaded to let me go only after one-and-a-half hours.

The needs of the poor countries are great and the expectations of UNICEF's help are high. At the same time, UNICEF is not a rich organization. Its contributions from donor countries and private citizens by the end of the 1990s were a little under US$1 billion a year for the organization as a whole – considerably less than the entire Norwegian development aid budget. The contributions are either for the organization in general or are earmarked for specific activities. The general resources are straightforward.

They are distributed to each country according to objective criteria and are used where the needs are greatest. But they cover only part of the expenditure. The rest has to be mobilized for each country from donor governments, UNICEF committees, voluntary organizations and private enterprises. The regional director assists with fundraising. In West and Central Africa many countries had problems. Few donors were engaged in the region. In addition, access to resources generally became more difficult in the 1990s. Many donor countries reduced their development aid, and the demands of donors were stricter than before.

Time for Reform

In the course of the 1980 and 1990s, UNICEF developed managerial difficulties. For Grant, the end was more important than the means. He managed the organization in his own personal, informal way, rather like a big family. As the budget expanded and the number of staff increased to nearly seven thousand worldwide, efficiency became more and more difficult to achieve with such a leadership style. The handling of issues became unsatisfactory and the control of funds insufficient. Staff were unhappy with the personnel management. Nor did the organization manage to keep up with technological innovations. Little by little Grant understood that something had to be done, and he introduced comprehensive management reform. But it was his successor, Carol Bellamy, who had to implement the necessary measures.

Bellamy has broad experience in American politics and finance, and was able to grasp UNICEF's management problems. She followed up the objectives and strategies developed under Grant and, in addition, initiated extensive internal reforms to make the organization more effective. It was not easy. Structures, procedures and attitudes all had to change. But gradually decisions became more participatory and the handling of issues more orderly. Financial controls and quality assurance became key functions. UNICEF moved to the fore in information technology. The question arose, however, whether some of the organization's creative flexibility was being lost. The administration of personnel did not change much – Bellamy managed personnel issues in much the same way as her predecessor. Processes remained unclear, and work in the field was at times hampered by unsuitable nominations and inadequate development of capacity. West and Central Africa presented special challenges. UNICEF was established late in the region and operations were not always up to standard.

Working conditions are tough in sub-Saharan Africa. There is not only widespread poverty and distress. The climate is harsh, distances are long, infrastructure poor and transport and communications difficult. In addition, national administrations often have inadequate capacity and professional staff are lacking. Grant created a very result-oriented aid organization. An extremely enthusiastic staff would work day and night, if necessary, to provide help to those who need it. But the impact of their efforts and the technical quality of the assistance could be improved. Here the regional director had an important task. Seminars and training courses were organized. Reacting to deficiencies in the handling of money and personnel was more delicate, requiring negative sanctions or even dismissals. In the case of political crisis or armed conflict, the regional director has a responsibility for the security of the UNICEF staff – at the very time that the needs of women and children in the country are particularly acute. Sometimes we had to evacuate country offices – that is, the international staff were evacuated. The UN has a special obligation to them, while locally recruited staff must take care of themselves. They are in their own country. As far as possible, they kept on with the work, often at considerable personal risk.

Part I

Working with Women and Children

'A child survival and development revolution' was Jim Grant's objective for UNICEF in the 1980s. The focus was on concrete measures for children, not a campaign for children's rights. When a Convention for Children was suggested, Grant's first reaction was lukewarm. He thought it would be a propaganda thrust without practical importance and, in addition, a politicization of the needs of children that could offend governments. But voluntary organizations actively supported the idea, and Grant was gradually persuaded that a convention could be used to improve the situation of children. He then engaged the whole organization in the elaboration of the text and the follow-up of the agreement. A World Summit for Children was intended to oblige heads of state to take the requirements in the convention seriously.

Historical Meeting

World history was made when 71 heads of state and 88 other high-level leaders met in New York on 29 and 30 September 1990. For the first time in history, a world summit had children on the agenda. Never before had a summit assembled so many heads of state. The family photo is impressive: long rows of men in black suits – white men, yellow and brown. In the front row the president of Mali stands out from the rest in his blue *boubou* (a wide African coat) with gold embroidery. There are three women: President Violeta Barrios de Chamorro from Nicaragua and the Prime Ministers Margaret Thatcher from the United Kingdom and Mary Charles from Dominica.

The summit was unusual. The heads of state were not allowed to give long speeches. They participated in working groups and round table meetings. There were children from all over the world everywhere. They escorted the participants, sang, attended the negotiations, read out the final declaration and made reports in the media. To remind the heads of state of the most important demands, the children gave them five objects. A gagged doll symbolized the non-acceptance of the rights of the child. A bag of seeds called attention to the significance of a safe and sustainable environment. A packet of oral rehydration salts and a piece of chalk pointed to the need for good health and education, and a false dollar bill with the face of a child underlined the necessity for structural adjustment with a human face.

The heads of state became strongly engaged, and stated that:

The well-being of children requires political action at the highest level. We

– the Heads of State of the world – are determined to take that action. We hereby make a solemn commitment to give high priority to the rights of children, to their survival, protection and development. This will also ensure the well-being of all societies. We have agreed that we will act together, in international cooperation, as well as in our respective countries, and we have adopted a plan of action to protect the rights of children and to improve their lives.

When the idea of a summit was launched, the Nordic countries were sceptical. We feared it would become just another costly public relations affair. But Grant turned the meeting into something more. The plan of action adopted by the heads of state not only included good intentions,

---

Box I.1 The World Summit for Children 1990

The major goals formulated by the World Summit for Children for the world by the year 2000:

a) Reduction of under-five child mortality by one-third or to a level of 70 per 1,000 live births, whichever is the greater reduction.
b) Reduction of maternal mortality rates by half.
c) Reduction of malnutrition among children under five by one-half.
d) Universal access to safe drinking water and to sanitary means of excreta disposal.
e) Universal access to basic education and completion of primary education by at least 80 per cent of primary school age children.
f) Reduction of adult illiteracy rate to at least half with emphasis on female literacy.
g) Protection of children in especially difficult circumstances, particularly in situations of armed conflict.

The Mid-Decade Goals were intermediate targets to be attained by 1995. They included measures such as:

- 80 per cent immunization coverage against the most important childhood diseases and 90 per cent against measles and tetanus for women.
- Utilization of oral rehydration therapy to prevent dehydration caused by diarrhoea in 80 per cent of the cases.
- Elimination of iodine and vitamin A deficiencies.
- Breastfeeding up to two years of age with exclusive breastfeeding for four to six months (without other liquids or food).

but precise goals for the countries of the world to achieve by the year 2000. Every country was supposed to adopt a national plan of action to implement the necessary measures. It was a first step in the process of fulfilling the Convention on the Rights of the Child.

A Turning Point

The year 1990 became a turning point. The Convention on the Rights of the Child (CRC) came into force. In the following decade, efforts related to children were concentrated on the CRC and the Plan of Action from the World Summit for Children. The CRC was widely accepted. Before 2002, the convention was ratified by all countries except two, and the USA and Somalia signalled their intention to ratify by signing it. The CRC naturally supplemented the Convention on the Elimination of All Forms of Discrimination Against Women (CEDAW), which was adopted earlier. But the CEDAW was more controversial and lacked a follow-up organization like UNICEF. It therefore took longer to ratify. By the end of 2002, CEDAW was ratified or signed by 173 countries – almost 90 per cent of UN members – including the whole of West and Central Africa. Niger and Mauritania joined in by the end of the century.

The African countries were broadly represented at the summit in New York, and West and Central Africa was the first region to ratify the CRC. In addition, the Organization of African Unity (OAU) adopted a special African Charter on the Rights and Welfare of the Child. In collaboration with UNICEF, the organization followed up with a large international conference in Dakar in 1992 to discuss assistance to African children. In the Consensus of Dakar the African countries confirmed their support for the decisions of the Summit for Children. In addition to the goals for the year 2000, they established Mid-Decade Goals to be reached by 1995. During the preparations for the International Women's Conference in Beijing in 1995 an African Platform for Action was also adopted.

My tasks were to follow up the conventions and plans of action and assist countries to implement them.

What Kind of Development?

Representing a donor organization in West and Central Africa, I entered a complex field of activity. The art of giving presents is difficult when you wish to satisfy the donors as well as the recipients. Usually, the donors have limited understanding of the lives of recipients. Nevertheless, a number of conditions are attached to the aid: what it should be used for and how it should be handled. The donors are in a position of power in relation to the recipients, and it is hard for the latter to raise their voices in protest. A precarious question is how to create a fruitful dialogue as well as ensure an appropriate use of resources.

I was supposed to help recipients 'develop'. But I came from a different reality, and 'development' is not a neutral phenomenon. It takes place within a context. When poor African countries make 'progress', it means that they take part not only in modern knowledge and technology, but also in Western thinking and behaviour patterns. A modernization of Africa is at the same time a Westernization. Many Africans want this, but is it positive for everybody? And does it entail the most constructive development?

UNICEF's mandate is generally accepted. Everybody wants to help children, at least in principle, and there is broad agreement about measures to promote the survival and health of children. Education is also widely supported, even if there are some reservations. Things start getting difficult in culturally sensitive areas, like family planning, gender equality and child labour. As an international organization, UNICEF has staff and board members from all over the world. Everybody knows what is going on. There are no hidden agendas or conditions. Recipient countries participate when the objectives and activities of the organization are decided on. There are extensive discussions about controversial issues. Conclusions are usually based on consensus. At the same time, Western countries are in a very strong position. They finance the operations, and the organization has a distinctive Western character. The senior leader has always been an American, and a majority of deputies are from donor countries. Decisions from the board and headquarters are usually global. They apply to the organization as a whole, and particular regional and local conditions are not much taken into account. Africa is sometimes discussed specifically, as are the programmes in different countries, but this takes place within generally accepted frameworks.

UNICEF's main partner at country level is the government presently in office. The UNICEF representative discusses the programme and activities with ministers and ministry employees. But how representative is the government of its people? And what capacity does the administration have to implement activities? As much as possible, UNICEF also collaborates with voluntary organizations and groups, district authorities and local communities. But the contact is necessarily limited, particularly with underprivileged groups.

An Abundance of Actors

The numerous actors providing development aid present a special challenge. UN organizations, regional groupings and bilateral donors (giving direct state-to-state assistance), international, national and local voluntary organizations – there is a real multiplicity, varying from one country to the next. All have their points of view and are engaged in different ways. Collaboration and coordination are necessary, but not easy. There were systematic efforts during the 1990s to improve collaboration within the UN system and among the donors contributing to specific sectors. But governments often lacked the motivation and capacity for comprehensive coordination, and donors had their own policies and guidelines. They sometimes had divergent opinions and a need to mark their own contributions. It was possible to organize joint action to solve concrete tasks, but strong donors in particular sometimes preferred to work independently.

In West and Central Africa, the use of limited resources was a key issue. What should have priority? The World Summit for Children adopted global goals for the health and education of women and children. But how can a particular region with multiple problems manage to achieve all these goals? The CRC did not simplify the task by presenting new demands related to children's rights. And in the course of the 1990s there was an increasing number of armed conflicts in the region at the same time as the HIV/AIDS pandemic was spreading.

It was tempting to do a bit of everything, but this would probably have little effect. At the same time, for every activity that was given priority, something else had to be disregarded. In addition to negotiations at country level, UNICEF engaged in regional discussions with professionals from recipient countries and representatives of donors. We tried to agree on common approaches and obtain a rational division of labour. Some progress was achieved. But at times, donors had different strategies and incompatible procedures, or the total donor contribution could be insufficient or coincide poorly with government priorities.

Recent decades have shown that it is not easy to promote development in poor countries. Many projects have been launched, but they have often been scattered and uncoordinated. The results have not always been as expected. Frequently everything collapses as soon as the donors pull out. We had numerous debates about strategies and practices to follow within UNICEF and in broader fora. We initiated reviews and evaluations of projects and programmes. How best to proceed? How could we reach those with the greatest need? And how could people take over and sustain the modern advances? Experiences varied. Sometimes they were stimulating and instructive, but often they were confusing and provoking. Quite often I became both perplexed and depressed. But doing nothing was never a solution.

THREE

Betrayed, Bereaved and Brutalized: The Merciless Realities of War

War is made by greedy men to prove that might is right.
(Proverb from South Africa)

I must admit that I was afraid the first time I went to Liberia. The country was at war, and nobody knew what could happen. I considered carefully if I, as regional director, should go. As a neighbouring country to the Ivory Coast, Liberia was not far away, and the UNICEF country office was badly in need of support. But I had never been there. The war was extremely complex, with different warring factions, and an important visitor could easily become an attractive target. But if UNICEF's regional director didn't dare visit the country due to the security problems, could the organization justify keeping an office there? I had to go, or the office would have to close down.

So I went. And once the decision was taken, I gathered more courage. When it came to it, the most dangerous moment during my trip occurred when I didn't have the least notion of it – during the landing at the airport in Monrovia. Due to the war, the big modern airport outside the capital was closed down. Instead, a small airport near the centre of town was being used. The aircraft were small and old: solid propeller planes taken over from the Russians. But the airport was not approved by the International Civil Aviation Organization. The quality of the runway was substandard. We were told that the American ambassador went out every other month with a wheelbarrow full of concrete to fill up the biggest holes. Even so, landing was not without risk. Shortly after my visit, a plane skidded right into the swamp. But I was happily unaware of all this, as I sat with a glass of juice on my way to Liberia, enjoying the luxuriant green landscape and the waves washing along the white sand beaches. In all this seeming idyll, where had the war gone to, I wondered?

Once on the ground, the war was a pressing reality. The airport was full of obstructions and soldiers. Outside were the notorious check-points of the regional peacekeeping forces, ECOMOG (Economic Community

Monitoring Group): a narrow, zigzag passage between blocks of concrete and barbed wire, some sandbags piled up around a booth and a handful of fierce soldiers, heavily armed and ready to shoot. You never knew what mood they were in, nor how they would respond to the diplomatic rights of UN personnel. Every transit was an ordeal. Seven check-points later, on the way from the airport to the UNICEF office, we were understandably weary.

The city was a depressing sight. It had the reputation of being one of the most beautiful towns in West Africa, a pearl by the sea. In 1995, nearly every major building was damaged or destroyed, and their bombed-out shells pointed towards the sky. The window glass was gone and the walls were full of holes. There were few cars. Numerous white four-wheel drives with 'UN' painted in enormous blue letters dominated the scene. On the pavements, there was swarming activity: people sitting and standing, chatting and doing business everywhere. The number of inhabitants in the city had doubled – from 500,000 to one million – during recent years, because people had fled from the fighting inland. Half of Liberia's population gradually huddled together along the narrow coastal strip around Monrovia. Every shed was packed, and camps were established in the ECOMOG security zone to receive those who had been internally displaced. UNICEF's representative explained:

> Work has become more difficult during the last year. The war changes all the time. We are getting less and less access to the countryside and are providing more and more humanitarian assistance to the Monrovia area. We hand out medicines, immunize and distribute vitamin A, iodized salt and rehydration salts against diarrhoea. We drill wells and build latrines. We take care of traumatized women and children and organize schooling. With 'school-in-a-box' we can teach under very primitive conditions. But the security is precarious, and fundraising is getting harder. Many donors don't think it is worthwhile giving support with the chaotic situation in the country. But the distress among people is not less. On the contrary.

A Female Voice from the Battlefield

I was in New York, attending a meeting of the UNICEF executive board, when the war in Monrovia exploded in April 1996. All of a sudden, the city was filled with outbursts of rifle fire and heavily armed military gangs, often young boys, riding stolen vehicles, in high spirits and fast on the trigger. A crisis team was immediately created at headquarters and daily conference calls established with the leader of the Liberia office. Every morning, the communication room was crammed full and the silence was intense when a clear female voice came in from the great nothingness, delivering the latest news from the battlefield. A British woman was responsible in Monrovia. She kept her head in a threatening situation. She found out where all the UNICEF staff and their families were, and provided assistance to those in need. She coordinated with the rest of the UN system. She organized food and drink for those who were stranded in the UNICEF premises, and provided water for the homeless seeking refuge on the neighbouring site.

Gradually, more than 400 people were packed into the UNICEF offices. Supplies were running out. Then armed gangs broke in and took what they could find, from provisions to computers and radios. The instructions from New York were unambiguous – don't resist! – and nobody was killed or hurt. Afterwards, there was only one thing to do: get out as fast as possible. American helicopters transported the international staff abroad, while the nationals had to hide as best they could among the local population. Some left the country and went to the Gambia, Ghana or the USA. A provisional UNICEF office for Liberia was established in the regional office in Abidjan.

After a while, the situation in Monrovia calmed down. ECOMOG regained the upper hand, and the humanitarian organizations started up anew. The UNICEF office had been looted five times in the course of a few years, and it was decided to move from the centre of town to a bungalow in the suburbs. Resources were dramatically reduced, and the number of staff was cut from 100 to about forty. A minimum fleet of cars was established (about ten cars instead of the previous 70). The new premises were cramped and cumbersome, but safer. In addition, the office was near the UN compound, *Riverview*, where all the international UN staff lived. It was a magnificent establishment with bungalows and gardens along the lagoon, a tennis court, swimming pool and restaurant – everything for a life of first-class luxury. Ten kilometres from the centre of Monrovia, the compound was never attacked during the warfare. But as Liberia was a 'non-family duty station', the houses were converted into lodgings for single people with joint living-rooms and kitchens.

None of the UNICEF international staff had the courage to start all over again – so much was destroyed of what they had struggled to build up, and the prevailing atmosphere was one of impunity. Property to the value of more than US$7–8 million – including 500 vehicles – was taken from the humanitarian organizations in the course of a few weeks. 'And Taylor drives around proudly in an official convoy of motor vehicles with cars evidently stolen from the UN system,' one staff member moaned. So, new international staff were recruited. But local staff returned.

In 1997, I was back again. There were even more bombed-out houses, black holes for windows and bullet marks. The local leader of the UN staff association declared:

> Liberia's history is a story of extreme determination to survive and keep life going. Behind the smiling faces here today are individuals separated from their families. Many of us sleep on the floor, because we are too afraid to purchase a bed for fear of being attacked and looted. Electricity, pipe-borne water, a good rest, family ties and support system, recreation, security and peace have all continued to elude us. In the office, we are starting from scratch, lacking basic equipment. And we are concerned about what could happen in the future. What if we are plunged back into war?

The Warlord Becomes President

When peace was accepted, presidential elections were held in July 1997. The warlord Charles Taylor won an overwhelming majority. 'This does not necessarily mean that we have confidence in him,' a Liberian explained. 'But it is the only way to get peace.' It was a delicate situation. To get peace, the people responsible for war crimes and atrocities were given amnesty and enjoyed impunity. One of them was elected to the highest leadership position in the country. Who, then, would ensure the legal protection of citizens and end the culture of impunity? At the same time, the president was elected with a large majority through democratic elections. The situation in the country would become impossible if the authorities did not manage to keep the peace and improve the living conditions of the people.

Liberia was in ruins. A new and inexperienced government was supposed to rebuild the country, consolidate the peace and govern with a budget reduced to a fraction of its pre-war level, a staggering debt overhang and an extremely weak administration. The immediate tasks were pressing. The warring factions had to be disarmed, demobilized and integrated into society again. War victims needed care and the displaced needed help to go home and resume a normal life.

What should the international community do? The bilateral donors adopted a waiting attitude. To resume aid, they demanded a broadly composed government, respect for human rights, reconciliation measures and proper management of resources. As long as these conditions were not being fulfilled, Liberia received much less assistance than requested, and the aid was preferentially channelled outside the government, through voluntary organizations. The UN system continued to work in the country. There was no good solution. We could not approve of impunity for war crimes. Nor could we abandon distressed women and children. In UNICEF we tried a two-pronged strategy. The country office collaborated with the authorities and voluntary organizations to help war-affected children and to rehabilitate the social services. At the same time, UNICEF stood up for the rights of women and children. Liberian human rights advocates received support. A group of eminent persons was nominated to promote the interests of children, and the government was confronted with the requirements of the CRC.

In the regional office, we kept as much contact with Monrovia as we could, so as to give advice and assistance. After some months, the atmosphere among UNICEF staff started to improve. Shock and depression gave way to eagerness and determination. Late in 1998, during my goodbye visit as regional director, the newly established choir sang 'Count it joy … joy … After the rain the sun will shine again', and 'Love will be our home'. In a touching way, the staff expressed their gratitude for the help they had received. They had written a long poetic speech describing how their lives had changed on 22 February 1995. That was when they discovered that they were not alone in their efforts to improve the lives of women and children in Liberia. They could get support and help when difficulties piled up, because people elsewhere cared about what was going on in their country! It took a while before I remembered that 22 February 1995 was the date of my first visit to Liberia. And they gave me a big pink-and-white cotton blanket, so I wouldn't freeze when I went back to the polar cold in the far north.

During the years to come, the staff needed all the perseverance and go-ahead spirit they could muster. Despite a peace agreement and democratic elections, the work of national reconstruction and reconciliation did not make headway. On the contrary – the humanitarian crisis worsened. Five years after the war, the economy was still devastated. Roads and telecommunications were in a lamentable state and there was no electricity or running water. Eighty per cent of the population lived below the poverty line, and half in abject poverty. As a consequence of the exodus of trained professionals, the shortage of health personnel and teachers was acute. Generally, the immunization coverage was low, but several polio campaigns were carried out and reached nearly all Liberian children. The lack of classrooms and teaching materials was critical. Thousands of children who had been left out of school during the war abandoned hope of being educated, and youngsters involved in alcohol, drug abuse, petty crime and prostitution hung out in the streets.

The demobilization was never completed and President Taylor was soon challenged by a new group of rebels: Liberians United for Reconstruction and Democracy (LURD), who were attacking and fighting in the north-western part of the country. In 2002, about one-third of the territory was unsafe and 100,000 people were internally displaced. Observers described a total disintegration of the sovereign state of Liberia, and the international community accused the government of taking part in illicit diamond trading and of supporting armed rebels in Sierra Leone. In May 2001 and again in 2002, the UN Security Council adopted economic sanctions, including an arms embargo and a ban on the diamond trade, to force President Taylor to change his policies. Donor aid was reduced to a minimum. UNICEF tried desperately to provide relief to those most in need and to curb human rights violations, but the organization had to function on a fraction of its funding needs. 'We try to be creative,' the UNICEF representative explained, 'but the condemnation of the government in fact often results in the ruin of Liberian children. Liberia must be among the worst places on earth to be a child.'

Women and Children as Targets

During the 1990s, there were 18 civil wars in sub-Saharan Africa. Each conflict is different. But in all cases, the civilian population became directly involved in a different way from before. In the past, there were very few civilian casualties. Now, they amount to 90 per cent, of which at least half are children. Civilians are not only caught in unexpected crossfire. Women and children have become important targets for warring groups. Maiming, rape and massacres have become part of war tactics. Nobody is spared or protected. Nothing is held sacred. The war in Sierra Leone became notorious for its brutality, and children suffered on an unprecedented scale. Nobody knows exactly how many people were killed. Estimates start at 40,000 and go upwards. Around one-half or perhaps two-thirds of the population was displaced. Sexual violence against girls and women was extremely widespread. In addition, mutilations became systematic. To terrorize the population, people's arms and legs were 'amputated' – cut off without anaesthesia, sometimes with blunt machetes (large knives). Many died. The others formed a new group of invalids, the 'useless', who had special needs for assistance.

It has become a characteristic of contemporary war that children suffer most. It is estimated that two million children were killed in wars globally during a decade, most of them in Africa. Six million were seriously injured or permanently disabled. Twelve million became homeless. They lost their parents, were kidnapped or forced to flee. Apart from physical injuries, many children have traumatic experiences. A nine-year-old girl from Liberia relates:

I saw 10 to 20 people shot, mostly old people who couldn't walk fast. They shot my uncle in the head and killed him. They made my father take his brains out and throw them into some water nearby. Then they made my father undress and have an affair with a decaying body. They raped my cousin who was a little girl of nine years old.

Such experiences leave lifelong emotional and mental scars.

'The statistics are shocking enough,' says Graça Machel, former minister and first lady of Mozambique and South Africa. The UN Secretary General asked her to make a report on the impact of armed conflict on children, which was finalized in 1996. She continues:

Even more chilling is the conclusion to be drawn from the statistics, that more and more of the world is being sucked into a desolate moral vacuum, a space devoid of the most basic human values, a space in which children are slaughtered, raped and maimed, where children are exploited as soldiers, starved and exposed to extreme brutality ... The time has come to call a halt. The international community must proclaim attacks on children for what they are – intolerable and unacceptable.

Corridors of Peace

Under armed conflict, thousands of children die from machetes, bullets, bombs and land-mines. But even greater numbers die of malnutrition and disease. Crops are destroyed and food supplies stopped. Social services close down. Local communities break up, and the population is dispersed. In 2002, there were around six million refugees and internally displaced persons in various African countries. It became a main task for UNICEF to assist the civilian population in crisis situations. New working methods had to be adopted when the fighting did not follow clear fronts, but moved around in unpredictable ways. It was difficult to plan and maintain ordinary quality standards. The staff had to show great ingenuity and be prepared to take risks. Together with headquarters, the regional office considered what should be done in different situations.

Access to the war-stricken areas often presented an acute challenge. UNICEF therefore launched an appeal for corridors or zones of peace to be able to reach destitute women and children. This practice began in El Salvador in 1985. The government and the rebels accepted three days of quiet, to allow 250,000 children to be immunized. This was repeated annually during the six years the war lasted. Similar arrangements have been made in Afghanistan and Sudan. In Liberia, the UN system and voluntary humanitarian organizations organized 'hit and run' expeditions. The warring factions guaranteed their security, so that they could go inland, deliver vital food supplies and medicines, immunize children and then withdraw. But the expeditions were not as frequent as we would have liked. If one faction refused safe passage, the whole operation had to be called off. It was also a bit haphazard as to who benefited from the visits. But it was better than nothing.

After the war was over, I visited a Lutheran missionary hospital in Gbarnga, in the middle of Liberia, which managed to function without interruption during the whole war. The hospital was bombed and shelled. Patients and personnel were looted and massacred. The doctor's mother was among the victims, when armed soldiers rushed in and shot wildly around. But the leader, a medical doctor from the district, was very dedicated. They didn't give up. Sometimes they got provisions. Sometimes the attempt failed. The funding stopped, but faithful supporters in other countries came to their aid. The equipment was destroyed. Still they continued with what they could get hold of. Crowds of people came to seek help, in spite of the primitive conditions.

In Sierra Leone, improvised feeding centres were established by voluntary organizations with UNICEF support up-country, in the two small towns of Bo and Kenema. There were attacks in the surrounding districts. People came staggering out of the forest, completely exhausted, and were assembled in big steel hangars that were emptied for the occasion. Hundreds of women sat and lay on mats on the floor, feeble and desperate, trying to feed their sick and undernourished children. Some kids were all big sad eyes and a stomach like a balloon, or swollen elephant feet with a small, petrified doll's face. It was nearly unbearable – and these were only those who survived and got food: a special mixture of wheat from surplus stocks in the United States which was called 'bulga'. It was completely different from what people were used to eating, so it wasn't always simple to swallow it down. Then they got medical care, and the children were immunized to prevent outbreaks of cholera and measles. Usually, people stayed for 45 days. The women received some training in hygiene and nutrition, but more could have been done. A few months later, the war suddenly overtook the two small cities. Everything had to be packed up in a hurry and moved to a safer place.

In Abidjan, we were involved in the assistance to refugees in an unexpected way. During the flare-up of the war in 1996, 3,000–4,000 people fled from Monrovia in a boat called *Bulk Challenge*. It turned out to be a sinking tub, packed with people, with only two toilets and practically no food or water. The authorities both in the Ivory Coast and Ghana shrank from receiving the refugees, so the boat drifted for days along the Gulf of Guinea with passengers on board becoming more and more panic-stricken. The whole UN system was mobilized, and tried to persuade the authorities to accept the distressed passengers and at the same time get water, food and medicines on board, until they could finally land in Ghana.

Child Soldiers

The Convention on the Rights of the Child requests governments to refrain from recruiting children under 15 years into their armed forces, and an optional protocol raises the minimum age to 18. Nevertheless, thousands of children are enrolled as soldiers in present-day conflicts. The development of weapons and the international arms trade have made light weapons very widespread. They are cheap, easily accessible and even small children are able to handle them. In some cases, children are forcibly recruited as fighters. In others, more subtle pressures are exerted. Under conditions of extreme poverty and starvation, where ordinary work and schooling are impossible and people are the victims of all kinds of threats, are arrested and tortured, joining a military group can be perceived as the most advantageous alternative. With a Kalashnikov, the boys can defend themselves and get hold of food, both for themselves and their family. In a group, they are no longer alone. Besides, it can be seen as exciting and manly to become a warrior. The soldier's life can open up new possibilities. Resistance against corrupt and exploitative power elites, or motives of revenge, may also play a role.

It is estimated that more than 100,000 children under the age of 18 served as soldiers in government or rebel forces in Africa in 2001. There were tens of thousands in countries like the Democratic Republic of Congo and Sierra Leone. They could be as young as seven to ten years of age. When they are recruited, the children are generally subjected to the same harsh treatment as adults – including brutal initiation ceremonies and training, where they have to endure violence and suffering and participate in mutilation and massacres. A boy from Sierra Leone explained that every year they had to have either a 'short sleeve' or a 'long sleeve' – that is, they had to cut off the arm of a victim either at the shoulder or the elbow. The children are given heavy manual tasks as camp assistants, cooks, carriers and messengers, but more and more frequently they are sent to the battlefield. They are put on front lines as cannon fodder or used as spies, forced to execute enemies or to man check-points. Before going to battle, they are often given drugs to make them brave and magic amulets for protection. Some factions have established special 'small boy' units, which are notorious for their cold-blooded and atrocious brutality.

Nobody comes out of modern civil wars unaffected, but children even less than adults. The Norwegian psychologist, Magne Raundalen, has worked extensively in the treatment of trauma and war experiences. He visited Monrovia a number of times for UNICEF, to teach local people how to take care of war-damaged children and youth. He characterizes the situation of child soldiers as very dramatic. They have been betrayed by adult society, because they have not received the protection and care that children have the right to get, and they have not been socialized into the basic values of society. They have been deprived of their childhood, their education and their closest family. In addition, they have been brutalized by their lives as soldiers.

Together with other organizations, UNICEF strives to prevent children from being enrolled as soldiers. When they are recruited, steps are taken to have them demobilized as soon as possible. In different phases during the conflicts in Liberia and Sierra Leone, child soldiers were released from both government and rebel forces. Programmes for reintegration into family and community were implemented. Often new warfare broke out, however, stopping rehabilitation efforts, and demobilized children were recruited into the armed forces again.

The rehabilitation of previous child soldiers is a demanding task. In most cases, both time and resources were insufficient. First of all, efforts were made to reunify the ex-combatants with their families. But perhaps these no longer existed, or they refused to accept the youngsters. 'Father said I would kill the whole family, if I came back,' one boy said. Another added: 'The village thinks I am possessed by the devil, because the rebels carved signs in my skin. They will lynch me if they see me.' If possible, the boys were taken care of for some months following demobilization. Besides medical treatment and basic education, they received psychosocial counselling and vocational training. The ex-combatants were returning to war-torn communities. It was not easy to start afresh. Many boys had known nothing but violence and the world of weapons for most of their lives.

There were heated discussions related to the use of Western psychotherapy or other methods for the treatment of war trauma and emotional problems. Therapy can be effective, but it is also demanding, and some people think it does not fit in an African context. At the same time, traditional rituals may be insufficient to heal the deep trauma left by war experiences. Therefore, our solution was to try both, as far as possible. Understanding adults helped the children to express their distress, agony and anger and narrate, draw or write about their painful experiences. Ceremonies related to religion and traditional customs were used for purification, healing and strength.

'Wartime Women'

Girls and women are given less attention in relation to armed conflict than boys and men. They may play different roles, but because of their gender they are more exposed and vulnerable, and their suffering is often more dramatic. Rape is particularly widespread, together with other forms of gender-based violence. Rape can be performed in an uncontrolled way, at random, by individual soldiers or militia. But it often functions as a form of torture and is used as a tactical weapon to humiliate and weaken the morale of the enemy and terrorize the population. While murder and torture have been classified as war crimes, rape was long considered more as an unfortunate, but inevitable, result of war. During recent years, the serious character of the abuse has emerged more clearly. When rape is used in massive proportions as part of a well-directed strategy, it is evidently a crime against humanity.

Some girls have been recruited into the war machine. They have been sent to battle or used as spies. Most often they have served as 'wartime women'. The girls are nearly always taken forcibly and raped. In addition to sexual services, they are forced to cook, wash clothes, get water and keep house in general. If they don't get pregnant themselves, they take care of the children of others, but many babies die under the harsh conditions.

The sexual exploitation has destructive effects on the physical and emotional development of the girls. They experience pain, anxiety and degradation. They may be infected by sexually transmitted diseases and become pregnant. In addition to the hazards related to an unwanted child, the young girls risk complications in connection with pregnancy, abortion or birth, and the health services are of even poorer quality during wartime than otherwise. After demobilization, it is not uncommon to see the girls rejected by their families as 'unclean' or 'spoiled' by the enemy and obliged to go into prostitution to survive. With a fatherless child, they are also considered an economic burden when they return to their communities. Reintegration is therefore more complicated for girls than for boys.

Different actions were taken to help the 'wartime women'. In Liberia, they established Sara's Daughters' Home, where young girls with soldier babies could be helped back to their home environment. They stayed in the institution for three months and were given counselling, literacy lessons and vocational training. Another organization created My Sister's Place. Here, women who had been sexually abused could receive counselling, be HIV tested, get help with child care and legal advice, learn how to start small businesses and obtain investment loans. But its capacity was small. Most women had to manage as best they could, without special assistance. In some camps, people from the same district got together to help the young girls. They organized traditionally inspired rituals, so the girls could be cleansed of all that had befallen them, and afterwards marry again.

Discrimination against Africa

Very many war victims do not get assistance. This is due to the security situation, but also to insufficient resources. Lack of funds leads to the reduction of aid programmes and the cancellation of life-saving measures. During recent years, the UN High Commissioner for Refugees has been encountering increasing difficulties in mobilizing the necessary resources to help the world's refugees and displaced persons. In addition, UN emergency appeals for Africa often get less response than appeals from areas geographically closer to the Western countries. A Norwegian aid worker coming back from West Africa noted that the refugee camps in Bosnia would have been paradise for refugees in Sierra Leone, for the Africans had nothing, not even the most fundamental assistance. The UN High Commissioner for Refugees stated in 1999 that the organization had received ten times as much money for every refugee from Kosovo than from Africa. Nearby Europeans were evidently more worth a helping hand than Africans.

Studying the figures more closely, considerable variations appear between countries. In Africa, some obtain a good response to their emergency appeals, while others don't. It is problematic that there are so many crisis situations in the region. The complex and long-lasting emergencies in particular have difficulties attracting the required assistance. If, in addition, the prospects for constructive development in the country are bleak, the motivation of donors wanes, even if the distress of the populations might be all the more pressing. In 2000, the UN obtained only one-tenth of what was needed to feed the two million refugees and displaced persons in the Democratic Republic of Congo. Lacking funds for assistance is a bitter experience for aid workers who are trying to bring relief under extremely demanding circumstances.

Few donor countries have budget lines for rehabilitation measures in war-devastated countries. When the acute crisis is over and the more long-term reconstruction begins, countries may experience dramatic cuts in international support. This was the case for Liberia, for example. In 2002, conditions here were described as a 'chronic post-war emergency'.

The media play an important role in international support to countries in distress. Even if Western newspapers, radio and TV generally are not very interested in Africa, they cover acute and dramatic events everywhere.

This has a great impact on the involvement of the public. Seeing suffering people on the TV screen immediately mobilizes sympathy and willingness to donate. But the focus is often brief. When events are no longer new and exciting, the countries disappear from news broadcasts. This 'CNN effect', as it is called, makes long-term and systematic support to people in distress very difficult, particularly if they live far from Western countries.

'Our Parents the Heads of State'

Children are among the most outspoken with regard to violence and war. In connection with the summit of the Organization for African Unity (OAU), in the capital of Cameroon, Yaoundé, in June 1996, a mini-summit against war was organized for children and youth with the support of UNICEF. Twenty teenagers from war-stricken African countries participated, together with a hundred children from Cameroon. The National Assembly hall was placed at their disposal, and interpreters were provided. First, the children discussed among themselves and elected chairpersons (a boy and a girl) and a drafting committee. Then, they fixed the themes for debate: child soldiers, land-mines, survival, protection and development of children during war, rehabilitation and reallocation of funds predestined for war. Everything was done very properly and in an orderly manner. I was a little worried that the children might be manipulated by the adult assistants, but I relaxed when these adults were requested to leave the hall, because the children wanted to talk among themselves.

It was tough, when war-affected children described their experiences, often stammering them out in poor English or French, or in a local language translated by a friend. A young girl made the deepest impression. She had been raped, and every time she opened her mouth to speak, she was unable to do so. She just swallowed and swallowed while her eyes filled with tears. Then, suddenly, one of the youngsters cracked a joke, and waves of giggling spread across the room.

The participants were allowed to question representatives of the adult society: the UNICEF executive director, the OAU secretary general, the chairpersons of the UN Commissions for Human Rights and the Convention on the Rights of the Child, in addition to three heads of state and government: the presidents of Mali and Eritrea and the prime minister of Ethiopia. The examination nearly became embarrassing, because the children were very direct: Why don't you stop the war? Why do you invest in weapons and soldiers instead of schools and hospitals? How do you help war-affected children? Why don't you ban land-mines? Why are children recruited to the armed forces? The fact that all three politicians at the time had contributed to ending wars on their own territories was very helpful. Otherwise the conclusions would have been depressing indeed. But two years later Ethiopia and Eritrea went to war against each other.

The mini-summit elaborated a declaration that was presented during the opening ceremony of the OAU summit. Here the children called on 'our parents the heads of state' to stop waging war, demobilize child soldiers, destroy all land-mines, ensure a minimum of care and protection for children under armed conflict, rehabilitate everybody affected by war, relocate the military budget for the social sectors and provide peace education. Seventeen-year old James from Uganda described how his family was killed and he himself kidnapped by rebels to become a child soldier. 'You are the leaders,' he told the summit. 'You are the adults who create problems for us.' And he made everybody in the audience rise to honour the child victims of war by a minute of silence. Thirteen-year-old Angelica from Sierra Leone concluded by urging everybody to do their best to ban the production of land-mines.

The hall was completely silent for several minutes. Then the applause broke loose. The heads of state rose and cheered, paying homage to the children. The representative of Liberia remarked: 'Finally some realities came into the picture – good!'

FOUR

Concealed Calamity: Stopping the Ravages of the HIV/AIDS Pandemic

Disease will wipe out a town faster than war.
(Proverb from Liberia)

'Africans must not become second-class citizens in the world!' The great audience is deathly still. Everybody is holding their breath in anticipation of what is to come. It is mid-December 1997, and 9,000 people are assembled in Abidjan to discuss one of the most painful issues in present-day Africa: the spread of the HIV/AIDS pandemic. More than thirty million people have been infected, and nearly ten million have died. Every day thousands of women and men contract the disease. All the time, the experts are obliged to adjust the numbers upwards, because the epidemic is spreading so fast.

The only Western country represented at high level at the AIDS conference is France. President Jacques Chirac himself is speaking during the opening ceremony. 'We are developing active drugs against AIDS. These cannot be reserved for the West, leaving Africa out. I suggest an international solidarity fund for treatment of HIV/AIDS victims in Africa to be managed by UNAIDS, the Joint UN Programme on HIV/AIDS.' The applause is spontaneous. But the atmosphere is a bit strange. The president of the host country at the time, Henri Konan Bédié, takes the floor: the French proposal is excellent. The Ivory Coast supports it. But it should be an *African* fund. New applause. The local newspapers are enthusiastic. It was a 'conference of hope' with 'renewed promises'.

But the strange atmosphere in the conference hall persists. On the UNICEF side, we have been deeply involved in the organization of the conference, but we have never heard of an AIDS fund. I take a quick look at Peter Piot, the director of UNAIDS, sitting on the podium. His face is as blank as a sphinx. But he doesn't seem relaxed. Afterwards, he observes that the fund is completely unknown to him.

Not only the procedural aspects create uneasiness. The fund itself does. Neither President Chirac nor Bédié said one word about money. In all probability the fund is empty – at least for the time being. And the focus is on treatment of the sick. The new drugs are extremely expensive: thousands of dollars a year for each patient, several times the fixed minimum wage in many countries. Developing countries will lag hopelessly behind. It is absolutely fitting to give them a helping hand. But first of all, the drugs should be sold at a reduced price. This has been done before with vaccines, where there are two markets: one in the North for those capable of paying, taking into account the development costs of the drugs, and a humanitarian one in the South, with the sole purpose of saving lives. More people could get treatment with reduced prices – but far from all of them. In poor countries, only a small privileged group would be able to benefit. The others would not have a chance. Even if the cure for AIDS were only a single glass of clean water, most HIV-positive people in Africa would still be doomed. So difficult are the living conditions, and so weak the health services on the continent.

Besides, increased emphasis on treatment might reduce the attention given to prevention of the pandemic. I remember one of the ministers of health in the region, who took me aside under a discussion of health for all and whispered: 'You know, Mrs Skard, the *real* problem is that it is so expensive to fly patients to Paris for an operation!' He looked as if he was serious. He definitely belonged to the (very) rich upper class, so this was presumably his problem. But what about ordinary people? What about the poor, who have difficulties ensuring the simplest meal from day to day, not to mention enjoying the most basic health services? And if the responsible political authorities don't give them priority, who will?

Undermining Progress

The AIDS pandemic has, in a short time, become a leading cause of death in sub-Saharan Africa. Were it not for HIV/AIDS, average life expectancy would be approximately 62 years instead of 48. At the turn of the century, more children were still dying from diarrhoea and malaria than from AIDS, but the numbers were increasing rapidly.

In June 2001, the AIDS threat was discussed in a special session of the UN General Assembly. The pandemic had not only become a major development crisis, but a truly global emergency. The number of infected people was 50 per cent higher than predicted a decade earlier. In Africa, many more people were dying from AIDS than from armed conflict. Millions of adults in their prime were being swept away. The disease fractures and impoverishes families, weakens workforces, turns millions of children into orphans and threatens the social and economic fabric of communities and the political stability of nations. Governance is undermined by the high death rates among the elites in both public and private sectors. Health workers and teachers are decimated. At the same time, the number of patients increases. 'In already unstable societies this cocktail of disasters is a sure recipe for more conflict,' the UN Secretary General, Kofi Annan, underlined, 'and conflict, in turn, provides fertile ground for further infections.'

By the end of 2002, 29.4 million people in sub-Saharan Africa were living with AIDS. The epidemic had not reached the same proportions in West and Central as in Eastern and Southern Africa. In some countries in Southern Africa, 20–30 per cent or more of adults were infected. In West and Central Africa, prevalence rates passed the five per cent mark in nine of the countries that had statistics. In a populous country like Nigeria, this meant that 3.2 million people suffered from AIDS. In three countries (Cameroon, Central African Republic and the Ivory Coast) ten or more per cent were infected. The disease was spreading quickly, assisted by mobility and migration, economic and political crises, increasing poverty and urbanization and a weakening of family and traditional social structures. Religious and cultural norms related to the status of women, extramarital sex and prostitution also play a role. At earlier stages, HIV/ AIDS was most widespread among urban, relatively well-educated people. Gradually, the poor are being hit the hardest. Poverty, combined with the discrimination against women, is explosive. Many poor women have no other option than to sell themselves to survive.

The consequences of the disease were being felt more and more. In the Ivory Coast, the defence, education, agriculture and private sectors were affected. In the Central African Republic, between 25 and 50 per cent of the teachers were expected to pass away by 2005. In Ghana, it was estimated that the health expenditure for treatment of AIDS victims would increase tenfold in the course of 15 years.

Family Disaster

AIDS has a different face in Africa from its face in the West. In Western countries, mostly men are infected. In Africa, women and children also contract the disease. In fact, more women than men catch it. Although HIV is more common among those who engage in high-risk behaviour and those with many sexual partners, most infected women get the virus from straightforward sexual relations with their regular partner. Due to the age difference between partners, women are usually infected at an earlier age and die before men. More than half of African girls are married before the age of 18.

In Africa, an AIDS tragedy is a family disaster. The husband usually catches the virus outside the marital relationship and transmits it to his wife, or wives, if he has several. The women must deal not only with their own suffering and impending death, but in many cases with that of their children as well. As the disease progresses, it becomes more difficult to provide a livelihood for the family. The adults cannot work. There is no social security. At the same time, the costs of medication and care rocket. Cattle and other assets are sold. Children are taken out of school. Relatives must contribute money and food. Female family members – the mother, a sister, older daughter or co-wife – must not only care for the sick, but take over child care, household tasks and economic activities. Soon the children lose both mother and father. Funerals must be organized and paid for. The grandparents, who thought they would be supported by their adult children when they got old, discover that the house is full of orphans who must be provided for. Children suddenly have to take over parental responsibilities and do the necessary work, look after younger siblings and care for dying family members. The number of households headed by children has grown dramatically.

For many African women, the AIDS threat begins with their lack of control over their sexuality: with whom, when and how they shall have sexual relations, and the sexual contacts their husbands have with other partners. The woman is usually subordinate to the man and has little to say regarding their sex life. Often such questions are not even discussed. There is a wall of silence surrounding intimate relations, sexuality and also AIDS. Conscious family planning through the utilization of modern contraceptives is very rare among couples in low-income groups in Africa. Condoms are not readily available, or free. Effective use also requires openness and collaboration between partners. It is a general trend that women have less access to health services than men, with the exception of mother and child care.

At the preparatory women's conference in Dakar in 1994, and at the International Women's Conference in Beijing the year after, the frank talk about sex by African women was a new and striking phenomenon. They demanded sexual rights, equal inheritance with men and protection of girl children. Not all were as radical. Some supported their conservative Catholic or Muslim leaders. But many African women perceived the demand for empowerment, which is the red thread in the Plan of Action from Beijing, to be a question of life and death. As one woman said: 'In intimate relations a woman must be able to protect herself, have the power to say no or at least request the man to use a condom.' The Dakar conference recommended that women be informed so they could practise 'protected sex', particularly when their partner did not. 'Men have to understand that their sleeping around has become mortally dangerous both for themselves and their family,' a woman noted. At the UN special session on AIDS the slogan was launched: 'Girl power is Africa's vaccine against AIDS'.

It is not easy to establish if a child is infected by HIV/AIDS. People refer to the 'slim disease'. Children lose their appetite, get chronic diarrhoea, fever and respiratory infections. But such ailments are common in early childhood. Parents may think the symptoms have a natural cause or are the result of supernatural forces. Health personnel with a long queue of waiting mothers may overlook the problems or hesitate to raise an issue that is usually taboo. When efforts to treat the child repeatedly fail, health workers may be obliged to draw the right conclusion, but what can they do? Modern medicine has little to offer. So mother and child are sent home. Here the child requires extensive care. The epidemic is more aggressive in Africa than in industrialized countries, because the burden of disease generally is greater and the resistance to infections weaker.

Fatal Mothers' Milk

Transmission of HIV infection from mother to child has been – and still is – a sensitive and difficult question. By the end of 2002, almost three million children and youths under 15 years of age were living with HIV/AIDS in sub-Saharan Africa. Most had been infected by their mothers. Not all children of HIV-positive mothers contract the disease, but the risk is higher in developing than in the industrialized countries. In the countries south of the Sahara, about one-third of the children acquire HIV from their mothers, and of these, one-third get it through breastfeeding.

Together with women's associations and health organizations, UNICEF has strongly supported breastfeeding of infants. Mother's milk is not only rich in nutrients. It protects the child from disease, and it is free. Breast-milk substitutes, as well as clean water, are very costly for poor families in developing countries, and often the hygienic conditions lead to infection. There has been – and still is – a bitter struggle between the defenders of children on one side and international companies like Nestlé on the other concerning the use of breast-milk substitutes. UNICEF and WHO have tried to strictly limit the distribution. 'Mother- and child-friendly hospitals' have been established that encourage breastfeeding and refuse to hand out free samples of breast-milk substitutes in maternity wards. But what approach should be taken to HIV-positive mothers who risk infecting their children through breastfeeding?

Experts recommend that health personnel provide HIV-positive mothers with the relevant information, so they can choose if they want to breastfeed their babies. So far, so good – but in a region like West and

Central Africa, most mothers do not know if they are HIV-positive or not. The possibilities for testing are extremely limited. In addition, many people have no access to clean water, or money to buy breast-milk substitutes. The risk of children falling ill is generally very high. Children who are not breastfed have a six times greater chance of dying than those who do. Of two possible evils, it is breastfeeding that overall entails the lesser threat to the health of the child. So we recommended it – where the AIDS pandemic was not very widespread. Drugs have been developed for pregnant HIV-positive women, which reduce the transmission of infection to the child. But the treatment is both costly and demanding, even if prices have been driven down recently. In poor countries, where regular prenatal and maternal/child care already represent a challenge, and the total expenditure on health amounts to less than fifty dollars per inhabitant, the costs of fighting HIV are prohibitive.

Nightmarish Scenario

There is a nightmarish scenario: 40 million starving, impoverished orphans in sub-Saharan Africa, with no education or employment, roaming the streets as excellent recruits for the criminal gangs, looting militias and child armies – like those that have slaughtered and maimed thousands of civilians in Liberia and Sierra Leone over the last decade.

Things have not yet come to this. By the end of 2001, the more than seventeen million people who lost their lives to AIDS in sub-Saharan Africa have left behind eleven million orphans, and the numbers are expected to double over the next decade. In the Ivory Coast alone there were around 420,000, and the numbers were increasing. The children often live in communities hit by poverty and distress. There are few support systems, and the solidarity of the established African family is subjected to great stress. Even if relatives and neighbours try to take care of the young, the burden may become too heavy: ten, 20, 30 or 40 children for a single provider, and the children are neglected. In addition to the painful experience of seeing loved ones die, in many cases they experience repudiation by the family and local community, exclusion from school, rejection by the health services and loss of inheritance rights. Many people are afraid of infection or believe that the disease is brought about by evil spirits or witchcraft. Numerous children end up in the streets, struggling from day to day to survive. The assistance offered by authorities and different organizations is like a drop in the ocean.

Among the street children, the AIDS pandemic has led to a worsening of sexual abuse. In particular, girls between the ages of 13 and 18 are exposed, and younger age groups are increasingly involved. Many men seek young girls for prostitution, because they are afraid of AIDS and believe the chances of infection are less. Some even think that sexual intercourse with a virgin will cure the disease. At the same time, young girls are more likely than older women to contract the infection. They have great problems persuading adult men to use condoms, and they are easily injured during the sexual act, permitting the virus to penetrate into the body. When they get sick, they have great trouble obtaining assistance.

Clementine from the Ivory Coast describes the situation of young girls living in the street:

> It is tough being HIV-infected, very tough. I lost my mother long ago, so I have nobody, absolutely nobody. It is five years since my family asked for news. When I force myself to visit them, and I use a glass, they immediately wash it. When I use a plate, they wash it. So I don't go there. It pains me too much. I get no support, no grant. If a man comes with money and wants unprotected sex, shall I refuse? He might become infected, but I need money to eat, to live. It is difficult. The money I had, I spent on housing. But then I had nothing for food. I struggled to keep the house and take care of my little daughter. But I didn't manage, and my girl died of malnutrition. I buried her myself, with my own hands. I could not pay for the necessary. Everything came to an end when I lost my daughter. She gave me the courage to live, to fight. I was thrown out of the house, because I couldn't pay. Then I was attacked by bandits who thought I earned a lot of money selling those small cigarettes. I was even raped. Now I live with a friend. I can't plan anything for the future. HIV has put up a metal wall in front of me.

A Far-sighted and Courageous Woman

However one looks at it, it is only by changing people's behaviour that the AIDS epidemic can be stopped. Many think it is impossible. The information and publicity campaigns that have been organized so far have not prevented spreading of the disease.

Behaviour change is difficult. AIDS is a new disease. People lack proper information and don't know what to do. We are dealing with one of the most intimate and delicate aspects of human life and a disease that brings widespread stigmatization. It is tempting to deny that the problem exists, for as long as possible. The cause of death for AIDS victims is often described as something else: 'pneumonia', 'fever' or just 'disease'. In addition, it is extremely difficult to change personal behaviour, even for people who are properly informed and acknowledge the threat. Deep-rooted family, kin and community traditions and norms are often involved.

In the 1990s, during discussions in the UNICEF executive board of activities in West and Central Africa, there was often criticism, particularly from some Western countries, that we focused too little on AIDS. Perhaps UNICEF was not insistent enough with regard to recipient countries. In headquarters, AIDS was long considered a regional problem, and in the region we were unsure how widespread the epidemic was and which strategy to pursue. On the other hand, African governments were rarely willing to give priority to activities related to HIV/AIDS, and international donors did not exactly line up to provide funds.

What should be done? It is of vital importance that political, religious and intellectual leaders are conscious of their responsibility, take the AIDS threat seriously and demonstrate resolute leadership. Some have done this, but far from all. In West Africa, some popular singers have even made the point that they do not believe in AIDS. But to fight the epidemic effectively, opinion leaders have to break the silence and help to overcome the stigma attached to the disease. They must speak candidly about the problems and make the combating of AIDS a priority. A feeling of crisis must be created, so people understand that unusual measures are required. If necessary, established customs and behaviour patterns have to be modified. There must be a free flow of information to enable people to acquire the necessary knowledge, and they must be able to understand the messages and how to react. Local culture and views concerning AIDS should be taken into account, for example that AIDS is because of witchcraft, social vices or the white man. It might be necessary to raise controversial questions relating to the roles of women and men, discrimination against women, poverty and inequality. Women and traditional and religious leaders should be encouraged to participate in exchanges of views. The fight against AIDS further requires resources for preventive measures and the strengthening of health services, especially in the treatment of sexually transmitted diseases.

It is possible to learn lessons from countries that have been hit less hard than others. One such example is Senegal. At an early stage, a systematic campaign against AIDS was launched. The initiative came among others from a woman, Professor Awa Marie Coll Seck, who headed the department for communicable diseases at the Dakar hospital. Later, she became the head of several voluntary organizations combating AIDS, joined UNAIDS for some years and then returned to Senegal as minister of health. As soon as the first cases were detected in 1986, a national committee to fight the pandemic was created. An action plan was elaborated, and a cross-sectoral action committee was mandated to follow up. A broad collaboration was developed with all concerned ministries, local administrations, voluntary organizations, youth and women's groups. The UN organization and bilateral donors contributed. Health personnel were trained. People were offered voluntary and confidential HIV testing and counselling. A programme against sexually transmitted diseases was introduced, and sex workers were advised to use condoms. Blood transfusions were controlled.

Very soon it was decided to organize an extensive information campaign aimed at the population as a whole: employees and the military, villages and urban neighbourhoods, politicians and opinion leaders. The president took the lead. Traditional and religious leaders were involved as well. AIDS was discussed on radio and TV. It was a theme in mosques and churches. Sex instruction and information about HIV/AIDS was given in schools and to youths outside of school. The objective was to stop the epidemic, and the slogans were 'abstinence, fidelity or protection'.

The Senegalese authorities regularly publish statistics of the number of infected people. The different measures are discussed openly, and the impact of the action taken is studied. The results have been encouraging. In 1997, the average age of women's first sexual experience had risen from about 16 to 19 years or older. The number of condoms sold had increased nearly ten times. Among men with casual partners, use of them had gone up from about zero to two-thirds. The number of pregnant women with sexually transmitted diseases had gone down. Factors like a relatively homogeneous population, less frequent extra-marital relationships and extensive control of sexually transmitted diseases, may have contributed to limiting the AIDS pandemic in a country like Senegal. But in any case, the authorities knew how to exploit the existing possibilities in a campaign which gave results. By the end of 2001, the spread of AIDS in Senegal was among the lowest in sub-Saharan Africa, with less than 1 per cent who were HIV-infected in the adult population. The efforts at mobilization and consciousness-raising continued, and special efforts were made to reduce HIV/AIDS among female sex workers.

'What Young People Don't Know, Can Kill Them'

In UNICEF, we were rather pleased before the AIDS conference in 1997. We were getting preventive activities going. Not least in the Ivory Coast, a number of young people were actively engaged. The scout movement used games, songs and sketches to spread information, and provided youth counselling. Comic strips and photo albums were made for use in schools and sold in kiosks. The Children's Parliament with 100 young people from Abidjan and other cities adopted a long recommendation. In it, they addressed 'our parents, the Government and His Excellency the President' and requested the adoption of all necessary measures so that the theme for the AIDS day 1997, 'Children in a world of AIDS', could be changed to 'Children in a world without AIDS'. It was recommended that children and youth should participate in the planning and implementation of measures against HIV/AIDS, and that parents and children should be encouraged to talk together about the pandemic.

UNICEF was not slow in following up. In collaboration with other organizations a seminar was organized on 'AIDS, health and children's rights'. An important issue was how to prevent children and youths from being infected. As one participant said: 'It is too late to help many adults, but young people still have a chance.' Two representatives from the Children's Parliament, a boy and a girl of 17–18 years of age, participated in the seminar.

> We must change the perception that young people create problems which must be solved. On the contrary, we are part of the solution. We have capacities and skills. We have a clear understanding of the problems. And we can communicate effectively with other young people. Youth must be informed about the epidemic, because what young people do not know, can kill them.

Together with the Children's Parliament, UNICEF engaged itself in the *Miwa* project of a voluntary organization in the second largest city in the Ivory Coast, Bouaké. *Miwa* means 'my child' in the local language. The project tries to create a system of peer educators, where children and youths help others of the same age and gender to understand the AIDS threat. Parents and teachers, but first of all boys and girls from nine to 15 in as well as outside of school, are informed about sexually transmitted diseases, HIV/AIDS and premature pregnancies. Groups and social gatherings are organized, where young people pass on the information. They show pictures and videos, discuss sexual behaviour and use role play. Many youths are very ignorant and have thought little about their own behaviour. They know of no way to protect themselves against HIV/AIDS and believe that a person looking healthy and well cannot be infected and transmit the disease. By the turn of the century, several hundred peer educators had reached out to thousands of children and youths. The number of premature pregnancies in Bouaké had been greatly reduced.

Christmas Coup

Generally in the Ivory Coast, things did not go well. The country has a socially and culturally heterogeneous population. There are great disparities between rich and poor, urban and rural areas. Migration and mobility are extensive. In addition, the measures taken by the authorities to combat AIDS were scattered and halfhearted, to say the least.

The AIDS conference in Abidjan created great attention in the media and in public opinion. Voluntary organizations, the UN apparatus, bilateral donors and involved professionals tried to strike while the iron was hot. There was no longer any discussion of curative versus preventive action. The situation was ominous, and as many measures as possible had to be implemented.

The national AIDS programme launched information campaigns in the schools, the police, the customs service and the military, and among sex workers and long-distance drivers. The appeal was 'careful love'. Twenty-two million condoms were distributed in 1999, compared to 700,000 five years earlier. The Chirac/Bédié solidarity fund also got some money. The Ivorian government allocated funds to subsidize the medical treatment of HIV/AIDS, while France, together with other donors, provided support to pregnant women. A reduced price for treatment was obtained. It benefited some thousand people. Assistance was further organized for abandoned orphans.

But HIV/AIDS was not made a priority in the country's national policies. And in 1999, external auditors reported that widespread abuse of funds had taken place in the state administration. Sizeable allocations, among others to hospitals and other health services, had been misappropriated. The report led to sharp reactions. Major donors froze their assistance. Just before Christmas 1999, President Bédié was ousted by a military coup and many activities stopped. There was a difficult transition phase. Then, in 2000, the newly elected president committed himself to give the AIDS issue higher political priority. A special ministry was created in 2001 to strengthen the public response and the national strategic plan was revised. But the country was struggling with serious economic problems and a troop mutiny in September 2002 led to a protracted crisis, unrest and violence. In the meantime, the Ivory Coast was the country in West Africa with the highest rate of HIV infection. Around 700,000 people or about 10 per cent of the adult population were affected.

FIVE

An Exploding Agenda: Chasing Childhood Killer Diseases

The Hare says: 'Walking slowly leads to death.'
The Chameleon says: 'Walking quickly leads to death.'
(Proverb from the Ewe people)

'You must come to the conference room immediately. A delegation from the US Congress is here to mobilize support for polio eradication, and the atmosphere is getting tense.' One of the secretaries ventures into the office of the regional director. A conflict between UNICEF and representatives of the US Congress is no joke. Through the door I hear an imperious female voice with an unmistakable American accent: 'Are you *opposed* to the eradication of polio?' No answer. Everybody looks at me. The faces of the UNICEF advisers are flushing red. The woman is the head of the American delegation. She is the wife of a congressman and accompanied by two health experts. She continues:

> We are concerned about the weak support for polio eradication in West and Central Africa. UNICEF must get more involved. In 1988, the World Health Organization [WHO] adopted a resolution calling for the global eradication of polio by the year 2000. Impressive progress has been made. The number of cases is reduced by 90 per cent. The Western hemisphere is polio-free. Now the rest of the world must follow up. We have only got four years left!

Her voice gets louder:

> Throughout history, polio has lamed and killed millions of people, very often children. Just imagine, being spared this suffering and agony! And we could use the funds we now are spending on polio, for other good purposes. In the US, our annual expenditures for polio prevention are greater than the cost of eradicating the disease on a global scale. Therefore, we are contributing to a worldwide campaign to get rid of the disease once and for all. WHO, Rotary International and the US Centers for

Disease Control and Prevention are participating, as well as a number of industrialized countries. Recently, the South African President, Nelson Mandela, launched the campaign 'Kick polio out of Africa!' Every effort must be made in West and Central Africa also. Our children should be relieved of polio and only read about it in history books!

It would undoubtedly be nice. I remember how afraid we were of polio when I was a child, and how happy we were when the Salk vaccine came. My best friend Brita and her brother were infected. Brita lay in an iron lung for weeks before she died. Her brother survived, but had to use crutches. One of the American health experts takes over: 'We have overviews showing the spread of polio in each country. In addition to routine immunization, national immunization days must be organized to stop circulation of the virus.'

The leader of the UNICEF health team can keep quiet no longer:

> It would be wonderful to get rid of polio, but children in West and Central Africa don't die first of all of polio. They die of diarrhoea and acute respiratory infections, of malaria and more and more of HIV/AIDS. Therefore, polio is not a priority. Routine immunization against polio and other infectious childhood diseases is carried out. But we still have not covered more than half of the children in the region. Great efforts were made up to 1990, and the campaigns gave results. But they were very costly, and a few years later coverage rates went down again. The health services couldn't follow up the new cohorts of children. Therefore, we are giving priority to the establishment of a primary health care system, so it will be possible to maintain preventive health care in the long term.

The American woman is impatient: 'So, you are against the eradication of polio?' The health adviser stutters: 'No, but ...' The woman insists:

> No country is free of polio, before *all* countries are free of polio. We will provide funds. Countries like India, China and Bangladesh have made enormous strides. Other poor countries should follow their example. The world managed to eradicate smallpox. And 80 per cent of the children in the world are immunized, even if people thought it was impossible when the goal was proposed.

Sure. There has been fantastic progress. When WHO launched the expanded programme on immunization in 1974, less than 5 per cent of the world's children were immunized against six child-killing diseases. Governments, international organizations (including UNICEF), development banks, political, religious and local leaders got started with what has been described as the greatest social mobilization effort in peacetime. Systematic disease surveillance was developed. Millions of health workers and volunteers were trained, global vaccine supplies established, 'cold chains' of refrigerators and networks of laboratories put in place. Not least, the price of vaccines was dramatically reduced through UNICEF's low-price procurement – down to US$1 for the most widespread diseases. In fact, immunization became one of the most cost-effective public health interventions. It was a revolution in child health.

The goal was to immunize 80 per cent of the world's children against six child-killing diseases before their first birthday. The goal was to be reached by 1990, and it was. An incredible achievement. The deaths of an estimated three million children were thereby prevented every year. Hundreds of thousands avoided becoming blind, crippled, mentally retarded or otherwise disabled. But these were global figures. In West and Central Africa, only a handful of countries reached the 80 per cent goal. Despite their efforts, the majority lagged behind. Of the three million children still dying annually from vaccine-preventable diseases, very many are in Africa.

I try a careful question: 'Has the American delegation been able to visit the field while you have been in the region?' The woman won't listen: 'We have got the technology. We have got the funds. It's no problem. We can do it. It is a question of will – nothing else.' *It's no problem – it's no problem* – the words whirl around in my head. Images file past my inner eye: desolate savannas as far as you can see, rainforests where cars disappear in the mud, women toiling in the fields from morning till night, looted health centres and offices with nothing but a dusty, rickety type-writer … *It is a question of will … nothing else?*

The woman doesn't understand the situation. I try again: 'There is no doubt that UNICEF supports the polio campaign. But there are obstacles in West and Central Africa which are not easily overcome.' The woman snorts: 'It's now or never. It isn't possible to eradicate all diseases, but we can eradicate polio. If we don't do it now, we will lose a unique opportunity.' A dialogue is evidently out of the question. It is best to end the meeting before I lose my temper: 'Thank you for the visit. We will discuss how to go forward.'

Shall Americans Decide?

We had quite a discussion. As soon as the Americans were out the door, everyone was talking at once. Why should Americans dictate the priorities in West and Central Africa? They are the result of extensive negotiations with ministers and health professionals in the region. Why should polio all of a sudden be a priority? Headquarters of UNICEF and WHO have so many priorities – a region like West and Central Africa can't possibly follow up all of them. We have to choose in relation to the local needs, and here other diseases are more important than polio. And why organize a new campaign? During the last decade, we have learned that it is crucial to consider the health services in their entirety. The most effective method is to create a well-functioning health care system that can deal with the whole spectrum of diseases. Otherwise, we will only be chasing one disease

---

Box 5.1 Little Darkie, 'Twas God Who Made Thee

Little Darkie, Little Darkie,
Sweet piccaninny,
Who made thee so dear,
And crowned thee with hair
So kinky and so frizzled?

Little Darkie, piccaninny,
I love thee so dear:
I know who made thee,
And crowned thee with hair
So kinky and so frizzled.

'Twas thee, 'twas thee,
    piccaninny,
God first created,
Ebon-checked dearie,
And God was delighted
To see thy pearly-white
    teeth.

So the Almighty Creator
Of all heav'n and earth
Dared to imitate
Thy darksome skin,
Thy milk-white teeth and
    robust lips;

He tried, but ere His self-giv'n
    task
The Omnipotent had done,
His water-colour
Grew faint and limpid:
Too pale to make another Darkie.

Thus came other sweet kiddies,
But not piccaninnies;
Red kiddies, and kiddies yellow
Did follow;

And last of all,
When God's creative colour
Had almost turned water,
He made another child
So pale and so mild:
'Tis he we call the white man.

Little Darkie, little Darkie,
Sweet piccaninny,
I know who made thee
And crowned thee
With hair
So fair
And so kinky.

(Michael Francis Dei-Anang, poet from Ghana: 'Wayward Lines from Africa', 1946)

after the other. Now it is polio, then it might be measles and tetanus, yellow fever and meningitis … .

The issue of priorities is touchy. At the big international and regional conferences, everybody wants to include their own preoccupations. The lists of priority tasks grow very long. Nobody dares delete something. Who will say some problems should *not* be solved? The poor countries have many problems. At the same time, the governments lack a proper overview of the resources they will receive. So they keep a long wish list, hoping to get as much support as possible. In the day-to-day work at country level, the agenda is all the time on the verge of exploding. Efforts are made to concentrate on some tasks, but new ones are constantly added. An un-expected situation arises requiring a reaction. A donor all of a sudden appears with a contribution – or something else. In most cases, there are neither human nor financial resources to deal with it all. At least, not effectively and not at the same time. In West and Central Africa, ministers of health and donors reached an agreement in the 1990s to give priority to the development of a primary health care system. But when it comes down to it, other tasks are also given priority. In the case of polio, the Americans came in with contributions which all of a sudden made it possible to achieve the goal of eradicating this disease.

As the frustration from being run roughshod over subsides, some of the regional health advisers venture to express differing views. It is clear that we have to give priority to the health care systems. But complete coverage of the region takes time. What shall we do in the meantime? A global campaign against polio has been launched. UNICEF supports it. One region can't stay out of it. For some countries in West and Central Africa, the eradication of polio will also be a step forward.

The reasoning is not easy for all to accept. After a while one of the African advisers comes up with a compromise: the Americans will go forward with polio eradication whether we like it or not. They are strong enough for that. The question is, shall we associate with it? The countries in the region have problems, because they lack funding for health activities. Perhaps we can use the polio campaign to strengthen the health services, renew the run-down cold chains and organize more routine immun-ization? If we base ourselves on the health centres, the campaigns can be a way of activating them.

I am not sure that the compromise will work in practice. But in the morass we are in, it seems to be the best solution. So we pursued the approach in discussions with WHO, the governments in the region and other donors. There were numerous reservations, but little by little the compromise was accepted – in theory.

Festive Drops

It is more difficult to eradicate polio than smallpox. Even if polio is very contagious, it rarely produces clear symptoms. Less than 1 per cent of infections result in polio paralysis. To establish protective immunity, everybody must be immunized not only once, but several times. Therefore a four-pronged strategy is developed. First, as many children as possible are included in routine immunization during the first year of life. During National Immunization Days (NIDs), supplementary immunization is provided to all children under five years. Effective surveillance is established to register all cases of polio. In the final stages, door-to-door campaigns ('mopping up') are organized in areas where the virus persists.

During the last few years, NIDs were organized, with the support of Americans and others, all over West and Central Africa, in many cases several times. Countries engaged in armed conflict were also involved. It was an enormous undertaking. The campaigns require months of preparations. Enormous distances have to be covered on roads that are often of extremely poor quality. People have to be informed, even in the most out-of-the-way places where they have never heard of something like immunization. Vaccines and equipment must be procured, and assistants mobilized.

The Democratic Republic of Congo (DRC) is the African country that in recent years has had the most cases of polio. At the same time, it is embroiled in a civil war that has affected one-third of the population. Hundreds of thousands of Congolese have been internally displaced or have fled to neighbouring countries, while refugees from these countries have arrived in the DRC. Roughly the size of Western Europe, the country has virtually no paved roads and transportation is practically non-existent. The weak health system has been degraded by looting and by fleeing staff. Nevertheless, in 1999 all-out efforts were made to eradicate polio. More than thirty million doses of vaccine were positioned in cold storage depots throughout the country. All kinds of transport were used: planes, bicycles, canoes and carriers. Nearly 16,000 vaccination posts were set up and 60,000 health workers trained. A national publicity campaign was launched to persuade the mothers of more than ten million children to come for immunization not only once, but several times. The bill amounted to about US$14 million in the course of one year.

In August 1999, there were complications. The warring factions promised to observe a temporary cease-fire, and this was respected, except in Kisangani, the third largest city. All of a sudden there was shooting and bombing. The humanitarian flights were grounded. Mothers and children had to go into hiding. Several hundred soldiers and many civilians were killed or wounded. Still the campaign continued. New rounds were organized and 9.5 million children were immunized.

But this was not sufficient. More rounds were needed to stop circulation of the virus. A coverage of 80–90 per cent is not enough. Pockets of virus can survive. And new children are born all the time. So three rounds of immunization days were organized in DRC in 2000 and in 2001, with special emphasis on children who are difficult to access, and displaced and refugee populations. The bill amounted to US$20 million in 2000 and US$28 million in 2001. Still the efforts must continue in 2002 and 2003 before the country is 'safe'. And recently some scientists have started wondering if it ever will be 'safe' – if polio in fact can be eradicated, technically speaking. Perhaps it can only be contained.

National Immunization Days are days of celebration. Everybody in the village is mobilized. The local leaders are all dressed up, and children line up with flowers. Prominent guests zoom in. There are drums and dancing. Often the immunization takes place outdoors, and long lines form in the heat. Sometimes the children are weighed, given vitamin A capsules or measles immunization together with polio. Mothers may have a chat with one of the assistants concerning the health of the child, but this is rare, and usually does not last more than a few minutes. So the children's health is strengthened, but the mothers are just as knowledge-able – or as ignorant – when they leave as when they came. Modern or traditional medicine – what is the difference? Both use incomprehensible magic power. It is not easy to judge the effect. After the immunization, mothers may get a sandwich and a soft drink. Then, next, please! Many hundreds may pass through an immunization post each day. The guests have to contribute. I became rather good at pinching a child's nose, and when it gasps for air, drip, drip, they get what they need.

Costly Success

During the last decade, not many cases of polio have been registered in West and Central Africa. But the countries in the region made a valiant effort to contribute to the global campaign. In October 2000, the greatest health action in the history of the region was launched to immunize 76 million children in 17 countries. Impressive progress was made. By 2002, all except two of the 23 countries in the region were polio-free, leaving Niger and Nigeria as the only endemic countries. The goal of eradicating polio by the year 2000, however, was not reached. The health systems, the routine immunization and the disease surveillance in the region were too weak, and the problems related to infrastructure, implementation capacity and mobilization of the population were too great. The endeavours must continue. The goal is adjusted for the world to be polio-free by the year 2005. It may well happen – if the political commitment is maintained in the face of an apparently disappearing disease, the children in conflict-affected areas are reached, and the necessary funds are mobilized. Globally, there were ten polio-endemic countries remaining by the beginning of 2001. It is estimated that US$1.5 billion have been spent so far on the eradication campaign and that an additional US$1 billion is needed in 2002–05 to complete the task.

The polio campaigns have already demonstrated that public health goals can be reached against all odds, when there is sufficient determination among national leaders and international donors. The eradication of polio will be a milestone in the history of humanity, and will improve the health situation in West and Central Africa. But what is the overall picture for the region, with gains and losses?

During recent years, the routine immunization stagnated or was reduced in very many countries. Some maintain that this was not because of the polio campaigns. The campaigns could be organized in such a way that they strengthened the existing health services. But in practice, these opportunities were often neglected. There were opportunity costs in contexts with weak implementation capacity and the campaigns were generally carried out in the form of isolated, costly projects. They gave results in relation to polio, but not real health benefits in general.

The same did not happen everywhere. In Benin, routine immunization was maintained at a high level during the campaigns. In Niger, the low coverage was further reduced. According to fieldworkers in West and Central Africa, the polio campaigns contributed to a strengthening of the health systems where these already were functioning well. Health workers were trained. The cold chains and means of communication were rehabilitated, and contacts between health personnel and the local population were improved. But in places where the health services were already weak, the special efforts to eradicate polio generally led to a deterioration of the service provision. The immunization days attracted great interest and resources. In many cases, the campaign costs were greater than foreseen. Other health interventions were neglected or interrupted. It was also demotivating to perform routine immunization with less attention and funds, equipment and staff than the special campaigns.

In the DRC, the polio campaigns could not prevent the dramatic deterioration of the health and nutrition of the population that took place over the last few years, even if efforts were made to use the campaigns for various health interventions. Child morbidity and mortality increased, due to malaria, diarrhoeal diseases and acute respiratory infections, malnutrition and HIV/AIDS, and there were numerous epidemics of measles, meningitis and even polio.

The polio campaigns had a trade-off. While some children gained life and health, others lost. How many and how much we do not know. It is difficult to get a complete overview. Not many campaign supporters are interested in reservations abou the campaign. The cost for Africa's children will probably never be known.

Both the progress achieved and the obstacles encountered during the efforts to eradicate polio contributed to an increased interest in immunization in general as a instrument of health promotion. In January 2000 a new initiative was launched: the Global Alliance for Vaccines and Immunization (GAVI), with a global fund for children's vaccines. The objective is to increase the use of existing vaccines and promote the development of new ones of special interest to the developing countries. The initiative is promising. It focuses on the world's poorest countries. New actors are involved, among others the World Bank and the Bill and Melinda Gates Foundation, in addition to WHO, UNICEF, other foundations, donor and developing countries. The initiative is elaborated at global level, but task forces are established in each region. Support is given both for vaccines and infrastructure. At country level, inter-agency coordination committees develop requests based on comprehensive, jointly prepared multi-year plans of action. It remains to be seen if a region like West and Central Africa will be able to catch up with the rest of the world with regard to immunization coverage – and at the same time make progress in the long-term development of effective health systems.

Persistent Mosquitoes

In the middle of the polio campaign came the malaria campaign. 'Roll back malaria' was launched by WHO in October 1998. A new, dynamic director general, Gro Harlem Brundtland, was responsible. A UN decade to combat malaria was supported by UNICEF, the UN Development Programme (UNDP) and the World Bank. African leaders endorsed the goal to halve deaths from malaria by the year 2010. Many health workers in West and Central Africa had difficulty responding. How should we cope with this as well?

There is no doubt about the need for increased efforts to fight malaria. During the 1950s and 1960s comprehensive campaigns were organized. DDT was used against the mosquito that carries the malaria parasite. People took chloroquine when they fell ill. In a decade, the number of malaria cases was dramatically reduced. But spraying was costly. It turned out that DDT was detrimental to the environment. Gradually, the mosquitoes developed resistance to chloroquine. Further, armed conflicts and massive displacement of people, changes in the climate and environment, in addition to inadequate health services, contributed to an increase in the spread and mortality of malaria, first of all in sub-Saharan Africa. In 2002, malaria was Africa's leading cause of mortality in children under five. Globally, at least 300 million people suffer from acute malaria every year. About one million die, mostly African children. Malaria hits the poor first of all, and the disease contributes to reduced income and increased expenditure. The cost of the disease amounts to billions of dollars every year. If malaria had been eliminated years ago, the national product of the African countries would be up to US$100 billion greater.

What should be done? During several decades, malaria research and control had low priority. In connection with the World Summit for Children in 1990, malaria was not included as a priority area of intervention. The need to fight the disease was evident, but effective interventions were lacking. According to UNICEF, the goals had to be 'do-able'. The spread of the disease led to increased focus on the problem. Impregnated bed-nets provided a new means of action. If the nets cover the windows and beds, research shows that 25 per cent fewer children die of malaria. It is not as effective as immunization, but it helps. The price of a mosquito net is about US$5–6. The cost of impregnating with insecticide is about US$1.50 a year.

Fortunately, 'Roll back malaria' did not become a traditional campaign. WHO noted the lessons learned from previous campaigns and listened to people in the field, UNICEF among others. The character of the disease also made it logical to place the health services in the centre of the strategy. Malaria is an acute illness that develops fast. It is vital to have rapid access to expert treatment, that is to a well-functioning health centre. 'Roll back malaria' therefore aims at strengthening the primary health care system in the different countries. In addition, preventive measures and appropriate treatment are to be implemented. This is more easily said than done. But industry and research are developing better drugs. And distributors and voluntary organizations are working to make bed-nets cheaper and simpler to use.

A New Campaign

In March 2001, WHO and UNICEF, in collaboration with the US Centers for Disease Control and Prevention, launched yet another initiative. This time the focus was on measles – an innocent childhood disease in Western countries, but a major killer in other parts of the world, particularly sub-Saharan Africa. Measles accounts for about half of the deaths due to vaccine-preventable diseases, and the objective of the Global Measles Strategic Plan is to halve this mortality by 2005. The virus is extremely contagious. Immunization coverage has to be above 90 per cent to stop measles deaths. In West and Central Africa, levels are below 50 per cent in nearly half of the countries. 'Africa helped the international community eradicate polio,' an African health worker remarked, 'now they can assist us get rid of measles.'

SIX

Mysterious Modern Medicine Men: Towards the Goal of Health for All

Suffer or pay the medicine-man.
(Proverb from Zaire)

Piercing screams. Ear-splitting drums. One woman after the other comes forward waving her arms and stamping her feet. 'Wawawawawawawa!' Fluttering shawls, swaying buttocks and glittering smiles: Welcome! A wrinkled old woman steps up and beckons me to join. When the rhythm takes hold, there is no end to the enthusiasm. 'WAWAWAWAWAWAWAW!' There are women all around, some carrying children on their backs, resilient, laughing and friendly. I am swinging in the middle of the crowd, and wherever we come from, we are sisters together.

All of a sudden, it's over. Under the shady crown of the palaver tree, the elders in the village are waiting – all men in colourful *boubous* (traditional wide tunics). The guests solemnly shake hands with everybody in the circle and get a welcoming drink, from a calabash bowl (made from a kind of pumpkin) filled with palm wine. Afterwards, the village chief rises, pours a little wine on the ground for the ancestors and speaks. Not far from the capital, most people speak only the local language. Even representatives of the local authorities often have to use an interpreter. The village chief is tall and thin, with a worn yellow *boubou* and a skullcap on his head. 'It is a great honour for the village to receive such prominent guests. We are very grateful for the assistance provided by UNICEF. The health centre is now put in order. People get help when they are sick. Not so many die of malaria. The children are also immunized. Everybody is happy.'

The representatives of the ministry of health and the municipality are all smiles. A young man in a white coat comes forward with a pile of papers:

The centre serves twelve villages with 13,000 inhabitants, mostly farmers. We are three staff. I am a health worker, and we have a midwife and an assistant. The centre has been revitalized. Now we can treat 40 patients a day. In addition, we immunize 55 children every month. We hope to reach 80 per cent of the children under the age of one before the end of the year. Volunteers go out on motorbikes in the dry season, when the roads are passable, and immunize in the villages. There were rumours some time ago, that immunization was black magic to make the children sterile. So we are going to organize an information campaign and go from village to village and talk with people. Those who are seriously ill present another problem. There is no place we can refer them. The nearest town is ten miles away, and the hospital is in very poor condition. Can UNICEF help us?

The health committee introduces itself: leader, deputy, treasurer and secretary, four men of different ages. The leader is relatively young and has a big account book:

I was elected head of the committee, because I have been to school and know how to calculate. But the deputy supports me. He has more experience. Besides, the whole committee has been trained. We were nominated by the village to take care of the money and make sure the health centre works properly. We have a stock of drugs, that we get at a very low price at the central medical store. People pay for the treatment. Malaria treatment costs 500 CFA francs (a bit more than half a US dollar) and an immunization card 50 CFA francs (about six or seven cents). A prenatal consultation costs 400 CFA francs (less than half a dollar).

He pages through the account book. 'We sell the drugs with a profit to cover operating expenses. Still, people pay less than on the market. The system works well. We have dug a well so the centre has got water. Still we have 500,000 CFA francs (nearly US$700) in the treasury.'

The committee leader is evidently proud. And it sounds impressive. But so far only men have spoken, while women use the centre the most. The space under the palaver tree is packed, but there are no women. The dancing group has disappeared. The midwife is gone. At a distance, a group of women is sitting with their children. I venture a question: 'What do the women think of the centre?' Deep silence. Everybody looks around. A woman, a woman! The regional director wants to talk with a woman! A few minutes. Then a young woman with a child on her back is shoved into the open circle. Poor lady – she looks completely at a loss. I regret my question, but it is too late.

'What do you think of the health centre?'

She squirms. 'It's very good. The children are immunized.'

'Do you think something could be improved?'

New hesitation. Then she replies with determination: 'I think it is expensive.'

The head of the health committee, who was happy because they were making a profit, looks somewhat uncomfortable. 'Did you know that women think the centre is expensive?' I wonder. He shakes his head: 'There are no women on the health committee.' 'What happens if somebody cannot pay?' I would like to know. 'Everybody can pay – it is so cheap,' he explains, 'and people help each other. If somebody has a problem, they get credit. And maybe the credit isn't paid back.' I can't resist: 'Maybe those operating the centre should talk with the women, so they are happy with the services?' Everybody nods silently – the authority has spoken. But the UNICEF representative should probably follow up what happens later.

Afterwards, we visit the health centre. It is a small concrete house painted yellow. Very simple, compared to institutions in a country like Norway, but much better than the dilapidated centres I have seen in many other places. It is clean and well kept. There are posters on the walls informing visitors about AIDS, clean water and family planning. The open waiting space is crowded with people, mostly women with small children. Fatoumata has brought little Souleymane, who is only eight days old. She has carried the boy five miles in the intense heat and is quite sweaty. She wants Souleymane immunized. Fatoumata has already lost two sons. The first died under delivery, and the other during a measles epidemic. 'We don't want to lose Souleymane also – we only have a daughter left!' she declares. Marie is sitting beside her with a thin one-year-old girl completely exhausted in her lap. She has had a fever for several days, has vomited and had diarrhoea. The traditional healer in the village sacrificed a hen to cast out the evil spirits, but it didn't help. Perhaps the health worker can give the girl some stronger potion?

The women say the health centre is fine, and nobody thinks it is too expensive. But one notes that it is far away (she has to walk seven miles), while another adds that it is difficult to get away from home, because there is so much to do. You wouldn't rather go to a traditional healer? I ask. Fatoumata replies: 'I think the health worker has stronger magic than the healer.'

Inside the house, there is one room for the health worker, one for the midwife and one for immunization. The assistant sits behind a counter, registering patients and selling drugs. The centre seems to function. The refrigerator works (using gas, as there is no electricity). There is some laboratory equipment (although not much), and the stock of drugs is nearly complete. Only 20 essential drugs are provided, but it should be sufficient to treat the most common diseases, and only a few are sold out. The head of the health committee pats his pocket and smiles:

> I have the key to the store room! Nobody can take out drugs without me. We are always two. I also sign disbursements together with the health worker. Once a month we go to town and put money in the bank. Everything is done properly. In another district, the treasurer and a bank employee ran away with the money, but this will not happen here!

In the room of the midwife I become worried. There is a desk with two chairs, a rickety examination bench and a poster about nutritious foods, but that is all. Doesn't she have more equipment? She pulls out a box with contraceptives donated by the UN Population Fund – for demonstration. Clients have to buy what they need from the drugstore in town. If the midwife needs a stethoscope, she can borrow the one the health worker has. In fact, there was not much to offer a pregnant woman in her fifth month who has had to walk many miles to get here. So, if the services of the centre are both expensive – and poor? The midwife admits that few women come for prenatal consultation. The great majority deliver at home.

'A Courageous Next Step'

I have not pointed out where the health centre is. It could be many places in West and Central Africa. A great number of centres were revitalized and reformed during the 1990s, on the basis of what is called the 'Bamako Initiative', and they function very much according to the same principles. The 'Bamako Initiative' refers to a meeting of African ministers of health in Bamako, Mali, in 1987. Its theme was the sad state of affairs of the health services after years of economic crisis and problems. The initiative was launched as model for a renaissance. It turned out to be a stimulating, practical and effective approach – although simpler in theory than in practice.

Actually, it started many years earlier. At a conference in Alma Ata in 1978, with participants from all over the world, a resolution was passed calling for 'health for all by the year 2000'. To achieve the goal, primary health care services were to be developed for the population as a whole. Afterwards, many countries invested strongly in their health systems, including sub-Saharan Africa, until the economic crisis became an unavoidable reality. During the 1980s, more and more countries struggled harder and harder. National budgets were cut and allocations to social sectors reduced. In 1990, two-thirds of African governments were spending less on health per person than they did ten years earlier. Buildings fell into decay. Health workers did not receive salaries. There were shortages of drugs and equipment. People became disillusioned and stopped coming to the health centres. Proponents of free health services for all understood that this was unrealistic. In Ghana, Nigeria, Senegal and Zaire (now the Democratic Republic of Congo) experiments with other solutions began to surface.

The experiences that provided the key to the final formulation of the Bamako Initiative started in Benin early in the 1980s. It was evident that many people spent considerable amounts of money on health. But they preferred to pay a visit to the traditional healer or to buy drugs (which were often outdated) sold by weight on the market. The pioneers in Benin assumed that if the health centres were better managed, it would be possible to provide people with better health for their money. They started experiments and research. On the basis of the lessons learned, UNICEF's executive director at the time, Jim Grant, challenged the African ministers of health in 1987:

> Africa faces economic hardships of unprecedented proportion. In spite of this, there is space for improving human welfare. Primary health care services are more urgently needed than ever. But we are still paying too much lip-service to the far-sighted approach of health for all. In most countries, the overwhelming majority of health expenditures remain on curative rather than preventive measures, and on major urban facilities rather than village and community health posts capable of serving the majority.

'Some of us have a vision,' Grant continued, 'a dream of what is possible – of a bold next step toward improving the health and well-being of people throughout Africa.' This step, according to Grant, was based on a dependable and affordable provision of essential drugs. There was evidence that health needs in Africa could be adequately catered for at a reasonable cost. The health authorities, in collaboration with local communities, should therefore be able to develop health services based on people purchasing essential drugs at low cost from the health centres, and the centres would use the revenue to finance preventive health measures, in addition to treating patients.

'Should this vision fade, or should it be actively explored and developed?' Grant wondered. The response from the ministers of health to this question was positive, and a resolution was adopted on the Bamako Initiative – Women's and Children's Health through Community Self-Reliance. The recommendation did not put an end to the discussion. On the contrary. There were numerous questions. Was there sufficient capacity at the local level to manage the primary health care services, and would local communities be able to participate in a meaningful way? What should the responsibility and role of the health authorities be? Would people be willing to pay for the health services, and would user charges prevent participation of the poor? Some thought cost recovery would never work, while others were opposed to a system where poor people who were sick had to pay for health services.

After the Bamako meeting, the World Health Organization (WHO), and UNICEF took action. Soon the Organization for African Unity (OAU), joined them, and gradually others: the World Bank, the UN Population Fund, the UN Development Programme, in addition to the European Union (EU), American, German, Dutch, French, British and Nordic donors.

Many African countries started revitalizing their primary health care services, based on the ideas of the Bamako Initiative. The initiative turned out to be a flexible model, which could be adjusted to different needs and possibilities. Various donors had different contributions. To a certain extent, they interpreted the initiative differently. It was quite a challenge for the governments to elaborate their own policy. In a review after some years, donors were requested to be more sensitive to the wishes of governments, to provide support with greater flexibility and continuity, to be more positive to coordination and to adjust their interventions to the health systems in each country.

UNICEF, WHO and the World Bank contributed to the elaboration of health strategies and the implementation of concrete measures. The World Bank was involved in structural adjustment and sector reform, while WHO gave advice in technical medical matters. UNICEF brought in field experience. Often countries began implementation in a limited number of districts. The World Bank could contribute to financing of the premises, while UNICEF delivered an initial supply of drugs and vaccines and supported the training of health personnel and committees. Other places, bilateral donors or voluntary organizations would assist. Gradually, each centre should be able to operate without external support, based on locally generated revenue and contributions from the authorities.

When the Ideal Cannot Work

Revitalization of primary health care services based on the initiative is past the stage of small, isolated projects. When the Bamako Initiative was launched, the objective was to create a sustainable health system for the country as a whole, and not only to provide health services to vulnerable groups.

The ideal arrangement with health for all free of charge had failed. The Bamako Initiative was an effort to implement the second best: a health system co-financed by the authorities and local communities. But the economic conditions in West and Central Africa were tough during the 1990s. Public administration was weak and poverty widespread. While external donors could provide support to small, scattered projects, this was neither possible nor desirable on a larger scale. The test of sustainability came when it was time to go to scale.

Most countries in the region were implementing structural reform programmes. Revitalizing the health services on the basis of cost-sharing fitted well with the reforms promoted by the World Bank. But it was difficult to strengthen the health services and at the same time reduce public expenditure. The principles of the Bamako Initiative were in line with a general trend towards more democracy and decentralization. The authorities had to support the health centres financially and technically, and allow local communities to manage locally generated funds. This last was painful for ministers of finance with a slender treasury. It was not easy, either, to maintain support from the centre when state finances were at a minimum. Strikes and demonstrations because of unpaid salaries became a part of everyday life for health workers in some countries.

To function properly, the Bamako Initiative depends on a reliable supply of essential drugs. It is no simple affair to elaborate a drug policy that ensures equal access to essential drugs, rational drug use and drugs of good quality. There is a multitude of competing drugs, and the interests of the population as well as of the pharmaceutical industry are affected. WHO gave important assistance, providing minimum lists of cheap and good essential drugs. It was already established that UNICEF's supply division could procure vaccines wholesale at low cost for poor developing countries. In every country, central medical stores for procurement, storage and sale of drugs had to be created. In several places there were heated discussions concerning the public or private status of these stores. Often the government preferred the former, while the World Bank endorsed the latter. In any case, the stores should not increase the cost or delay the supply of drugs.

At the end of the century, the great majority of countries in West and Central Africa accepted the approach as a national strategy, some in a revised form. Several were implementing reforms on a large scale. Benin and Guinea were pioneer countries. Ghana, Mauritania, Senegal and Togo soon followed, and gradually Mali and Niger as well, to mention some that made special efforts.

Ten Thousand Health Centres

The Bamako Initiative evoked considerable enthusiasm and dynamism. Around 10,000 health centres were revitalized in West and Central Africa in the course of the 1990s. Millions of people got health services they would not otherwise have.

Everything is not perfect. The supply of drugs sometimes fails. Preventive measures may be given lower priority than curative ones. Health personnel may experience problems with motivation, qualifications and salaries. At times, the support of the local community runs short, or monitoring on the part of the authorities is insufficient. Nevertheless, it is clear that the revitalized centres generally contributed to greater availability of primary health care services and improved quality of care in rural areas.

Benin and Guinea have been implementing the initiative the longest. When they started in 1986–87, health services in rural areas were practically non-existent, or at best sporadic. Only 5 per cent of one-year-olds were immunized in Guinea and 12 per cent in Benin. In the course of a few years, 300 centres in Guinea and 400 in Benin were revitalized. In the target areas, immunization rates improved dramatically and in a sustainable way. Prenatal consultations increased from practically none to nearly half of all pregnancies. Many more people got medical treatment, also among poor segments of the population. The revenue of the health centres varied. Devaluation, price increases and other economic factors had an impact. In both countries, 75–80 per cent of health centres nevertheless managed to cover their operating costs.

By 2001, the national immunization coverage (for diphtheria, whooping cough and tetanus, or DPT) was 40 to 50 per cent in Guinea and 80 per cent in Benin. In both countries, there was a reduction in child mortality during the 1990s that was much greater than average in the region. In all, the under-five mortality rate was reduced in sub-Saharan Africa from 180 per thousand live births in 1990 to 173 in 2001. In Benin, the mortality fell from 185 to 158 during the same period and in Guinea from 237 to 169. Many factors influence mortality rates, but revitalization of the health services has certainly contributed to the reduction. Other countries in the region that applied the Bamako Initiative on a larger scale often experienced a marked increase in immunization rates and reduction in child mortality, although this varies from country to country.

What about the Poor?

As in other parts of the world, cost-sharing was a sensitive issue in West and Central Africa. How much could the local population be expected to pay? Funds were needed to operate the centres adequately. At the same time, people should not be deterred from utilizing the services. Generally, during the 1990s the centres managed to deliver an integrated primary health care package for about US$1 per person per year, of which salaries accounted for about half. The sales of drugs provided the main revenue. The drugs were usually sold at 2 to 2.5 times the purchasing price, and the revenue was used to replenish the stocks of drugs and vaccines and to pay operating costs. Salaries of the health staff and procurement of equipment and vehicles were seldom covered by locally generated revenues. The authorities had to take care of these costs. Such an arrangement could work in many communities. But the poorer the population, the more difficult it was to get contributions from the patients. The minister of health in Mali, who is responsible for an extensive Sahelian country, estimated by the end of the 1990s that they could manage to cover 60 per cent of the population with the existing arrangement. The remaining 40 per cent would need further subsidies.

To begin with, I was sceptical towards the Bamako Initiative. I was afraid the poorest would be excluded. I gradually became more positive, even if the access of the poor remains a challenge. In the rural areas in West and Central Africa, poverty is extremely widespread. Often half of the population or more is poor. Without well-functioning health centres, few or none have access to heath services. When the centres are revitalized, many poor people get access, often more than before, but not necessarily all and not necessarily the poorest, even if they often have great needs. In Benin, some years ago a survey showed that the poorest used preventive health services as much as others. But the user fees excluded 5–10 per cent from treatment on a permanent basis and 30–40 per cent temporarily. Imagination and political will are needed to reach the poorest. The health centres often level out prices, so everybody can benefit from preventive measures. In addition, the poorest are treated free of charge or at a reduced price, according to an approximate assessment. But who shall be included? The poor are hit if too few are exempted. The revenues of the health centre suffer if too many are. Quality and sustainability have to be balanced against equity and access. In several countries, efforts were being made by the end of the century to develop different forms of health insurance or risk-sharing to obtain an equalization of costs.

Laborious Participation

The Bamako Initiative is actually a top-down arrangement. The authorities try to reduce morbidity and mortality by ensuring people's access to health services. But the initiative is based on active participation by the local communities. Before a health centre is revitalized, a general meeting is usually organized to discuss the promotion of health and elect a health management committee. In some places, the population is easy to mobilize. In other places, where there is no tradition for this kind of organization, there is more resistance. In any case, it is a challenge both for the health staff and the committee not only to acquire the necessary technical skills to operate the centres, but also to be accountable to the population, in recognition of their right to health and dignity. A genuine dialogue between service providers and consumers is rare. The population is seldom invited to present proposals for the promotion of health for all. If the health services had been organized from the bottom up, it would have been easier to mobilize the population – but then the services probably had been different also.

In communities where the majority of the population is illiterate, the health committee and staff can exert great influence. Effective control on the part of the community may be weak. Where most people are poor and corruption widespread, a strict management of financial resources presents a special challenge. Effective monitoring by the authorities is required.

The traditional division of labour, with men as the heads of the household, results in health committees usually being made up of men. This issue was first raised seriously after I came to the region and started a systematic monitoring of women's issues. It is not easy to find arrangements permitting women to participate in health activities in a constructive manner. In some places, they have elected one or more women to the health committee or established a special women's group. But women have little influence in areas where they have lower status than men, and according to tradition are supposed to keep silent in male-dominated gatherings. The most promising efforts are taking place where the local leaders have been persuaded to hand over the tasks of the health committee to a women's cooperative. This has not happened in many places. Where it has been done, the management of both funds and drugs has worked very well. Health staff have received assistance. Contact with the population has improved and more women have visited the centre.

Different Worlds Meet

Many people utilize the revitalized health centres. But not everybody. Towards the end of the century, the health centre coverage in Benin and Guinea was 80 per cent or more. But only about one-third of the population actually utilized the services. There are multiple reasons for this. People do not always need them. It is difficult to get away from home.

The distance is long. People are dissatisfied with the services or have problems paying the fees. They might also prefer other solutions, such as drug vendors on the market, traditional healers or others.

'We are not received with understanding and respect,' some women complain when asked what they think of the health centres. There exists a real cultural gap between modern Western health services on the one hand, and established African views of life on the other. Modern medicine breaks with traditional approaches to illness and health. Traditional healing has also been discounted by the medical science of our time. WHO started not long ago to work systematically with African medical herbs and drugs. In West and Central Africa, as far as I know, only Mali has included traditional medicines on the list of drugs. At the same time, the health centres generally carry out few information activities related to health and nutrition.

When a traditional healer receives a customer, it usually happens in an

---

Box 6.1 Traditional Healing

A year passed, and no child came. Efuru did not despair. 'I am still young, surely God cannot deny me the joy of motherhood.'

Efuru was very worried in the second year of her marriage.

She did not sleep one night. Early in the morning before the cock crew she got up, dressed and went to her father. She opened her heart to her father. 'Something must be done, my daughter. It is not in our blood. Our women are productive. There must be a reason for this. We shall see a *dibia* [traditional medicine man].'

Efuru and her old father went to see a *dibia*. He was a very old and dirty man. He was almost blind and was unable to walk.

A mat was spread on a mud-bench in the room and the two visitors sat down. Some *kola* was brought in a saucer.

When they finished the *kola*, the *dibia* cleared his throat. 'I am sorry about your daughter, Nwashike, but you have come in good time. Your daughter is not barren. She will have a baby next year if she will only do what I am going to ask her to do. Again she has not many children in her womb. Some women are like that. It is not their fault. It is not God's fault either.'

Father and daughter were astonished.

'How did you know the object of our visit?' Efuru ventured to ask. The old man laughed.

'You are children. You cannot understand. You will not understand. Nwashike, this is what your daughter will do every Afo day.

ordinary hut. He or she takes time to chat, sometimes going far back in the life history of the patient, and relates to the person as a whole. The health centres are in modern concrete buildings. There are often many patients. The health worker cannot spend too much time on each. Attention is focused on the symptoms and their treatment. In many places, confidentiality is not properly respected. In Africa, as in the West, the medical profession is dominated by men. The health centres frequently have a male health worker and a female midwife. It is particularly delicate for male health workers to deal with female patients. The health worker may have higher status. And in societies that are clearly segregated according to gender, there are often strong norms related to the female body. Some health workers are sympathetic and discreet. Others may be 'professional' and quite arrogant in relation to 'ignorant' women. The cultural gap is all the more noticeable when health workers come in from the outside and have little knowledge of the local culture and language.

She is to sacrifice to the ancestors. It is not much, but she will have to do it regularly. Every Afo day, she is to buy *uziza*, alligator pepper, and *kola* from the market. Uziza must be bought every Nkwo day from a pregnant woman. Every Afo day before the sun goes down or when the sun is here,' and he pointed to the direction, 'she should put these things in a small calabash and go down to the lake; there she will leave the calabash to float away. So, go home young woman and be cheerful. Next year during the Owu festival if nothing happens to you, come back to me. Go in peace.'

Efuru was happy because she had so much faith in what the *dibia* had told her, and did not worry so much about her state. But her mother-in-law was still worried.

About three months passed after Efuru's visit to the *dibia*, and nothing happened. She started to despair again.

The Owu-festival at last ... and on Afo day Efuru did not see her period. She told her mother-in-law, who began to dance. 'God heard me. God has heard me. My daughter, you are pregnant.'

Efuru did all that the *dibia* had told her. Every Afo day, she bought the things she was told to buy and did as she was told.

One night she felt some pains ... and in about half an hour she delivered her baby – a baby girl.

(Extract from *Efuru* by the Nigerian writer Flora Nwapa, 1966. Reprinted by permission of Heinemann, part of Harcourt Education Ltd.)

When in exceptional circumstances female health workers are recruited, the quality of services frequently improves and more women come to the centres. The recruitment and training of health staff are therefore main challenges in the further development of the health services.

Building One Stone upon the Other

I became deeply involved in the Bamako Initiative. It aims at ensuring people's right to health under difficult circumstances, and does so in a way that encourages popular participation. The implementation of such a system is neither rapid nor easy. My predecessor as regional director – a very knowledgeable and experienced man from Benin – supported the initiative warmly, because it implied a democratization of the health services. At the same time, he admitted that the greatest weakness in the implementation was the limited involvement of the population. Seven years later, I agree with him. It is a major challenge to increase the involvement of the communities, particularly the women, in the health services. If this succeeds, the Bamako Initiative may turn out to be the best health system and not just the second best.

No progress in a region like West and Central Africa can be taken for granted. Continual efforts are needed to maintain and improve the quality of services in the revitalized health centres. At the same time, thousands of centres remain to be revitalized – in addition to all the communities where there has never been a centre. The Democratic Republic of Congo and Nigeria present special challenges, due to the size of the countries and their problems of governance. Much remains to be done before primary health care services can ensure health for all in the region. Unfortunately, there are no short cuts. One must always be prepared for setbacks. But it is possible to make progress and to create a sustainable system, if stone is laid upon stone, slowly but surely, without allowing oneself to be distracted by isolated, short-term activities. The Bamako Initiative has made many people do just that.

SEVEN

Motherhood and Martyrdom: Breaking Centuries of Silence and Neglect

Pregnancy is a gamble and giving birth is a life-and-death struggle. (Proverb from the Bambara people)

I was circumcised when I was 11 or 12 years old. They gave me presents and flowers. It was fine until the old woman came with the razor blade. Four women held me. I don't remember much of what happened. The pain was unbearable. There was no anaesthetic. Afterwards, they tied my legs together to make the wound heal. But it kept on bleeding and bleeding. If my mother's sister and her husband had not showed up and got me to a doctor, I would have bled to death.

Aminata is talking with a low, monotonous voice – as if all this really doesn't concern her, in spite of the dramatic and personal content of her story. But the theme is not something ordinarily talked about. We are driving together. I am visiting a project in Burkina Faso, and she has come from the ministry for women's affairs to guide me. She is an experienced woman in her mid-30s, who has gone to school and been trained as a health worker. Now she is working with a women's project in the capital of Burkina, Ouagadougou. We have just talked about circumcision or female genital cutting (also called female genital mutilation, FGM) with a group of women from one of the town districts. Aminata doesn't look at me, but just keeps on driving, silently, for quite some time. Then she continues:

Having seen what happened to me, my mother decided never again. So she refused to let my sister be circumcised. My father's mother was furious. It meant breaking away from tradition. No man would marry a woman who wasn't circumcised. Often it is the father's mother who takes the decisions relating to circumcision and the like. But now my father supported my mother, so my grandmother had to give in. Father's brother also wanted my sister to be circumcised. We are a royal family, and some of the sacred rituals can only be performed by women who have been cut. But there are others who can do this. Personally, I started to combat circumcision during my training as a health worker. Then I learned that the girls risk not only bleeding to death, but getting infections and shock. They may become sterile, have problems with menstruation and urination and experience difficulties in connection with sexual intercourse and delivery.

Seven Women

The aim of the women's project in Ouagadougou is to improve living conditions of the families in one of the town districts. The World Bank finances infrastructure for water and drainage, while UNICEF helps mobilize the women to achieve better hygiene and health standards. Women playing an active role in the local community were selected – seven to begin with. They were trained, and then sent home to organize other women in the neighbourhood, spread information and promote new behaviour patterns.

I met the seven women in 1995. They were extremely proud of what they had learnt in a couple of weeks and held forth about the progress they had made. We didn't know each other before, they said. Now we meet regularly. Everybody sweeps their yard, which we didn't do earlier, and we make sure the drinking water is clean. Even small children use the latrines. We didn't know that the faeces of children could be dangerous, but now we have learned that they can carry infection. Before, we thought the neonatal milk was harmful for the child. Now we know this is wrong and have started to breastfeed immediately after delivery. We have also understood that children must wash their hands before they eat. We take the kids to the health centre for immunization, and we go when they are ill. We didn't dare do this before.

The women had made up a song about health and hygiene. They form a circle, clap their hands and sing: 'ORT – clap, clap, clap, ORT – clap, clap, clap, against diarrhoea – clap, clap, clap!' ORT means oral rehydration therapy, or the use of a solution of sugar and salt to prevent the children from becoming dehydrated during diarrhoea. The rhythm is catchy and the message clear.

One day the women started discussing female genital cutting. Some said the practice represented a health hazard. Was it really necessary? The women went to the imam (Muslim religious leader) to find out. He confirmed that the Qur'an says nothing about cutting. In the village, the elders underlined that women wanted the operation. Then, the women took action, got the equipment used for cutting, presented the secret rituals publicly, danced and sang. Thus, they performed a ceremonial burial of both the equipment and the cutting. Afterwards, they hoped the practice would end!

Two years later, I met the women again and wondered how things were going. The network of seven had now expanded to 121. In addition to nutrition, hygiene and immunization, the groups discussed sexually transmitted diseases, family planning, the upbringing of children, juvenile delinquency, prostitution and drug abuse. What about genital cutting? I wanted to know. Few talked about it after the burial, the women say. They think it has stopped. A man wanted to send his wife away because she was not cut, but the women persuaded him to keep her.

Two of the old women who did the cutting are members of the network. One is present, a small wizened woman with a shy smile. She explains that she thought a child would die if it touched the clitoris, and that the operation was necessary for girls to become proper women. Now, she realizes that this is not so. She lost her means of livelihood, though, and has learnt to weave to earn money. Unfortunately, the price of thread is going up all the time, so it is hard to cope. According to traditional belief, the women who do the cutting go blind when they grow old, and the other woman is, in fact, blind. She lives in a little hut where she sits on the floor amidst a lot of mess and disorder. She seems quite lost, but is all smiles when she understands she has a visitor. The women's network makes sure somebody passes by every day to give her food. A granddaughter takes her out at times.

Abandoning Genital Cutting

Female genital cutting has roots far back in history and cannot be related to any religion, be it Christianity, Islam or traditional religions. The custom has been practised in many places in the world: the Amazon, the Middle East, the Pacific Islands and Australia. Today, it exists to a certain extent in Asia, but above all in Africa. Here it is observed in 28 countries, from Senegal in the west to Somalia in the east, affecting from 5 to 99 per cent of the female population. The practice is customary in some ethnic groups, but not in others. It is estimated that around two million girls are subjected to the operation every year, some as infants, others in connection with puberty or the first pregnancy. In total, more than 130 million African women are living with the consequences of the cutting.

When the feminist movement in Western countries became more dynamic in the 1970s, female genital cutting was brought into the open. The veil of secrecy was broken, and the custom condemned as barbaric and oppressive. Many Africans (mostly men, but also some women) reacted strongly against this, not only because they found the statements indecent, but because they could not accept such 'Western cultural imperialism'. The situation was delicate. We were dealing with an ancient, deep-rooted tradition ingrained in African culture. Shouldn't this be respected? At the same time, the practice was a violation of universally accepted human rights, above all the right to health and personal integrity. The issue was raised in the big international conferences on women, human rights and population that were held during the 1980s and 1990s. During the discussions, the Western feminists acquired more respect for African culture, while Africans came to appreciate better the Western reactions. In the first round, a compromise was found by condemning 'all practices harming the health of women and children'. By focusing on the general health aspects of circumcision, the cultural context was toned down and the matter could more easily be followed up. The World Health Organization (WHO) organized technical seminars on measures to improve women's health, and gradually the message got through. Later, a human rights perspective was introduced and circumcision was considered to be one of the various forms of violence against women.

African women themselves started to promote the abolition of female genital cutting, first individually, in a rather haphazard way, then in a more organized manner with the support of UNICEF and the UN Population Fund (UNFPA), in addition to WHO and bilateral donors. Regional and national voluntary organizations were created against 'harmful traditional practices', and information campaigns were launched against female genital cutting. It took time, but little by little the women were heard. Politicians and authorities condemned circumcision publicly. National committees were created of health professionals, women and religious leaders. A regional symposium of religious leaders confirmed that circumcision is not based on any of the Holy Scriptures, and the Organization for African Unity (OAU) adopted a declaration about violence against women. By 2002, twelve countries had taken legal action against cutting, but there was often little action to stop the custom in practice.

In Burkina Faso, 70 per cent of women are circumcised. Women started to combat the practice in the 1970s. Fifteen years later, a public committee was appointed, and in 1996 the operation was prohibited by law. Lawyers and police are involved in extensive information campaigns. A crisis telephone line is established: 'SOS circumcision'. People can call and ask for help from the police or a doctor. Several people performing the operation, have been brought to court and sentenced.

A 'Miracle'

Traditional customs will not change if only the urban elites are active against them. Ordinary people in rural areas must also start reflecting on their practices. This is happening in some places. In addition to the women's network in Burkina Faso, women's groups have taken action against cutting in Senegal, among other places. About 20 per cent of Senegalese women are cut, and the practice exists in several ethnic groups, including Bambara. In 1996, in the village of Malicounda Bambara, 45 miles from Dakar and with around 3,000 inhabitants, 40 women participated in a basic education project called Tostan ('Breakthrough') in 1996, supported by UNICEF among others. They learned about human rights and the negative health consequences of cutting. During the programme, the women decided to stop cutting the girls in the village. They managed to convince their husbands, the village chief and the imam to support the decision and it was made public in July 1997. The media and authorities were informed, and immediately came to the village to learn how such a 'miracle' could take place in a very traditional culture, where circumcision was an established practice. The women explained that they started to share their experiences with cutting during the education project. They realized what pain, suffering and ill health the tradition entails. At the same time, the president of the republic condemned circumcision publicly, underlining the emphasis that religion places on women's physical and mental health. So there was only one thing to do: stop the cutting.

Women from other Tostan classes went further. They set up a travel-

---

Box 7.1 You Gave Birth

You, who gave birth to a boy,
You, who gave birth to a girl,
You are wearing the birthbraid,[1]
The dance of joy is yours.
Haayo[2] victory is here,
Haayo we have won.

1. Ceremonial braid that women make after every birth   2. Expression of joy

(Lullaby from the Soninké people in Mali, Mauritania and Senegal, translated from French by Torild Skard. From Aliou Kissima Tandia: *Poésie orale soninké et éducation traditionelle*, 1999)

ling theatre show dealing with human rights and the risks involved in circumcision, and contacted women in other Bambara villages. After intensive discussions, 50 representatives of 13 villages met in February 1998 to discuss the issue. They decided to stop circumcision and to make the decision public. Gradually, more villages followed. By the end of 2002, the number had passed 708. In addition, the authorities passed a law against female circumcision, and a national plan of action was adopted to abolish the practice by the year 2005.

Such events are encouraging. The mechanism is interesting. It is extremely difficult for an individual family to stop cutting, because this is required for a respectable marriage, according to the social norms. Women who are not cut risk being excluded from a proper marriage. But when the community as a *whole* agrees to abolish the practice and commits itself publicly, then everybody can stop at the same time. The decision must include all the groups that intermarry.

Another question is *how* to stop. In some communities in West and Central Africa the operation is done without special ceremonies. In others, it is part of initiation rituals that mark the transition from child to adult. Even if cutting is abolished, the rituals should not necessarily be discontinued. Often they have important functions, such as transferring knowledge from one generation to the next and creating a special room for women's culture and mutual assistance without interference from men.

The abolition of female circumcision in West and Central Africa is still far away. One only had to go to the neighbouring country of Senegal, the Gambia, and hear the president declare in 1999 that he would not ban FGM, that it was part of African culture. Campaigners against the practice were being called 'enemies of Islam'.

Invisible Hardship

In some Asian countries baby girls may be killed simply because they are female. I have never heard about such a practice in sub-Saharan Africa. It may happen that newborn infants are killed. But this is because they are deformed, or people believe they are bewitched, not because of their gender. In general, we know little about the reception infants usually get. There is reason to believe that they generally are given a warm welcome. They represent a new generation and a valuable labour force. Many infants are, however, weak when they are born, as a result of the widespread poverty or unsatisfactory care. Infant mortality is high. But it is not particularly high for girls. On the contrary. It is usually higher for boys, as is the case in most regions.

Social and cultural factors influence the care of children, and African girls are generally considered to be socially inferior in relation to boys. Some claim that boys get better food and care than girls, but existing statistics do not reflect this. We therefore have no basis to state that girls generally suffer more than boys in early childhood. But from the age of five or six years African girls face special problems. They have to help their mothers cook, clean, fetch water, care for younger siblings, and assist with farming tasks and generation of income. Often the workload is very heavy, much heavier than that of boys. A great amount of time and energy is required, but the food the girls get rarely has sufficient nutritional value.

Box 7.2 The Joys of Motherhood

The people of Ibuza were never to forget the night the people of Umu-Iso came for Nnu Ego. Her father excelled himself. He sent his daughter away with seven hefty men and seven young girls carrying her personal possessions. There were seven goats, baskets and baskets of yams, yards and yards of white man's cloth, twenty-four home-spun lappas, rows and rows of Hausa trinkets and coral beads. It was indeed a night of wealth display.

Nnu Ego and her new husband Amatokwu were very happy: yet Nnu Ego was surprised that, as the months passed, she was failing everybody. There was no child.

'What am I going to do, Amatokwu?' she cried to her husband, after the disappointment of another month.

After a while, Nnu Ego could not voice her doubts and worries to her husband any more. It had become her problem and hers alone. She went from one *dibia* (traditional healer) to another in secret.

She was not surprised when Amatokwu told her casually one evening that she would have to move to a nearby hut kept for older wives, because his people had found him a new wife.

'I cannot fail my people … I am a busy man. I have no time to waste my precious male seed on a woman who is infertile. I have to raise children for my line.'

Amatokwu's new wife became pregnant the very first month.

On the eve of the day Amatokwu's second wife was giving birth, the pain hit Nnu Ego with such force that she could stand it no longer.

Her father was summoned, and he took his daughter home.

(Extract from *The Joys of Motherhood* by the Nigerian writer Buchi Emecheta, 1979)

About half of African girls are married before the age of 18. In several countries, many girls are married as young as 10–14 years old. The prevailing view is that the value of a woman is demonstrated first of all by her fertility. Childlessness is considered a catastrophe, and family planning is widely resisted. African women have the lowest use of modern contraceptives in the world. As a result, the continent has the highest birthrate in general and of teenage pregnancies in particular. On average, every woman gives birth to five or six children. More than half give birth in their teens. The young girls are often physically immature and ignorant about their bodies and health. Many are overworked and undernourished. When they are forced into sexual relations and procreation before they are ready, the consequences are often tragic. Complications in connection with pregnancy and delivery are the most important causes of death for girls of 15 to 19 years. The children they give birth to are often weak and vulnerable.

The hardships of African girl children were 'invisible' for a long time in the public debate. It was a challenge for UNICEF to draw attention to the girl child and support measures to improve her situation. During the African preparations for the Women's Conference in Beijing in 1995, we contributed to giving emphasis to the girl child. The African women requested the elimination of negative cultural attitudes and practices against women and girls, and the end of discrimination in the areas of education and training, health and nutrition. They stated that the capacities and esteem of girls must be enhanced, and they must be sensitized about social and economic issues. A special chapter on the girl child was included in the international Platform for Action. But afterwards, implementation was weak and intermittent in West and Central Africa, despite the efforts of women's groups and organizations. The demand for basic education for girls had the greatest impact, and positive measures were carried out in a number of countries.

World Record in Maternal Deaths

West and Central Africa has the highest rate of maternal mortality in the world. One woman in 13 dies as a consequence of pregnancy or childbirth. Some die of unsafe abortions. For every 100 live births, one mother dies. The risk of a woman dying of pregnancy-related causes is many times higher in sub-Saharan Africa than in industrialized countries, where the ratio is one in every 4,100. In no health area is the discrepancy between poor and rich countries so great.

Maternal death is only the tip of the iceberg. For every woman who dies, between 30 and 100 suffer from serious injuries that are often painful and long-lasting. A problem which is little known, but very traumatic, is vesico-vaginal fistula or VVF. It is estimated that there are more than two million VVF victims worldwide, with a considerable proportion in sub-Saharan Africa. It mostly hits young, poor women with a small pelvis, or women who have been genitally cut, so that labour during childbirth becomes obstructed. An opening might be created between the vagina and the rectum or the bladder, so that the faeces or urine go straight out through the vagina. The result is tragic. The women become soiled and smell bad. Infections are frequent. Many become social outcasts, rejected by husbands and families and expelled from the local community. They have to manage as best they can on their own, and usually live in great misery.

At the hospital in Niamey, the capital of Niger, a voluntary organization has established a centre for VVF sufferers, with the support of UNICEF and other donors. It is only a single room, where the women sleep on the floor. They eat a porridge that they cook outdoors over an open fire. Fifty women can receive help here for nine months. Some are treated. The operation to close a fistula is supposed to be simple, but often it fails because the women come too late. So they get rubber panties designed to improve their hygiene, and they receive counselling to repair their damaged self-image. They learn to sew and embroider, in order to make a living. The women organize themselves to be able to provide mutual assistance and support. Unfortunately, such help is remote for most poor women in Africa today.

When a woman dies, or is permanently disabled by childbirth, this not only brings human suffering, but is also a loss for social and economic development. The women perform important tasks, are responsible for the welfare of their families and contribute to the life of the community. Children suffer the most. When the mother dies, the chances increase that the newborn infant also will die within a short period. Complications during delivery can also lead to permanent physical or mental disabilities among those children who survive.

Shall Birth Mean Death?

In spite of the central role of women, maternal mortality attracted little attention for many years. It 'only' concerns women, and in many cultures pregnancy and birth are not a theme for public discussion. Many consider the death of a woman during childbirth practically as a natural event – something unavoidable. Gradually, pregnant and childbearing women have been brought more into focus. In 1987, WHO, the World Bank, UNFPA, the UN Development Programme and UNICEF launched a global initiative for 'safe motherhood', together with voluntary organizations and bilateral donors. The objective was to halve maternal mortality by the year 2000. At the International Population Conference in Cairo in 1994 and the Women's Conference in Beijing in 1995, reproductive health was an important item. It was stated that maternal deaths are morally unacceptable, and it was noted that they can be prevented by surprisingly simple means. The overwhelming majority of maternal deaths, half of infant deaths and the painful and often permanent disabilities that millions of women suffer from in poor countries, can be prevented by well-targeted interventions at an annual cost of about US$3 per person. It sounds reasonable. But this does not mean that these are easy to implement in a region like West and Central Africa. Women have to have access to basic health services that include family planning and prenatal consultations. They must get satisfactory nutrition before and after birth, and qualified assistance during delivery. Finally, they must have access to emergency obstetric care in case of complications.

Controversial Measures

Despite increasing attention to maternal mortality, few countries in West and Central Africa elaborated national programmes to tackle the causes of maternal deaths during the 1990s. In collaboration with WHO and UNFPA, we in UNICEF tried to create interest and encourage involvement. But it was not easy to make women a priority or to obtain financing. African authorities, as well as bilateral donors, had a tendency to think that other groups were more important. The misery of mothers was too 'special' and birth-related complications too 'complex'. Some measures were also controversial.

Family planning has been a delicate matter for UNICEF. Many member states, including the Nordic countries, have been of the opinion that the UN Children's Fund should actively promote family planning. Others have seen it as paradoxical that an organization for children should support birth control. The Vatican has exerted pressure to prevent UNICEF from involving itself in family planning and abortion. UNICEF's solution was 'family spacing'. The organization promotes safe motherhood, and births that are too early, too close, too many or too late threaten the health of both women and children. Family planning thus becomes an important part of mother/child care, which UNICEF supports. But the organization does not take a stand on different methods of family planning and does not support abortion. Nor does UNICEF purchase contraceptives. This is the task of UNFPA, to the extent that the organization has funds at its disposal. But the USA withheld its contribution for several years. On the other hand, the US Agency for International Development (USAID) distributed condoms in many countries.

One of the most important measures for reducing maternal and infant mortality is to ensure the presence of a professionally skilled person during delivery. But in West and Central Africa, only a traditional birth attendant or a member of the family attends at least half of all deliveries. The traditional birth attendants have created considerable controversy. They are usually elderly women from the community who assist on the basis of traditional knowledge and medicines. Many who are responsible for health think they should not be utilized, because they are not familiar with modern medical methods. Nor does additional training necessarily reduce the risk of maternal deaths. But the attendants know the local community, and the women giving birth, usually have confidence in them. As it has turned out to be impossible to provide sufficient numbers of health personnel with a modern education, the training of traditional birth attendants has nevertheless been organized. The objective is limited. The birth attendants are prepared to deal with normal labour and deliveries, to realize when something is going wrong, to perform necessary emergency measures and to assist during transfer to a district hospital. The expectant mothers are given simple birth equipment so that they can contribute to preventing infections.

To save lives, a well-functioning district hospital must exist within a reasonable distance, and have a qualified medical doctor, delivery room, equipment and drugs, so that effective emergency care can be provided, including, if necessary, blood transfusion and a Caesarean operation. This implies that the health services at district level in many countries have to be revitalized. By the end of the century, only a few were taking seriously the challenge of birth complications. Analysis of the situation in Mali revealed that the technical competence of the district health personnel was essential. But the main bottlenecks were related to the organization of work of the health teams at local and district level, the means of communication and transport between the two levels, and the possibilities of financing an evacuation or an emergency intervention. The problems have to be solved in collaboration with the local population. Malian communities tried setting up radio communication systems, so that health centres could call the district hospital. An ambulance was available and gas was stored in case of need. Different kinds of cost-sharing, solidarity funds and mutual benefit societies were introduced to help poor families pay for the services. In the course of a few years, the number of emergency evacuations and Caesarean operations increased several times, particularly from distant villages. In Benin, a 'bush ambulance' has been created, consisting of an adapted motorbike with a piece of wax cloth stretched behind the driving seat, to be able to bring childbearing women to the hospital.

Mother-friendly Societies?

The low social status of many girls and women in West and Central Africa is an essential factor affecting maternal mortality. Women often have poor education and limited access to modern knowledge in the areas of health, hygiene and nutrition. They are economically active, but often have little money for their own needs or for help in an emergency situation. They have little freedom to make choices related to sexuality, and difficulties gaining access to family planning and health care. The result is repeated pregnancies, with all the risks these entail. Further, for social or economic reasons, women are often denied help when they need it. Work overload and poor nutrition contribute to birth complications.

Specific measures aimed at reducing maternal mortality must be considered in relation to more general efforts to strengthen the social and economic status of women. Like other UN organizations, UNICEF also elaborated a strategy for women in development, and studies and training were carried out during the 1980s and 1990s. Many in UNICEF thought the issue was straightforward, because women and children are the main target groups of the organization. But the insight into the situation of women and children was often limited, and women were perceived mostly in their role as mothers, not as citizens in their own right.

When I arrived in UNICEF in West and Central Africa, the staff had not reflected much on the gender aspects of the organization's work. They developed mother/child care, but did not emphasize the involvement of women in the elaboration of the health services. They supported basic education for girls, but did not realize how much the course content and working methods of the school had to be changed to be able to achieve the goals. Gradually, UNICEF became an active partner in many countries, mobilizing political will and support not only for the rights of the child, but also for the rights of women. UNICEF assisted women's groups and supported legal assistance, training and income-generating activities for women.

At the end of the 1990s, a movement was launched for 'Mother-friendly Societies'. The objective was to promote legal reform to strengthen the status of women and children, establish mother-friendly services and encourage a positive approach to safe motherhood. Particular efforts will be made to mobilize local communities with the involvement of husbands, mothers-in-law, families and neighbours in order to ensure the life and health of women.

EIGHT

Searching for the Excluded from School: Experiments with New Forms of Education, Particularly for Girls

Knowledge is better than riches.
(Proverb from Cameroon)

'No, I want my daughter out of school! Immediately! Her mother needs help with the household chores. Besides, girls who go to school become stubborn and spoiled!' It's a very angry outburst, but people laugh. We are in a village near Thiès in Senegal. Everybody is assembled under the palaver tree to watch the youth group. They are attending a basic education programme, and are now going to show what they have learnt. The focus is on the Convention on the Rights of the Child, and the facilitator – a woman in her thirties – has put up a drawing of a girl who is fetching water and firewood, carrying a younger sister or brother, sweeping in front of the hut and giving her father a sleeping mat. She explains that children have the right to education and not to be overworked. She speaks in the local language, but I have an interpreter. Now some of the young children act a sketch. It is a family scene. A small boy of 12 or 13 is the father, dressed in a *boubou* that is too big, with a skullcap on his head. He goes back and forth waving his arms, yelling in the deepest voice he can muster: 'I cannot accept any more schooling for my daughter!'

Laughter again. The young boy plays with such impressive commitment. But the young actor is not distracted: 'When my daughter spends all her time in school, I have to drink water from dirty calabashes!' The audience roars. The boy's remarks are pertinent indeed. A teenage girl plays the role of the mother. Sitting on the ground with a scarf around her head, she looks humbly down. Beside her is another girl, who is probably the daughter. The mother ventures a meek protest. 'My husband,' she implores, 'Mareem is my only daughter. I will work harder so the calabashes are clean. If you permit, I will sell the goat my uncle gave me, to pay for books and writing materials.'

The father doesn't listen. 'Worst of all, the girl will get her head full of ideas and be impossible to marry off! She doesn't learn how to be a good wife and mother at school.' The daughter can stand it no longer: 'But, father, I am one of the best in my class!' The mother explains: 'Mareem will be a much better wife if she knows how to write and count.' The father explodes in fury: 'Do you dare to contradict me? Have you forgotten that men decide, while women obey? I will show you!' And he lifts his arm, threateningly – but both rapidly pick up their skirts and disappear.

People are thrilled, clap and laugh. Some men support the father: that's a real man! The womenfolk must not get the upper hand! The facilitator turns to the youth group. 'What do you say?' A forest of hands from both boys and girls. 'Beating is not allowed.' 'Mareem can make money if she knows how to count.' 'If a woman can read and write, she is able to understand letters and fill out forms.' 'If they get an improved stove, Mareem can go to school instead of fetching firewood.'

A man in the audience breaks in: 'I can tell you. It's very costly to send a girl to school – and what do you get for it? At the end of the day, somebody comes and snatches her away.' Another man adds: 'And we can't even raise the bride-price, because she is educated.' All of a sudden everybody is talking. Support, protests. Everybody has a point of view. But one sentence penetrates the commotion. A frail but determined female voice repeating over and over: '*My* daughter shall at least be able to learn, so she can manage better than *I* have done!'

When the noise subsides, the facilitator points at the table. Several written texts are displayed, and a girl picks one, which she reads aloud: 'CHILDREN HAVE THE RIGHT TO EDUCATION'. A boy selects another: 'CHILDREN HAVE THE RIGHT NOT TO WORK TOO MUCH'. Both texts are put up on the palaver tree. Finally, a young girl comes forth and reads a poem written by a group of girls. It is about a girl who has to work all the time and has no time to play. The poem ends like this:

> Why do I have to do all this work?
> Because I am a girl.
> I work from morning until evening,
> And at night, when I finally fall asleep,
> I think and think and think about my life.
> My heart is so full and
> I start to cry,
> Because I do not know
> When all this suffering will end.

It is so quiet you can hear a pin drop. Some adults seem embarrassed.

Others are evidently proud. They clap and cheer. What a clever youth group! They have never been to school, and in a couple of months they have acquired all this knowledge!

Street of Knowledge

The youth group participates in the Tostan programme. Tostan means 'breakthrough' in the local language. It is a basic education programme teaching people not only literacy and numeracy, but also ways to improve their daily lives. The programme is based on African culture and tradition and explores new methods of achieving literacy. Only one-quarter of the women and one-half of the men in Senegal know how to read and write. Sixty to 65 per cent of the children go to school. New initiatives are needed to reach the objective of basic education for all. Tostan is one such initiative. A key person in the programme is an American woman, Molly Melching. She came to the country in 1974 to complete a master's degree in African literature and never left. She studied oral traditions, learned the local language (Wolof) and worked with underprivileged children.

The Tostan programme started in 1988. Through experiments with people in the villages a course of 18 months to two years was developed, with three two-hour sessions a week. Since women are the most important caregivers in the Senegalese family, as well as being the least educated group in the society, the programme focused on them. Each class consists of a maximum of 30 students, and sessions are organized according to the available time. The programme is developed with support from UNICEF, the UN Educational, Scientific and Cultural Organization (UNESCO), and the Canadian and the Netherlands governments. During the first eight years, the programme reached a total of 20,000 adults in four regions in Senegal. Courses were also developed for children and youth.

Tostan is the most radical school experiment I have seen in West and Central Africa. It has not only changed the organization and content of teaching, but its whole methodology. In Senegal, they say the methods are 'new', but they were familiar to me. They reminded me of the progressive education launched in the USA in the 1930s under the slogan, 'learning by doing'. Instead of the teachers presenting knowledge for pupils to memorize, they ask questions and learn while searching for the answers. It is a fascinating and effective way of learning. I experienced it myself as a child in school in Washington DC, and studied it later in teachers' college in Oslo.

The Tostan programme is based on everyday experiences of the participants. They analyse situations and find solutions to problems. The slogan is: 'You never teach people anything; they learn because they want to learn.' Learning to read, write and do maths comes little by little as part of the process. Instead of memorizing letters, the participants start by writing their own texts with the help of a facilitator, and then read them. Ordinary teachers are not used, but facilitators from the villages who get special training. More than half are women. Through dialogue and conversation, they stimulate and guide the participants. Within four to five months, most of the women can read and write simple texts. They are encouraged to create a literate environment in the villages, using signs to identify trees, houses and alleys, like the 'The tree of life', 'Street of knowledge', 'Medicine hut' etc.

The programme has been evaluated twice. In both cases, it was noted that the participants were very motivated, and the training led to significant changes not only in the lives of the women, but in the whole local community. The women became more self-confident, dared to express their views, took initiatives and improved their daily lives. Besides learning how

---

Box 8.1 Joal

At the first call of prayer
I climb over my husband
And go straight to the sea
Greeting the morning dew and wind.
Keccax, yeet and tambaje[1]
Have liberated me,
Have transformed my world...
Their putrid odour is now for me
The smell of life.
I no longer need to wait for a man
To give me money.
I am independent
And can take care of my family.
When I finish my work on the beach
I go to this shed
Which once was used to store dried fish
And today has become our temple of knowledge,
Our school
Symbolizing the rebirth
Of our national languages.

The children are sucking
My breasts and my sweat.

to read, write and do maths in their mother tongue, they acquired insight in health and hygiene, individual and group finances, the environment and project management. They established health committees, introduced improved stoves, planted trees and obtained mills to grind millet. In some cases, they decided to abandon female cutting in the villages.

A critical issue is the financing. Developing the Tostan methodology has been relatively costly, including guides for the facilitators, textbooks and other material. Testing the courses also requires funds. Without UNICEF support, it would not have been possible to develop the Tostan approach. The government was critical at times, because of the programme's high cost and independent management. Those responsible for administering it have underlined that a good and sustainable educational programme requires a certain amount of time and effort, especially to begin with, but that then the costs drop. Once they are up and running, the Tostan courses are cheaper to implement than other courses. Nevertheless, in 2002 the

---

The school waters my mind
And becomes a mother
From whom I suck knowledge
Until I am drunk.

I am here in my ngemb[2]
Wrestling with our era
Which pins me down, yes,
But which I am sometimes able to pin down too.
Yet I know for certain that now
When I meet my husband's gaze
I will no longer lower my eyes.
If I have a problem
I can solve it myself
And don't need to wait for his judgement.
And so at this first call to prayer
I go to the sea
To breathe in my myrrh and my incense...
Keccax, yeet and tambaje.

1. Joal is a place in Senegal where women dry and sell different kinds of fish called keccax, yeet and tambaje to make money. 2. Ngemb are the loincloths worn by traditional wrestlers.

(Written by a female participant in Tostan literacy courses in Senegal. Translated by UNICEF)

programme still depended on considerable external funds. Transfer of the Tostan methodology to other voluntary organizations initially created some difficulties. But little by little, more than 20 voluntary organizations have included the Tostan modules, in their original or adjusted form, in their programmes for rural development both in Senegal and other countries.

Education for All

Tostan is one of many initiatives in West and Central Africa aimed at achieving the objective of the 1990 Jomtien Conference in Thailand, called Education for All. The conference was organized by the World Bank, UNESCO, the UN Development Programme and UNICEF. In spite of global efforts, the number of illiterate adults and children without access to schooling was on the increase, particularly among girls and women. It was necessary to focus on basic education and to renew the commitment of governments and decision-makers.

West and Central Africa is one of the regions causing the most serious concerns. Following independence, considerable efforts were made in the area of education. But the population growth was so rapid that it was hard to keep up. When the economic crisis developed in the 1980s, things became really difficult. Expansion of the educational system stagnated. It was hard to maintain the quality of schooling. The number of children without access to school increased quickly. The situation was not the same everywhere, and the statistics are not very reliable. But in sub-Saharan Africa as a whole it was estimated that around 54 per cent of children were enrolled in primary school (net enrolment) in 1990. About half of the adult population was literate. More boys than girls went to school, and the majority of illiterate adults were women.

After Jomtien, more and more countries accepted the concept of education for all. This was not the case before. The colonial powers never had such an ambition. After independence, the new African leaders held the view that higher education was the key to development. Well-educated experts would modernize African societies. Gradually, it was realized that expert knowledge was necessary, but far from sufficient, to achieve this.

Most countries in West and Central Africa tried to strengthen basic education in the course of the 1990s, some in connection with system-wide educational reforms. It was an exciting process. The challenges at times seemed overwhelming. In many places, schools and teachers were lacking. Classrooms were overcrowded and buildings dilapidated. Where school enrolment was high, repetition rates tended to be also, with many pupils repeating one or more grades. Nearly everywhere boys dominated. In some places there were very few girls. The quality of teaching was often poor. Learning materials were lacking and teachers unqualified. Schooling is generally costly, with high expenditure particularly for teacher salaries – in spite of the fact that teachers have lost much of their status during recent decades. Some countries had great difficulties paying recurrent costs, resulting in schools being closed down for months at a time. Where the HIV/AIDS pandemic was widespread, many teachers fell ill and eventually died. In a context of increasing poverty in the population at large, numerous parents found it too costly to pay for school uniforms, books and writing materials. In particular, many families had to manage without the valuable assistance of girls with domestic chores while they were in school.

Nevertheless, comprehensive reforms were started around the region with the support of the World Bank, UNESCO, UNICEF, bilateral donors and voluntary organizations. School management was reorganized, curricula were revised and new types of school and teaching methods were tried out. Buildings were constructed or rehabilitated, teachers recruited and learning materials procured. Mobilization campaigns were launched and special incentives introduced, especially for girls. The extent and effectiveness of the efforts varied. The situation was usually characterized by stagnation or decline in Sahelian countries, or countries with economic recession or political unrest. In other countries, however, trends began turning upwards. Some showed remarkable results, like Mauritania, where school enrolment for girls, as well as for boys, increased by more than 50 per cent in a decade.

In 2000, the World Education Forum in Dakar assessed the progress made since Jomtien and noted that the goal of education for all had not been achieved. There had been progress, but not enough. Overall, the expansion of schooling in sub-Saharan Africa had caught up with the population growth and coverage had increased towards the end of the century, but not much. Sub-Saharan Africa remained the region with the weakest school system. In 1998, 60 per cent of children were enrolled (net enrolment) in primary school. But as the cohorts of children grew larger, the number of children out of school also increased. Among adults, literacy rates rose, although much still remained to be done. So the Dakar Forum adopted new targets, requiring all children to have access to and complete free and compulsory education of good quality by 2015.

What Kind of School?

One of the greatest challenges for ministers of education in West and Central Africa is education policy. The persistent resistance to educational reform is intriguing. The great majority of those who have gone to school

– and people in high-level decision-making positions have all done so – evidently hold the view that 'school' is what they themselves have experienced, and something different seems inconceivable. Thus, well-educated Africans often promote the type of school established by the colonial power, even if it represents a Western culture and the teaching is both theoretical and authoritarian. However, the lack of education on the continent gradually became so dramatic that finding new solutions became imperative. A broad consensus emerged that a new and different school must be introduced, to be able to achieve education for all. The school must be more relevant and effective for ordinary African women and men. Instead of expecting people to adjust to the school, it is now accepted that the school should adapt to local needs. But what kind of experiments should be encouraged, and to what extent? What should a good school in Africa actually look like?

I discussed this with a seemingly endless number of ministers of education. I tried to stimulate innovation and experimentation. Many were afraid to 'let the school go'. They would lose control of developments. In countries with marked social and cultural differences, a comprehensive school represents a unifying force. At the same time, it was clear that the school was reaching too few people. Little by little, the thinking moved towards a school more adjusted to local needs, but within the framework of a unified national system. The public authorities must be responsible for education as a whole, and elaborate common guidelines and core curricula. Then private organizations and local communities can operate within and outside of this. What the school will look like in practice depends on the local conditions.

A particularly important but touchy question relates to the use of local languages. From a pedagogic point of view, it is undoubtedly an advantage for children to start school using their mother tongue, as they learn much better. But African countries have tens and hundreds of local languages, many of which do not exist in written form. It is practically impossible to provide learning material in all languages. Children also need to learn the national language. I remember a discussion between the minister of education from Mali and his colleague from Cameroon. They were in strong disagreement. 'We *have* to use local languages in schools in Africa,' the Malian stated, but the Cameroonian protested: 'We can't.' And the explanation was simple: while Mali has 'only' 12 languages, there are around 237 in Cameroon. There are generally fewer languages on the plains than in the forests along the coast. In the Sahel, local languages are increasingly being used in written form. They are not seen as an alternative to international languages. They have a value of their own and emphasis is placed on 'functional trilinguism'. People learn to read and write their mother tongue, thereafter an African language with wide diffusion (like Mooré, Wolof or Bambara) and finally an international language like English, French or Arabic.

Closely related to language is the question of the local culture in school. This was rarely a theme for discussion. Most ministers of education seemed to take the Western character of the school for granted. Perhaps they considered it a necessity to ensure access for the young to modern society, or they did not attach much significance to traditional African culture. They might also hesitate giving too great importance to ethnic specificities, or take the view that children received sufficient introduction to their local culture at home. In any case, there was very little learning material based on African realities. The most profitable method was often to buy textbooks wholesale from Western countries. I met only one minister of education who saw transmission of the history and cultural heritage of his country as a main challenge, and he had great difficulty understanding how it could be done in an effective way. In UNICEF, we were more preoccupied with the teaching of life skills than the cultural aspects of education. In a certain sense, we saw ourselves as culturally 'neutral' and supported different kinds of schools, among them Qur'anic schools in several West African countries.

The attitudes of people in West and Central Africa varied. In some places, parents were extremely interested in modern education and were prepared to make considerable sacrifices to get their children to school. In Chad, for example, where the civil war destroyed most of the administration and the school system, people organized themselves and started 'spontaneous schools'. A person who had been to school simply got going and taught the kids what he or she knew, as well as he or she could, often under miserable conditions, with a minimum of guidance and teaching materials, but with impressive commitment and effort. In 1990, 3,500 classes were created in this way. When the war was over, the authorities started improving the quality of teaching, with the support of UNICEF and other donors. In Togo, parents organized 'clandestine schools', because they were dissatisfied with the public service – until the schools didn't have to be 'clandestine' any more, because the authorities became more tolerant. In Mali, UNICEF was approached by groups of street children, hundreds of boys and girls who wanted to go to school. 'We have to earn money,' they explained, ' so we must know how to read and count. Otherwise we will be cheated!'

In the past, I took for granted that school was something valuable and attractive to everybody. But in West and Central Africa some people had reservations. Particularly in traditional and Muslim societies, large groups felt that the modern school represented an alien culture. They perceived it as a continuation of the colonization process, marked by the language and reality of the colonial power and part of an undesirable modern-ization of society. In other places, parents reacted to the impoverished state of the school. They found it both costly and of poor quality. They failed to understand how the school could ensure a better future for their children, especially as it was no longer the case that education guaranteed a job in the public administration.

Non-formal Schools

During the 1990s, extensive innovation took place around the region, even if it was not always very systematic and coordinated. New initiatives popped up like mushrooms in rain. Some 'experimental' schools had started earlier, operated by religious communities and voluntary organiza-tions, but these initiatives were often scattered and random and had little contact with the educational authorities. The approach of the authorities also varied, from ambivalence and reluctance towards private initiatives, to positive appreciation of constructive interventions. Gradually, the view developed that the education services in a country should be considered more as a whole, and that innovative activities should be included in collaborative efforts. To an increasing extent, schools were established and operated in partnership between the authorities, local communities and national or international donors. The authorities paid teacher salaries, for example, and gave technical guidance, while the local communities chose school committees, constructed buildings and hired school assistants. UNICEF – or other donors – delivered equipment and provided training for committee members and local personnel.

The involvement of UNICEF in the field of education was relatively limited for a long time, and concentrated on the training of women. After Jomtien, the organization became more engaged in the development of primary education. UNICEF could contribute constructively to school reform on the basis of experiences with community-based health services and an unconventional, practical approach to learning. The involvement was all the more necessary as UNESCO was often weak at country level.

The range of innovative experiments was broad, both good and not so good, within the existing primary school and supplementary to it. Often the experiments were based on Western school models, but people were also inspired by other developing countries: BRAC in Bangladesh and Escuela Nueva in Latin America, as well as by colleagues in West and Central Africa. An important task for UNICEF was to promote exchanges of experiences across the borders and between different milieus. Very many experiments related to 'non-formal' schools. These are aimed at children of school age, particularly girls, and try to give them basic knowledge, so that they can enter the formal educational system or get a job. There are 'village schools', 'common schools' or 'pilot schools' near home for 7–9-year-olds, who otherwise would not go to school. And there are educational or developmental centres for 9–15-year-olds who have never been enrolled or left too early. These may combine basic education with some vocational training.

The comparative advantage of the non-formal schools is their capacity to adapt to local conditions. They are mostly developed in close collaboration with the local population. School committees, parent–teacher associations and groups of 'mother educators' are created. The curriculum is practically oriented. In some cases local languages are used. The schedule and sessions are flexible. Often they require less time in the classroom than the ordinary school, so children can help their parents during the planting and harvesting seasons. Many of the schools have difficulties, though, in meeting rigorous standards of quality. Evaluation of learning achievements is rarely done in a systematic way. The teachers also constitute a very heterogeneous group and their status, salary and competence frequently entail problems.

'I Want to Make a Future for Myself!'

In the village of Souly, east of the capital of Burkina Faso, less than 10 per cent of the children were enrolled in school. The villagers organized a campaign to get a school of their own. The chief established a committee, and a building was constructed, a single concrete room with a blackboard, tables and benches. The authorities were contacted, and they requested assistance from UNICEF and Save the Children. Long discussions ensued. What kind of school should it be? The wishes of the villagers were considered, as well as the conditions set by authorities and donors. The result was a 'community school' for children of school age who had never been to school, of whom at least half should be girls. Classes would last four hours a day for five months of the year. Teaching would start in the local language (Mooré instead of French) and include health and hygiene, community life and the rights of the child, as well as practical skills, reading, writing and arithmetic. The village chief would himself give lessons in local history and culture. The school started in January 1995, with 22 boys and 22 girls. By 2001, 245 non-formal schools of different kinds were established around the country, mostly 'satellite schools' for 7–9-year-olds.

In Guinea, UNICEF, in collaboration with the school authorities and local communities, created what are called 'NAFA-centres' – centres for a new chance, or 'the school without a school'. *Nafa* means 'useful' or 'advantageous'. Up to 2001, a total of 125 centres for 10–16-year-olds, mainly girls, were created. Instruction is provided 360 hours a year for three years, distributed according to local conditions. The students learn to read, write and do maths, are given information about the environment and health, society and rights, acquire problem-solving skills and are offered vocational training, sewing and embroidery. 'I thought I would never go to school,' one of the girls says. 'I was so old. Then this opportunity turned up, all of a sudden. I'll learn to read, write and calculate very fast, so I can gain my freedom!' Another adds: 'I want to make a future for myself! I am learning how to handle money and sew, so I can earn a living.' Most of the girls are content to complete the NAFA course, and they should be able to make a living in the local community afterwards. About one in five continues in the ordinary school. In the long run, the authorities want the centres to become self-financing by selling student products. It is also hoped that the ordinary school will pick up elements from the 'NAFA-centres'.

In Benin, the authorities have tried to improve the ordinary primary school and raise the low percentage of girls. The Education and Community (EDUCOM) programme for 'district-friendly schools' was developed with the support of UNICEF and other donors and started in the six poorest districts in the country. The situation in each village was analysed, and an agreement was reached concerning the measures to be implemented. These could include anything from more school benches and running water to reduction of the workload of mothers. Simultaneously, the curriculum was changed, placing greater emphasis on life skills. The teachers were trained in gender relations, child-centred teaching methods, monitoring and evaluation. To support the girls in school, a sponsor scheme was introduced, called 'girl for girl', with older students taking care of the younger ones. School report cards were designed, with graphic drawings, to show illiterate parents how their children are behaving and performing. In two years, the gross enrolment rate of girls increased by 23 per cent in the six project areas. The authorities also tried to establish village councils with a responsibility for community development in general. To begin with, local female assistants were engaged and given special training in helping to get things going. At the same time, they served as models for new female roles. Gradually, the local community is supposed to take over.

Education for Girls?

Getting girls to school is more complicated than one might think. It involves overcoming deep-rooted sex roles, changing certain attitudes towards the development of society and appreciating the whole concept of education – and in addition, a number of practical problems arise.

Since the first UN World Conference on Women in Mexico in 1975, numerous resolutions have been adopted to improve the status of women. The World Bank has prepared cost–benefit analyses, and the message is clear: educating women and girls is the most effective investment in the developing world. Education reduces maternal and child mortality and contributes to a lower birthrate, better health for family and children, more education for children and higher productivity and income for women. Canada and Norway played a special role in West and Central Africa in recent years through their support for basic education for girls. Government partners noted with surprise that Western countries were willing to allocate funds for such a task: this was serious business!

To influence public opinion, the authorities in the region, together with voluntary organizations and international donors, organized information campaigns about education in general and girls' education in particular. The Forum for African Women Educationalists (FAWE) played an important role. Radio and TV programmes, articles and pamphlets were produced and lecture and theatre tours organized. In Burkina Faso, the play, *Malo – pilot* was shown in hundreds of villages around the country. Malo is a girl who wants to be a pilot, but her father intends to take her out of school, have her circumcised and married off. The mother, however, allies herself with the teacher to help Malo run away and go to her uncle in town, where she can continue her schooling. The plot is simple, but the audience gets very involved. After the performance, there are lively discussions.

In Guinea, the rural radio would broadcast live from outdoor meetings, where contests were organized to choose the best song or poem about girls' education. The atmosphere is vibrating with *balafons*, drums and dancing. People join in the competition with enthusiasm and courage. Not all have a proper grasp of the task, though, and it created considerable merriment when a man solemnly sang a psalm, while a woman tried 'Frère Jacques – Brother Jacob'. The winner in this case was a twelve-year-old girl. She received a radio as a prize. Her poem emphasized that girls should be educated, so that they did not become a burden for their husband and parents.

In Niger, the traditional and religious leaders actively collaborated with the authorities. Niger is one of the countries in the region with the lowest percentage of girls in school. One-third of the boys were enrolled in primary school and only one-fifth of the girls. Both sociocultural and economic factors explain this. Zinder is one of the districts with the lowest enrolment. It is in the heart of Hausaland, towards the Sahara desert.

The population is Muslim and makes a living from grain cultivation and cattle breeding. In June 1999, the ministry for social development organized a seminar on girls' education, The seminar was chaired by the sultan of Damagaram. The sultan is the traditional leader of the province and heads a hierarchy of local leaders. The office carries religious as well as spiritual and administrative responsibilities.

In Zinder, the view of the traditional and religious leaders is that the school does not prepare the girls properly for their role as mothers and subordinate wives. In the worst case, it is a 'place of perdition' for young girls. Many parents fear that schooling will prevent early marriages. In addition, there are problems finding a safe place to stay, and maintenance for children who have to leave home to go to school. The opinion of the sultan, however, was that education was necessary for a harmonious development of society. At the seminar, he advocated that more children, and especially girls, should be educated. No sooner said than done. The sultan mobilized administrative and traditional leaders, village chiefs, parents, imams and marabouts (holy men). In every district, a committee was established with representatives from the school authorities, the traditional leaders and the Muslim Society to spread information and implement measures. In the villages, classes were organized in huts of straw, and in some districts 'mini' secondary schools were created. Every school had close contact with the parents and local leaders, who make sure that it transmits the right moral values and gives an introduction to daily life in the community. To get funds, efforts were made to sell student products from practical classes. The local population could choose if they wanted a school that taught in French, in French and Arabic plus Muslim culture, or local language for the first years before French.

In Kaduna in northern Nigeria, a meeting was held to discuss girls' education. Women from different backgrounds described how they managed to get an education. The important role played by one or more adults supporting the girl child was striking. The only female member of the state government, a charming woman wrapped in green from head to foot, except for her face, was commissioner for water resources and rural development. Her father had insisted that she should go to school. When she married, her husband had to promise to let her complete her studies. She was his second wife (so far he had three). He accepted her taking a university degree and obtaining paid employment – besides giving birth to nine children. Her husband was very proud when she was asked to assume political office and join the state government. But he laid down the condition that she should come home every evening (from Kaduna to the neighbouring city, Zaria).

In Kaduna, women have taken matters in their own hands. The

Federation of Muslim Women's Associations in Nigeria (FOMWAN), is working to strengthen women's basic education and health. The efforts of the educated to assist their less privileged sisters were impressive. The women have to be careful, so that they are not accused of opposing Islam and of promoting 'Westernization'. It is essential to respect the Qur'an and, among other things, to dress traditionally. Only when they are perceived as 'one of us', is it possible to get in touch and transmit information and assistance. FOMWAN was engaged in health services and a hospital, a school, seminars and vocational training. The school had three classes for children and four for adult women. An important task was providing insight into the Qur'an, what it says and what it does *not* say. When I visited one of the classes, the theme was the approach of the Qur'an towards breastfeeding.

As the debate on girls' education catches on, and measures are implemented, the need for comprehensive measures to overcome the barriers becomes clear. The workload of mothers must be reduced, by better access to water pumps and improved stoves, or by obtaining access to credit. The cost of girls' education must be reduced, by eliminating school fees for girls or providing scholarships. The school environment must become more girl-friendly, by employing female teachers or assistants, letting the girls wear long skirts, building schools in accessible and safe locations and installing proper water and sanitation facilities. Women must be respected and the needs of girls met, by making the curriculum more relevant for women, eliminating gender discrimination from the textbooks, changing inappropriate attitudes among male staff and providing training in women-friendly teaching methods. It is important to get girls to school, but there must also be a positive atmosphere. It is neither liberating nor stimulating if the girls experience new forms of depreciation and discrimination in the curriculum, from teachers and schoolmates. Before I came to the region, I did not understand how physically exposed African girls can be. But the high number of schoolgirls being sexually abused, becoming pregnant or infected with AIDS by male teachers, is alarming in some places.

During the 1990s, efforts were made in many countries in the region to increase the education of girls, and the number of girls in school increased. But so did the number of boys – at times even more. So the gender gap was not closed. On the contrary, it became wider. In fact, from 1990 to 1998 it increased by 10 to 12 percentage points for net enrolment in primary schools in sub-Saharan Africa. Among literate adults, women did not catch up with men either, even if more women learnt how to read and write. Here the difference was around 15 percentage points by the end of the 1990s. There is still a long way to go. Both political will and comprehensive measures specifically targeting girls and women are necessary to achieve equality between women and men.

Sustainable?

It is too early to evaluate the different educational experiments carried out during recent years. Activities have expanded rapidly. The number of pupils in primary school in general, and the number of girls in particular, have increased in a noticeable way in the countries making serious efforts. But the progress has not been sufficient to change the overall picture of educational crisis in sub-Saharan Africa. Questions remain: how far is it possible to go, and how sustainable are the different interventions? Success or failure will be measured on the basis of access and quality, cost and financing. Will we get good and useful education for all, at a reasonable price, funded in a sustainable way?

Education costs money for the society – and it costs more in Africa than in Western countries, because there are more children. By the end of the twentieth century, more than half of the population in sub-Saharan Africa consisted of children and youths under the age of 18. At the same time, the cost varies considerably from one country to another. The differences have only become known little by little, and they have led to discussions about how to reduce costs. School buildings can be built using local materials (clay and straw) instead of concrete. Textbooks and supplies can be produced locally, and money can be saved by establishing lending schemes for books, instead of each family buying its own. Teacher salaries represent a high proportion of expenditure, however one looks at it. But teaching staff can be better utilized by introducing double-shift schooling and multigrade classes, reducing the number of classes for each pupil and increasing the number of pupils in each class. In some schools, classes are overcrowded, but on the average, the number of pupils does not exceed 35–40 in sub-Saharan Africa. It is considered possible to go up to 40–50, without necessarily affecting the quality of teaching negatively. Assistants can also be hired. If it is possible, in addition, to reduce the repetition rate (often one-quarter of pupils), considerable savings can be made. It is maintained that educational productivity can be improved in many African schools without increasing the cost, by strengthening the motivation and competence of teachers, increasing the demand and control by the local communities and improving the availability of necessary learning materials.

However, the cost of a proper primary school cannot be reduced beyond a certain point. According to UNESCO, the absolute minimum cost per pupil (with the exception of teacher salaries) should be about

US$5 a year: $1.50 for textbooks, $1.50 for writing materials and $2 for teacher training. But by the end of the century, the expenditure in sub-Saharan Africa only amounted to about $4.

Whatever the cost, it has to be paid – but how? It is easy with small projects, but how to do it on a larger scale?

The first requirement is that countries themselves give priority to education, and in particular to basic education – in relation, for example, to military expenditure, infrastructure and non-profitable state enterprises. An important factor here is debt relief, so that countries don't have to spend considerable amounts on interest and loan repayments. It is important that local communities contribute to the school. They already do this to a great extent. How much is it reasonable to expect? People's appreciation of the school and sense of ownership are crucial. In any case, poor parents with numerous children, not to mention orphans, will have difficulties contributing. It might be easier to provide in-kind contributions or labour. Still, the amount cannot be very large. External donors cover part of the total expenditures for education in sub-Saharan Africa. The allocations are not very large, relatively speaking, in the overall picture, but they play an important role, and support for basic education should be given higher priority in the years to come. Some estimates indicate that the amounts should increase six or seven times.

NINE

The Lost Children: Ruthless Exploitation of the Weakest

Children are the reward of life.
(Proverb from Zaire)

It was the number of children that first made the police suspicious. It could not be a school outing when three well-dressed men in Porto Novo, one of the coastal towns of Benin, were looking for buses to transport 90 small children to Gabon. Some of the children were no more than eight years old. In fact, the children had been bought from families in Togo and Benin for about US$30 per child. They were going to be sold in the capital of Gabon, Libreville, for a profit. If they were lucky, the men could get $300–$400 per child. In Gabon, the kids would be put to work as domestic servants, cattle herders or prostitutes by their new 'owners'. They would be beaten, forced to work all day and would scarcely receive enough food to survive.

This was in 1997. It wasn't the first time the police in Benin had arrested people dealing with the purchase and sale of children. Some weeks earlier, a truck full of small girls was stopped at the border between Benin and Nigeria. In the course of two months, no fewer than 300 children had been intercepted by the immigration authorities. They were mostly girls between eight and 15, whom slave traders tried to smuggle illegally out of the country. The events created a stir. The media became involved, together with local and international organizations, including the International Anti-Slavery Organization. In UNICEF, the efforts to combat child labour suddenly took on new regional dimensions. We immediately contacted the regional office of the International Labour Organization (ILO), also situated in Abidjan, to organize a joint response. This turned out to be less straightforward than we expected. The approaches and working methods of the two organizations were very different. But I was familiar with the ILO from the past, and we found ways to collaborate and complement each other constructively. UNICEF could deepen ILO's knowledge of the informal sector, while ILO demonstrated the usefulness of formal labour standards.

The first task was to clarify the situation. It became apparent that a lucrative and brutal trade with children had been established during recent years. It was acquiring frightening proportions in West and Central Africa. Some children were plainly kidnapped. The majority were sold by their parents. When well-dressed middlemen came to poor families living in isolated districts, and said that they would ensure a better future for their children, many parents sent them off in good faith. A sum of money, some cotton cloth or bottles of alcohol were also tempting.

In Lagos in Nigeria, a 'labour camp' for children was discovered in a five-storey house called the 'children's market', or the 'slave-dump' by people in the neighbourhood. The emaciated, undernourished children were aged from seven to 17, mostly girls. Thirty new children were delivered every second month. Middlemen fetched them from Benin and Togo. People who wanted cheap labour came to the camp and chose the children they wanted. The girls were engaged as domestic workers, while the boys were assigned to carry goods, wash cars or collect fares on minibuses.

In the Ivory Coast, it became known that many of the labourers in the mines and the cotton and corn fields were children from Mali. There were thousands of them, mostly boys, who were picked up on the street in cities and towns by middlemen promising them the moon. They were smuggled across the border at night and transported to cities like Korhogo and Bouaké. Here farmers came to get manpower at a low cost. The commission for the middlemen and transport costs were deducted from the children's salaries, which on average were very low, between US$100 and $200 a year. Sometimes the boys were not paid at all. They were assigned physically hard work, twelve hours a day, with a minimum of food. Most of them were illiterate. Many did not understand where they were or what had happened to them. Those who tried to escape were abused, and in some cases locked up.

Girl Slaves

The regional trafficking in young girls was particularly extensive. It was an old tradition in several coastal countries that rural families sent young girls to relatives in the city. It was part of family solidarity. The urban relatives took care of the girls and gave them an education. But the system was distorted by the economic crisis. Poverty made ordinary people desperate for income, and officials pliable. It became a matter of urgency for many rural families to send pre-teen children to other caretakers. At the same time, urban families were happy to acquire cheap and ready labour. As a consequence, the children often worked long hours and received little or no education. The girls were the first to get up in the morning and the last to go to bed, and not only cleaned, cooked, washed clothes and cared for children, but assisted with petty trade and other tasks outside the house. At times, they were sexually abused by men in the household.

The girls were alone and helpless, at the mercy of the host family. The worst, says nine-year-old Kasarachi, who worked for a Nigerian family, was that she was treated differently from the other children. 'They got two meals a day, while I only got one. The house mistress beat me every day, and the other children laughed and beat me too'. Fifteen-year-old Jeanne also got beaten when her employer from Benin was dissatisfied. But the greatest problem was the 23-year-old son in the family, who regularly raped her. If she resisted, she was beaten up. In Togo, the great majority of children who quit their jobs as domestic workers, said the reason was a 'cruel boss'.

The problems first surfaced in Benin. It took time to obtain a proper overview, because the abuse took place in the private sphere, protected by the four walls of the home, and the participation of girls in household chores was generally accepted. The authorities at first refused to admit that there could be maltreatment. The minister of health gesticulated and declared: 'I have had young girls in my house for years, and as far as I know, we have taken care of them well!'

Little by little it became clear that there were no fewer than 100,000 children under the age of 15 who were placed with others, *vidomégons* (child maids), as they are called. Most were girls. Every fifth child was under ten years of age. Many stayed with relatives, but not all. Some girls were placed in the family of a creditor, as payment for a debt. Others were sent to traditional priests, as a kind of present or propitiatory sacrifice. The studies documented widespread exploitation, even if it was not always the case. On average, the children worked 14 hours a day and were grossly underpaid, if they were paid at all. US$7 a month was not unusual. The younger the children, the longer they worked, the less they were paid and the more they were abused. Ninety per cent of them had never been to school.

Public opinion was stirred up in support of the girls. Fuel was added to the flames when an organized commercial trade was discovered, that placed girl children not with relatives, but with complete strangers; and not in Benin, but in other countries. They were sent from Ghana, Togo and Benin to the Ivory Coast and Nigeria, or from Togo, Benin and Nigeria to Gabon. Abroad, the girls were not only brutally exploited, they felt completely lost. The ancient name, 'The Slave Coast', suddenly took on a new meaning. All concerned parties in Benin were mobilized to help the *vidomégons*. Information campaigns were launched about the rights of the child, and the abuse of the children was described. A law was passed prohibiting children under the age of 14 to leave the country to work, so that the smugglers could be prosecuted and sentenced. Centres for homeless children were created and special educational services organized for domestic workers. In addition, efforts were increased to ensure basic education for girls.

To stop cross-border trafficking of children, a close collaboration had to be established between different bodies, both nationally and regionally. Authorities had to be mobilized, which didn't ordinarily deal with the well-being of children. The Benin government was willing to take the lead. In July 1998, a major conference on the trafficking of child domestic workers was organized in Cotonou, with more than a hundred participants from 17 countries. There were representatives of ministries of labour, justice, family, health, social affairs, women, the interior and external relations. In addition, participants came from trade unions and employers' associations, international, regional and local voluntary organizations, research institutions, donors and the media. The organization of working children and youth (AMWCY) sent two participants. One had been a child domestic worker herself in another country, and her sober account left no doubt that we were dealing with a ruthless exploitation of defenceless minors.

The issues attracted much attention, and the conference adopted a number of recommendations. Special emphasis was placed on teaching about child rights to teachers, health and social workers, judges, police, media people and work inspectors, as well as the children themselves. Regional organizations were requested to take up the problem of trafficking in children, and diplomats, customs officers and police in the different countries were asked to collaborate closely. In particular, it was suggested that a new conference should be held for Central Africa, as the Cotonou conference mainly covered West Africa.

Two years later, a conference was organized in Libreville, Gabon. This time there were more than two hundred participants. Nearly all the countries in the region were represented, along with some others. The regional organizations for West and Central Africa respectively now joined in. The conference dealt both with the prevention of child trafficking and the reintegration of children who had been victims of the trade. It was estimated that some 200,000 children were trafficked every year in West and Central Africa, to work as domestic labour, in farming, fisheries or the sex trade. An appeal was launched to elaborate an international instrument against child trafficking, and governments were called on to devise national and joint regional programmes to combat the phenomenon. In 2001, the

Economic Community of West African States (ECOWAS) adopted an action plan against trafficking in persons.

The publicity began to disrupt the child trade. Warned by their governments, parents in Benin and Togo started to seek news of their expatriated offspring. In Libreville, embassies tried to track down child domestic workers and hundreds were sent home. The police made efforts to cut off the trade at its source, but they often lacked resources and personnel. In 2000, the Togolese authorities blocked the transfer of 337 children and charged 30 adults with trafficking. In Benin, some 1,200 children were stopped before smugglers got them on board a ship for Gabon. Several traffickers have been prosecuted, but have been given only suspended sentences.

The Most Intolerable

African children have traditionally begun to work alongside their parents. The concept of a childhood in which children could be exempt from work, so that they can devote themselves exclusively to school and recreation, reflects an essentially Western attitude that appeared gradually during the last century. A childhood separate from working life and adult responsibility is quite alien to Africa. The educational systems evolved by African peoples regard productive work, apprenticeship and culture as inseparable. But as a consequence of increasing economic problems and poverty, the work burden of children has increased. Some even note that the perception of the child has changed. Children represented the supreme value of traditional society. Now, for a large number of families, they have become a stepping-stone to survival. They are sent out to work, they are 'placed' and exploited. The 'child-king' has become the 'child-servant'.

Work performed by children, particularly girls, has assumed large proportions. Usually, girls start helping their mother as soon as they are perceived to be big enough. The household chores, farming and other income-generating activities easily take up most of the day. When they are ten to 14, girls spend at least seven hours more per day than boys of the same age performing different household tasks. Boys spend more time playing or exploring their surroundings, if they don't assist the father with his work or go to school.

The concept of 'child labour' is not altogether simple in an African context. When does the work stop being useful training and start becoming exploitation? It is not easy to answer, and accusing somebody of child abuse is a delicate matter. There are no 'child factories' in sub-Saharan Africa like those that exist in some Asian countries. In Africa, much of the child labour is invisible, necessary and, moreover, socially accepted.

Most takes place in the rural areas, where the children are unpaid family workers in agriculture, help with household chores and contribute to small family enterprises. In some places, children can be found in mines extracting iron, gold or diamonds. In the towns, children don't only work as domestic workers, but also as assistants in shops and workshops, as garbage collectors, street vendors, prostitutes and beggars.

A special type of child labour has come into existence in Muslim milieus. Some of the marabouts, who are traditionally responsible for Qur'anic schools, encountered problems providing for the children placed in their care. More and more had to leave the countryside and go to the towns, especially Dakar, to make a living. They took all or some of the children with them, and sent them out on the streets as beggars to get money, food and clothes, not only for their own needs, but also for the marabouts. Most of the children, usually boys, are under 15. They live under unbearably harsh conditions with regard to nutrition and sanitation, and regularly suffer beatings and other forms of physical mistreatment. Education, whether religious or any other form of instruction, does not take place and the children become the victims of dangers and violence in the streets.

According to the ILO, 'child labour' does not encompass all work performed by children. Child labour slated for legal abolition includes labour performed under the minimum age, that interferes with the child's education or is 'hazardous' in the sense that it is harmful to the child's health, or physical, mental, spiritual, moral or social development. The estimates are uncertain, and household work is often not included in surveys or routine reporting systems. In 2002, the ILO believed that there could be around 48 million economically active children between the ages of five and 14 in Africa. In absolute numbers this was less than in Asia, but in relation to the total child population it was more. Twenty-nine per cent of African children could be considered as economically active, both boys and girls. Not all, but probably the great majority were engaged in forms of labour marked for abolition.

The situation was frightening. It's true that many children were working part-time, but the duties often prevented them from going to school or benefiting from the teaching. A considerable number were less than twelve years old, which in many countries is the legal minimum age for light work. In addition, the activity was often detrimental to the children's mental and physical health. Because of their immaturity, children are less aware than adults of potential risks involved in their occupations. At the same time, they are physically more vulnerable and tire more easily. In agriculture, children are exposed to burning sun and rain, heavy lifting, sharp tools, toxic chemicals and dangerous engines. If they guard cows or sheep, they may be attacked by wild animals, snakes or insects. The toil and stress of domestic work, especially when combined with isolation from family and friends, can lead to psychological problems. In addition, sexual abuse threatens the physical safety and health of the children and seriously damages their emotional development.

It was impossible to tackle the whole range of child labour, at least not in the short term, with the enormous number of families depending on the earnings of children for survival, and the few alternatives that existed in the form of educational and social services. But resigning oneself to the poverty seemed untenable. The extreme cases of child exploitation that were revealed towards the end of the 1990s called for an immediate reaction, and bilateral donors and voluntary organizations were prepared to become engaged. UNICEF and the ILO decided to concentrate on the most intolerable forms of child labour.

In June 1999, the ILO Labour Conference adopted a convention prohibiting the worst forms of child labour and demanding immediate action to eliminate them. The convention addresses slavery and forced labour, including trafficking of children and their recruitment for use in armed conflict, in commercial sexual exploitation, and in illicit activities and work that harms the health, safety or morals of the children. The ILO and UNICEF followed up by mobilizing public opinion, carrying out studies and developing programmes of action in interested African countries. Voluntary organizations, particularly employers' and labour unions, universities and media were involved. The focus was first of all on serious breaches of ILO standards. It was only the tip of the iceberg. Still, it was a challenge. Legal systems were inadequate, and enforcement mechanisms very weak. Nevertheless, some measures were introduced. Besides assistance to child domestic and plantation workers, the dangers that children were exposed to in small coal and diamond mines were taken up in six Sahelian countries.

The primary task is to get the children out of an exploitative workplace and into school. In many cases this is difficult. The children have to earn money, there are no schools nearby or they cannot offer useful learning. An alternative is to prevent the work from being hazardous for the child and to organize non-formal education alongside it, if necessary on a part-time basis. Such educational interventions can be effective. The children get an anchorage point outside the workplace and are better placed to handle their problems. But the interventions require resources and must be organized in an appropriate way. In the long term, it is essential to strengthen basic education in general. Children should not be forced into labour due to the lack or poor quality of schooling. And a school of good quality can enable children to satisfy their needs and contribute to society.

Child Workers Organize

The Association of Working Children and Youth (AWCY) became a constructive actor in the area of child labour. In 1992, a group of girl domestic workers went to the island of Gorée, outside Dakar, to relax and discuss their working conditions. As one girl explained: 'We are treated badly. We are underpaid. We are given tasks we cannot endure. We have no days to rest. We have no time for training. We have to demand our rights from the employers!' They were determined young women, and people with experience in organization gave them a helping hand. It was May 1. The girls decided that they wanted to join the demonstrations. It took time. But two years later, they participated in the First of May procession with posters and slogans. The child workers were given broad television coverage. Contacts were established with young workers in Mali, the Ivory Coast and Benin. At a meeting in the Ivory Coast, they agreed upon twelve rights of particular importance for child workers:

> The right to be taught a trade,
> The right to stay in the village,
> The right to work in a safe environment,
> The right to complain and be treated fairly,
> The right to rest when we are ill,
> The right to be respected,
> The right to be listened to,
> The right to perform limited and light tasks,
> The right to health care,
> The right to learn to read and write,
> The right to play and enjoy ourselves, and
> The right to express our views and organize.

These rights are presented in a book with text and drawings by child workers, called *Voice of African Children*.

In many African countries, child workers, domestic girls, self-employed street workers and apprentices organized themselves into AWCY, with the support of African NGOs, churches and civil servants and organizations like ENDA Third World (Environmental Development of the Third World), Caritas, the ILO and UNICEF. It was essential that the children could express their views. With a little assistance, they managed more than could be expected. At regional meetings, they discussed their situation and adopted recommendations. AWCY organizations published information and initiated literacy courses and private health insurance for their members. Gradually, activities have developed in 40 cities in 16 countries. In 1996, an international movement of child workers was created.

AWCY members in West Africa ask,

Who will ban child labour? The campaign is important, because some children work under intolerable conditions. But they are a minority. The majority of the child workers are proud to help their parents and take care of themselves. We are obliged to work. We don't have any choice. To help us, adults have to combat poverty and improve our working conditions. And then we in AWCY will participate under the palaver tree and present our views!

TEN

Dangerous Food and Drink: Progress with Simple Means

The hungry boy eats the fruits with the worms.
(Proverb from Nigeria)

Africa's misery and distress are well known. The media seldom inform about things that go well. Nevertheless, there have been some remarkable achievements, although they might not be very numerous or impressive. The story of Guinea worm disease is an outstanding success – or near success.

Guinea worm disease, or *Dracunculiasis*, existed far back in history, at least from the fifteenth or fourteenth centuries BC, in ancient Egypt, India and Persia. There were also cases in Russia, China and Latin America. In the twentieth century, the worm was mostly found in Africa and Asia. In some countries it has been extremely widespread, with millions of cases. But on the threshold of the twenty-first century, it is on the verge of eradication, thanks to systematic efforts in many countries.

Right after the Second World War, a total of 47 million cases of Guinea worm were reported worldwide. In 2001, this was reduced to 60,000 cases, all in African countries. In West and Central Africa, the number of Guinea worm cases was reduced by 95 per cent during the 1990s. Of the ten infected countries in 2001, half had fewer than five hundred cases. Ghana and Nigeria had the most, with around 5,000 affected people each.

How was such a dramatic reduction of Guinea worm cases possible? Guinea worm, or the fiery serpent as it is also called, is a parasite that can grow to three feet long, although it is only a fraction of an inch thick. It is the biggest parasite attacking human tissue, and when mature, emerges from the victim's body, usually the legs, causing great pain, fever, nausea and vomiting. After it has left, a blister is created in the skin, which is easily infected. The disease is not fatal, but victims are disabled for weeks and sometimes months. Farming and other income-generating activities become impossible. Children miss school. A whole village can be devastated by a serious outbreak.

Guinea worm is the only disease that is transmitted exclusively through drinking water. The worm that works its way out of the human body is a female, carrying hundreds of thousands of microscopic larvae. When the human host steps into a pond or shallow well, washing or collecting water, the larvae are dropped into the water. The water is polluted for several weeks. The larvae are eaten by an intermediate host, a small crustacean known as a water flea, in whose body they mature. When the water is drunk and the crustaceans enter the human body, the larvae are released. The male worm dies soon after mating, while the female worm grows and after a year starts penetrating the tissue of the victim in an attempt to get out.

There are no medicines that can prevent or cure Guinea worm disease. When the head of the worm emerges through the skin, people laboriously roll it up, inch by inch, around a small stick until the whole can be removed. If parts remain, there can be serious infections. It is a long and painful process. The only way of avoiding the disease is to make sure the larvae don't enter the human body. The Guinea worm is extremely vulnerable. Only human beings can uphold its fragile life cycle. If the transmission via humans is broken, the worm dies out.

Death of the Fiery Serpent

To begin with, nobody understood where the Guinea worm came from. Even when people knew the cause of the disease, many had difficulty understanding that apparently clean drinking water could lead to the painful Guinea worm twelve to 14 months later. They frequently believed that the worm was caused by a divine curse, evil spirits or black magic. The disease is still endemic in poor, remote villages, where there is a shortage of water and technical remedies, including modern wells and pumps, and the population is to a great extent illiterate.

What has been done to reduce the number of Guinea worm cases? Most important has been drilling wells to provide people with safe drinking water, so that they no longer have to depend on unclean water. Unprotected water sources have been treated chemically, to kill the small crustaceans. But people sometimes resist treating the ponds and prefer to drink unsafe water, through force of habit or because they think it tastes better. People have also been taught how to use filters when they drink from unprotected, possibly contaminated sources. They filter the water when it is poured into the water pot, or use straws fitted with a filter.

Before measures can be implemented, the spread of Guinea worm has to be mapped. It is necessary to know in which villages it is endemic. Health maps have been created, which have turned out to be very useful for other diseases as well. A main strategy has been to organize village committees and volunteers, who report on the number of cases, inform the population, distribute filters and make sure that those who suffer are cared for in a proper way. It is of special importance to prevent those who are infected from contaminating nearby water sources.

Impressive mobilization and information campaigns have been carried out, often in poor and remote districts. Traditional and religious leaders, village taskforces, local organizations, teachers and school clubs have actively participated. Series of posters are shown during general meetings in the villages, explaining what the worm is and how it can be combated. Volunteers go from house to house talking with people. Messages in local languages are transmitted by radio. Students perform plays. People are given filters and shown how to use them.

The organized campaign for the eradication of Guinea worm started early in the 1980s, following a proposal from the Centers for Disease Control (CDC), in the USA. In 1988, African ministers of health gave their support. At the beginning of the 1990s, most countries in which the worm was endemic launched campaigns for its eradication. Central co-ordination teams were established and district supervisors appointed. The need for co-ordination was great. The campaigns were first of all supported by the WHO, the Organization to Combat the Great Endemic Diseases (OCCGE), the American Peace Corps and UNICEF. In addition, different multilateral and bilateral donors and private enterprises contributed. Global 2000 from the Carter Center in the USA, and former US president Jimmy Carter, played an important role, together with the former President of Mali, Amadou Toumani Touré.

Nothing to Report

Towards the end of the 1990s, there was a slowing down of the campaign against Guinea worm. The reduction of cases stagnated. In some countries there was even an increase, for several reasons. As the disease became less widespread, motivation waned. Donors provided less support. In addition, there were practical implementation problems.

Guinea worm should have been eradicated by 1995. But governments as well as donors were slow to make the necessary efforts. Measures were delayed, or only partially carried out. There were difficulties due to the remoteness of the endemic areas, understaffing and high logistical and maintenance costs. In 2002, the great question was if sufficient will existed internationally and locally to eradicate the disease. Resources were scarce and the campaigns against polio and malaria required their share. In Sudan, which had 80 per cent of the remaining Guinea worm cases, the war created serious obstacles. But with so few cases left, it would be unfortunate not to get rid of the disease for ever.

The results achieved owed a good deal to the commitment of village committees, volunteers and supervisors. Villagers who saw the Guinea worm disappear displayed a touching involvement. In one village, they hung up the last worm, together with the water filter, in the palaver tree in the middle of the village, as a symbol and reminder of their victory over the disease. Villagers like these are the best missionaries to others in the same district.

Before a country can be declared Guinea worm-free, three years must pass without any cases. The strategy during this phase caused disagreement among donors. It is difficult to maintain an extensive surveillance system to report on an absence of something. We in UNICEF therefore tried to get the committees, volunteers and supervisors to take on other tasks and mobilize the villagers to improve their hygiene, strengthen the children's nutrition, provide ORT salts during diarrhoea and use impregnated mosquito nets. To continue making progress in the reduction of child mortality, interventions must focus particularly on the community and village level, providing people with appropriate knowledge to improve their health. The campaigns against Guinea worm demonstrated that this is possible. But representatives from the Carter Center, among others, were afraid that an extension of the tasks would reduce the attention given to Guinea worm and weaken the final effort. The controversy was all the more difficult to solve because the Carter Center did not accept the coordinating role of WHO in technical matters. Different countries have therefore pursued somewhat different strategies.

In Ghana, a comprehensive disease surveillance system was put in place. Local supervisors were mobilized to eradicate Guinea worm in the northern districts. A total of 7,000 volunteers, mostly illiterate, were trained to count the number of Guinea worm cases, to teach people how to use water filters and to help bandage Guinea worm wounds. As the Guinea worms disappeared, they were taught to count births, deaths and cases of meningitis, polio and measles. They also noted exceptional events, like outbreaks of cholera or yellow fever epidemics. The supervisors report the findings to the nearest health team, which takes action, investigates the problem and tells the population what to do. Thus the local population is activated to a greater extent in protecting its own health, and health statistics become more accurate.

Struggle for Water

Because it targets women and children in particular, UNICEF should not be a central actor in the campaign against Guinea worm. The disease can strike anybody, not only women and children. But UNICEF was engaged at an early stage in the efforts to provide people with clean drinking water. It was evident that child malnutrition, illness and death were caused, among other things, by a lack of proper hygiene. UNICEF tried to improve conditions in the poorest villages, and thereby found itself in the middle of the Guinea worm problem.

Considerable efforts were made during past decades to provide people in West and Central Africa with access to clean drinking water and adequate sanitation. During the International Water and Sanitation Decade, from 1980 to 1990, conditions improved. But during the 1990s progress stagnated. At the end of the century, more people were without adequate services, as a result of population growth. Nearly half of the population was without clean water and satisfactory sanitation facilities, especially rural populations and slum dwellers in the cities, who were living in medieval conditions.

Previously, UNICEF had contributed extensively to the drilling of wells and installation of water pumps. But in the 1990s, limited resources reduced the efforts. The focus was moved to less costly interventions that might have a snowball effect: development of new technology and experiments to find cheaper and more sustainable solutions. Improved techniques reduced the per capita cost of clean water to perhaps one-thirtieth of its 1970 level. Similar efforts were now focused on the installation of water pumps, maintenance of hand pumps (up to one-quarter of the installed pumps broke down) and building of latrines. The most recent invention consists of simple concrete latrines ('Sanplat'), which are easy to produce, cost less and are simple to clean.

The inhabitants in several city slums now have cheap and clean water, thanks to UNICEF and other partners. The efforts were particularly successful in Nouakchott, the capital of Mauritania. The city is located on Africa's Atlantic coast at the edge of a vast desert. Low square houses are scattered across a desolate plain of sand. A well about 60 km away supplies the city with water. Large water pipes have been placed along the main streets, but there is a shortage of distribution networks, especially in the areas inhabited by the city's poor. Donkey-cart water vendors bring the water round, and sell it at a price that is often too high for poor people. Even before the water arrives, it is often no longer clean.

In three districts in Nouakchott, UNICEF took the initiative to create cooperatives among poor women so that they could manage the water supplies themselves. Each cooperative included 100 female heads of household. They learnt how to make a cooperative work. They elected a board and signed an agreement with the municipality of Nouakchott and UNICEF determining their rights and duties. The women were given their own water standpipe and organized the distribution of water. They thus cut the cost to one-third, and at the same time the water quality was much better. Household water consumption increased by 40 per cent. In one cooperative, they fenced in the area surrounding the standpipe, planted trees and built a small house with a meeting room, community latrines and showers. They used the profit from the water sales to organize literacy courses, training in health and hygiene for the members and a day nursery for the children. A children's garden was planted. A savings and credit system was set up and a small shop established, which could sell basic necessities cheaper than the local merchants. The president of the co-operative was a woman who had endured the harsh realities of poor urban life. Filled with pride, she stated:

> We make savings, and the group can address all problems. If we do not find solutions, we send a delegation to speak with the mayor. We have told him that we need a better system for refuse collection in the city!

The pilot projects were the first stage of a four-year negotiation process between the authorities, donors and traditional water vendors. The results of the projects generated much discussion. A water lobby was created at the donor level and at the level of national decision-making. The aim was to spread the message: 'Clean water at an affordable price for Nouakchott's poor communities.' In 1998, the municipality of Nouakchott and the local administrations involved – with support of other partners, including UNICEF – decided to reorganize entirely the management system of standpipes. Fifty-one standpipes spread over eight of the city's poor communities were to be rehabilitated. The strategy was to replace the owners and managers, who were only interested in making profits, by new managers: NGOs and unemployed university graduates. The pilot projects were implemented in the newest areas, far from the merchants' 'territories'. In the extended project, there were stakeholders in the existing distribution system who might oppose a change, and must be neutralized. User committees were established at community level to monitor the cost and quality of the water. In 2000, the cost of drinking water for the entire distribution system still remained too high at the household level, but significant steps were being made towards progressive regulation of prices and control over the distribution network. The example from Nouakchott is being followed in other cities in the region.

A Vital Substance

Iodization of salt is another success story. When I went to Africa for UNICEF, I had no idea that I would be dealing with salt production. But UNICEF's regional office had to map where and how salt was being produced. I visited salt ponds in Ghana, the Pink Lake in Senegal and salt mines in Mauritania. The biggest commercial production of salt in West and Central Africa takes place in Ghana and Senegal. In Ghana, salt is obtained along the long flat coast by channelling sea water into big square ponds, mile after mile. They are like enormous salt fields. As the water evaporates, the salt can be scraped from the bottom, collected and sold to consumers. The process is nearly industrial. A single enterprise can harvest large areas. The Pink Lake, on the contrary, is a natural phenomenon. It is not far from Dakar and is fed by sea water penetrating the ground. The salt concentration in the water is so high that the salt forms layers on the bottom. Women and men from the village nearby wade out with small pirogues (a traditional canoe), cut loose bits of salt and transport them to the shore. The landscape is moon-like, full of pink salt piles close together all along the shore. Each family has its own piles. Middlemen come and buy, to sell all over the region. In Mauritania, salt is extracted from deposits underground, where there are thick layers.

Why did I have to acquaint myself with all this? Because malnutrition is a major problem for women and children in sub-Saharan Africa, and UNICEF tried to find cheap and simple ways of improving the diet. One of the most widespread and serious forms of malnutrition is iodine deficiency. Iodization of salt is the best way to solve the problem. A person needs very little iodine – a teaspoon is sufficient for a lifetime, consumed in tiny quantities every day. But if it is lacking, the consequences are serious.

Nearly half of the population in West and Central Africa risks not getting enough iodine. Until recently about every sixth person has suffered from goitre due to iodine deficiency. The problem arises when plants grow in soil bearing very little iodine, so people don't get the quantities they need. Where cassava is a staple food, as is the case in many places, the problem can be aggravated, because the plant often contains cyanide, which destroys iodine. Additional quantities must then be obtained from other sources. 'From ancient times, we have always eaten our *attiéké* (cassava) with fish,' an Ivorian from the coast explains. 'But inland people eat the root vegetable without anything else or with other trimmings – and then they can acquire iodine deficiency.' In the Central African Republic, where people live mainly on cassava, it is estimated that about two-thirds of the population have suffered from iodine deficiency.

You can see it immediately when you come to a village: people with a big, bulging ball on the front of their throats, the sure sign of iodine deficiency. The thyroid gland swells up without iodine. Among pregnant women, iodine deficiency increases the risk of abortion, stillbirths and deaths during delivery. The physical and intellectual growth of children is impaired. They become tired and sluggish in their movements and thinking. In serious cases, they can become mentally retarded. Even moderate iodine deficiency can lead to a loss in intelligence of 10 to 15 points among children, as well as adults.

The Salt of Life

Adding iodine to salt is a simple procedure, involving a small mixer that sprays liquid iodine on the salt before packaging and sale. The cost is no more than two US cents per person per year. The control is also simple. If you drip a special chemical fluid on the salt, the iodized salt immediately changes colour, while the non-iodized remains the same. It is just as magical every time. A few drops of clear liquid on the white salt, and suddenly it turns intensely blue.

UNICEF raised the issue of iodization of salt with the health authorities in different countries, and they contacted the ministries of industry and thereafter the salt producers. It was rapidly agreed that all countries in the region had to introduce the same rules, if we were to succeed. The regional organizations for economic cooperation were involved. Here, the member states decided to adopt laws making the iodization of salt compulsory. The customs authorities should monitor the imports and ministries of industry the production. UNICEF and other donors should help in providing machines to add iodine and to package the salt in a proper way. A single machine can serve a population of about one million people. There was a need for information, so that people understood the importance of iodized salt.

Everything worked well as long as the authorities were dealing with large commercial producers like those in Ghana. But in many places there were small producers and importers who could not afford machines of their own, and who could not easily get together in a joint enterprise. At the Pink Lake, there was a great fuss when a collaboration between the producers was suggested. Those extracting the salt felt that it would interfere with their status as autonomous enterprises. The middlemen feared it would reduce their profit. When the salt is extracted from deposits underground, it is usually sold in big blocks that have to be crushed before iodine can be added. This makes the process more costly. In some cases, the consumers were also sceptical about the new salt. It was more expensive (although not much). The packaging was different, and some thought it didn't taste so good. So there were publicity campaigns, negotiations and consultations.

Beside the governments in the region and UNICEF, several international organizations became involved. Kiwanis International made the campaign against iodine deficiency a main objective. Little by little, people were convinced. By the end of the century, all the countries in West and Central Africa had adopted laws concerning the iodization of household salt, and three-quarters of households in the region were consuming iodized salt. That was not bad in the course of a few years. It is to be hoped that time will prove that the results are sustainable.

Part II

A Journey in History and Society

Moving to Abidjan, I thought that living in one of the most central cities in West and Central Africa would give me first-hand knowledge of people and conditions in the region. I learned a lot, but there were fewer possibilities for exploration and social contacts than I had expected. The beginning was tough. The third night in our new house we became the object of an armed burglary. Bang! all of a sudden, somewhere in the dark. Then a piercing piping – ihhhhhhhh! It is the warning whistle of the night guard. The sound penetrates to the marrow. Before we realize what is going on, the street is full of people – at least sixty gesticulating black men. What is happening? Burglary? Robbery?

It doesn't take long before the car patrol of the security company is on the spot. Our night guard explains: 'Three men tried to break into the house. When they saw me, they fired a shot and ran.' Everybody starts looking around. One of the burglars is discovered in the neighbouring garden. The crowd immediately falls upon him. The man would have been lynched if the security company hadn't driven off with him. We don't want trouble in our street – it is a decent neighbourhood!

We are rather shaky afterwards, both the night guard, my husband and I. The guard trembles like a leaf, even if the shot didn't hit him. My husband and I look at each other. We were prepared for security problems when we came to Abidjan. But armed burglary? It is a bit more than we bargained for. Our luxurious bungalow is well protected with high walls, iron bars and guards both day and night. A really handsome prison. Still, somebody tried to break in with a gun in his hand.

The day after, the security company inspects the house and the garden. The walls are raised and the entrance fortified. We get walkie-talkies so we can call for assistance when we need it. It helps. But we feel the shock a long time. We only start to relax when we get a dog. Rina is a pure Ivorian dog, white and brown, the size of a collie. She lies by the entrance all night and starts barking at the slightest sound, so wakes up both the night guard and us.

The instructions for rich foreigners in Abidjan are that we have to be careful when moving around in the centre of the city and the popular districts. We should dress as if we don't own anything (no jewellery, no expensive watches, handbags, clothes), in order not to attract robbers. After dark, we should not travel outside of the central parts of town. We have to keep the car windows and doors locked and park only in guarded parking lots. It is rather complicated. Even so, several of my UNICEF colleagues were robbed while they were shopping in the centre of town in the middle of the day. In one case, a man and his little daughter were driven out in the countryside by armed thieves, who took the car, their clothes and money, even the wedding ring, before the two victims were dropped off to find their way home as best they could. Fortunately, they were not hurt.

Just before we arrived in 1994, the CFA franc, which is used in the Ivory Coast, was devalued by half. This created serious economic problems for many people. Crime rates rose. The authorities took drastic measures. In several cases, people who were caught in the act of committing a crime were shot immediately, without trial and sentence. But the situation did not improve much, and tensions increased further before the presidential elections in 1995. For formal reasons, the most important candidate from the opposition was prevented from running for the presidency. People protested. The opposition declared that they would boycott the elections. There were demonstrations in the streets, even though these were forbidden. The police and gendarmes were placed on the alert. Suspicious-looking people were arrested. Several demonstrators were killed. In the UN system we prepared for crisis, hoarding water and foodstuffs, checking communications and updating our security plans. But we didn't need any of it. The elections took place in a peaceful and orderly manner. The Acting President, Henri Konan Bédié, won with a great majority. Afterwards, the security situation in the city was much better – until economic mismanagement and political tensions at the end of the 1990s led to the military coup in 1999, which brought increased insecurity and crime.

Rich and Isolated

It was understandable, in a way, that people might want to break into our house. It was a gorgeous two-storey bungalow with a flourishing garden, a swimming pool, refrigerator and stove, telephone, radio and TV. Everything that belonged to a life of luxury, which is completely out of reach for most Ivorians, whose daily lives were marked by hardship and deprivation, more than by wastefulness and abundance.

Everything was arranged so that UNICEF's regional director should enjoy a comfortable life. But it was a puzzle to me how I, living in such affluence, could get a proper understanding of the living conditions of the great majority of Africans, who lived in much worse circumstances, not to mention the poor, who were the primary target group for UNICEF. And that was not all. Due to my status as director and the security problems, I mainly stayed within what has been called the 'VIP bubble'. I not only lived behind high walls but nearly always travelled in a car with locked windows. When I went out, it was mostly to restaurants for the rich. Our shopping mainly took place in the Western-style supermarkets for the upper class. I never took an ordinary bus or train, and at the airport I bypassed all the queues to go to the 'VIP room'.

I met many people in connection with my job. But conversations, meetings and receptions were usually brief and superficial. In regard to Africans, my husband and I came into contact mostly with the staff in the office and our servants at home. The servants changed frequently, so we did not get to know them very well. We often invited the office staff to our house, but they never returned the invitation. One of them explained: 'We Ivorians, we cannot use the informal "tu" ("you" in French) and your first name like others do, when they speak to the regional director. We have to be more formal. We cannot meet privately, either – the social distance is too great.' I only went to the homes of local staff on visits of condolence. We associated with the small Norwegian colony in Abidjan and a few international families. Some of these were from other African countries. During my travels in the region, I was often invited home to the UNICEF representatives, including those from Africa.

In a strange way, I was in Abidjan – and yet not in Abidjan; in Africa – and yet not in Africa. It became a definite challenge to break out of the 'bubble' and get in touch with Africans of different backgrounds and see different aspects of African reality.

'A Security Risk'

We had only to go to our closest neighbours in Abidjan to catch a glimpse of the sub-standard living conditions of many urban Africans. Our bungalow was located in one of the most expensive development areas in the city, but there were a number of sites where no houses had been built. Here, people just came and settled down. They were from other districts or nearby countries, had practically nothing and tried to manage as best they could in the big city. Our neighbouring site lacked water, electricity and sanitation. People set up houses of boards and tin plates, fetched water from taps in the neighbourhood and did their cooking over open fires. The smoke could sometimes shroud the whole neighbourhood. They also acquired hens and sheep, so we were often woken up by cock crows and baa-ing in the morning.

The security company said the neighbours represented a 'security risk' and underlined that we must be careful. We were also uncertain. It didn't seem quite natural to ask for a guided tour of the neighbouring site or invite the neighbours for coffee. So we just said '*Bonjour*' in passing. At times, they asked if we could get them a job (which we unfortunately were unable to), and that was it.

As regional director I did not stay very much in Abidjan. I travelled extensively around in West and Central Africa. I visited all the countries in the region, most of them several times. I always went out in the field to see how people lived, and to inspect projects that were being implemented. In this way I visited a lot of villages, small towns and urban slums, health centres and schools, income-generating activities and social services. I talked with presidents and ministers, civil servants and professionals, representatives of the UN system, bilateral donors and voluntary organizations, local leaders and women's groups, children and young people. It was extremely informative, but the circumstances rarely made it possible to go into much depth. Time was short, and there were welcoming rituals with drums and dancing, palm wine and greetings under the palaver tree. To talk to ordinary people, I usually had to use an interpreter, and conversations with a high-level foreign guest easily took on a certain formal character. It was necessary to supplement these experiences with studies and reading.

Hidden Knowledge

Like many development organizations, UNICEF considers that knowledge of local conditions is a valuable qualification, but not particularly important for international experts. The organization does not, therefore, offer introductory courses in local language, history and culture. Those interested must find it out for themselves. This is not always easy. Few museums in West and Central Africa have particularly rich collections. The media in the region are weak, and book production is very limited. I found some literature in Abidjan, Dakar and Lagos, but most of it was in Paris and New York, where I visited museums and bought books.

Language is an extremely thorny question in sub-Saharan Africa. All the local African languages present special problems. In addition, the national (or international) languages create complications. In West and Central Africa, the countries use Arabic, English, French, Portuguese or Spanish as their national language. Usually, only the educated elite has a good command of it, and very few know more than one of the languages. As a consequence, the region is divided according to language. Official UN documents are always translated. Apart from this, in research, literature and the media, there is, for example, an English-speaking world and a French-speaking world, each with its own documentation, approaches and analyses. English-speaking people get to know very little about the French-speaking countries, and vice versa.

Even in a global organization like UNICEF, language is a sensitive issue. Six international languages are used in official documents and governing bodies, and the working languages internally are English, French and Spanish. But most documents exist only in English, and many staff understand only this language. In headquarters, all meetings, except board meetings, take place in English. In West and Central Africa, it is impossible to manage properly without French. Otherwise in UNICEF, this language is not much used, and documents in French have a very limited circle of readers. I carried on a stubborn fight to increase the emphasis on French, but with few results.

Regardless of language, I often experienced a noticeable lack of information. People have lived in West and Central Africa for thousands of years. But the history is little known in modern times. A widespread view among Europeans has been that Africans are 'primitive' and 'pagan' peoples, worth studying only by missionaries and colonial representatives who are supposed to 'civilize' them. When British students in the 1960s began demanding African history at the university, a famous professor of history in Oxford replied:

> Maybe there will be an African history in the future. Now there is none. There is only the history of the European in Africa. The rest is darkness – and darkness is no theme for history.

Not everybody held the same view, however. Another British historian, Basil Davidson, started studying Africa in the 1950s, travelled extensively on the continent and wrote a number of books to place Africa in world history.

Scientifically, it has been a problem that little archaeological material is preserved in sub-Saharan Africa. Written sources relating to the lives of Africans are lacking to a great extent. From the Middle Ages, there are Arabic accounts, and later European travellers' tales and reports. But more comprehensive written African documents are available only from the last part of the nineteenth century. Western observers have usually had limited access to indigenous customs and ways of thinking. They have described events and utterances according to their own judgement and standards, which in many cases has led to misunderstandings and disparagement. On the other hand, few Africans have had the opportunity to study and transmit in written form their knowledge of cultural and social conditions on the continent to a broader audience. There are important writers, like the historian Joseph Ki-Zerbo from Burkina Faso, the philosopher Cheikh Anta Diop from Senegal and the storyteller Amadou Hampâté Bâ from Mali. I discovered fascinating novels and poetry by female authors, like Mariama Bâ from Senegal, Buchi Emecheta from Nigeria and Ama Ata Aidoo from Ghana, in addition to the better-known male writers. These are valuable contributions, but none the less modest in the total picture.

In 1964, the UN Educational, Scientific and Cultural Organization (UNESCO) initiated a large project to collect and present African history from pre-history to modern times. It took time. The last volume was not finished until 1999. This series of books has become a basic work of reference. Still, very much of the social and cultural history, including women's history, is lacking in written form. It is estimated that there are as many as 10,000 different ethnic groups in the world. Anthropologists

---

Box II.1 The World Summit for Children 2002

A decade after the World Summit for Children in 1990 the United Nations organized a review of progress. On 8–10 May 2002 a special session of the General Assembly on Children was convened in New York to evaluate the results and renew the commitment of the international community. More than seventy heads of state and government participated. They adopted a final outcome document, with 21 goals intended to promote healthy lives, provide quality education, protect against abuse, exploitation and violence and combat HIV/AIDS. The goals included: reduction in the under-five mortality rate by two-thirds by 2015 and in the maternal mortality ratio by three-quarters; elimination of gender disparities in primary and secondary school by 2005; ensuring girls' full and equal access to and achievement in basic education of good quality.

During the end-of-decade review it was noted that the children of sub-Saharan Africa had the most acute needs in 1990. Yet the least progress had been made in this region. By the end of the century, sub-Saharan Africa still had the highest child death rates in the world. While over a hundred countries during the 1990s reduced mortality rates for children under five by 20 per cent or more, the rate for Africa declined by just 5 per cent overall. The mortality rate in 2000 of 175 per thousand – or one in every six children – was 30 times higher than that of children in industrialized countries. Immunization coverage generally decreased in sub-Saharan Africa during the 1990s, and by the end of the decade less than half of the children were fully immunized against diphtheria, pertussis and tetanus. Important progress was made in combating polio and Guinea worm, but the weakness of the public health systems led to a resurgence of major child killers, such as malaria and cholera. Less than half of the children with diarrhoea were treated with oral rehydration therapy.

have supposedly studied 700–800. Much remains to be done, not least in sub-Saharan Africa.

Up-to-date social science reports and statistics from the African countries are relatively few in number and dispersed. There is little current and reliable information. Most of the documentation is produced in the West, sometimes by African professionals, but mostly by Western experts. They can be competent enough, but their insight is necessarily limited. Not

---

In addition, African children were beset by two largely unanticipated calamities: AIDS and war. Africa was the epicentre of the HIV/AIDS pandemic, leaving millions of children without one or both parents. The armed conflicts and violence that consumed some regions not only wiped out advances for children, but led to death and debilitation, suffering, hunger and disease.

At the beginning of the twenty-first century, sub-Saharan Africa had the highest maternal mortality in the world, with women facing a 1 in 13 lifetime risk of dying during pregnancy and childbirth. In industrialized countries the ratio is one in 4,100. The number of malnourished African children climbed during the 1990s, despite notable success with regard to salt iodization and the widespread distribution of vitamin A. It is estimated that by the end of the twentieth century one in eight babies was born underweight each year – the second highest level after South Asia. In spite of modest gains, families in sub-Saharan Africa still had the world's poorest water supply by the end of the 1990s. Slightly more than half of the population had access to safe drinking water. Sanitation coverage was better in Africa than in Asia, but only half of the Africans had access to sanitary means of excreta disposal, there having been no gain in this area since 1990.

Net primary school enrolment in sub-Saharan Africa rose from 54 to 60 per cent from 1990 to 1998. However, coverage was the lowest in the world and no progress was made in closing the gender gap. Sub-Saharan Africa accounted for one-third of the world's children out of school, who were vulnerable – increasingly, it seemed – to every kind of exploitation and abuse. More adults became literate during the 1990s, but by the end of the century nearly half of the women and one-third of the men were illiterate. Only South Asia had more widespread illiteracy.

(Source: United Nations Secretary General: *We the Children*, 2001)

all acknowledge this, unlike the Norwegian historian, Jarle Simensen, in the last chapter of his African history, where he notes that the future challenge for history is to penetrate more deeply into African ways of thinking.

Unanswered Questions

The longer I worked in the region, the more questions arose that it seemed urgent to clarify. Since 1990, UNICEF regularly drew up a balance sheet showing the progress of nations in relation to the goals set by the World Summit for Children. It was depressing. I arrived in headquarters from the field with strong impressions of the efforts made under difficult conditions – only to receive the confirmation that the year 2000 goals remained out of reach for most people in West and Central Africa. There was progress, but not enough. Some countries achieved some goals, but none achieved all of them. Perhaps the year 2000 goals were unrealistic. But comparisons with other regions were also discouraging. Most African countries found themselves at the bottom of the global ranking list, the poorest in the class.

Why is it so difficult to improve the conditions of women and children in a region like West and Central Africa?

Africa is the cradle of humanity with thousands of years of history behind it. Great empires and highly developed civilizations have been created in West and Central Africa. But Africans today rarely pride themselves on their past and their identity. What has happened? An insight into African history might provide an answer.

West and Central Africa is richly endowed by nature. There are forests and cultivable land, oil and minerals, gold, silver and diamonds. Still, most of the countries are classified among the poorest in the world. What kind of economic development has led to this situation?

When the African countries gained their independence in the 1960s, there was great exultation. Now there would be progress! But 40 years later, people are struggling with authoritarian regimes, civil wars and states in disorganization. An analysis of events in the political arena might give a better understanding of the problems.

In the past, West and Central Africa was famous for its female chiefs and commerically successful women. Today, African women are mostly presented as poor, powerless and pregnant. How can this be? An in-depth description of the roles of women in the past and the present seems to be warranted.

Western media often transmit an image of Africans as primitive and underdeveloped. But a visitor is rapidly impressed by people's practical skills and artistic creativity. It is necessary to take a closer look at religion, crafts and traditional culture.

Everywhere in Africa there are great disparities between urban and rural, traditional and modern, African and Western. How can people relate to all this in a sensible way? What type of adjustments exist between old and new?

While my journey through history and society cannot give complete answers to all these questions, it might conceivably contribute to a better grasp of an extremely varied and dramatic reality.

ELEVEN

From Emperors of the Desert to the White Man's Yoke: Centuries of History with Greatness and Humiliation

'Whoever disregards what he was yesterday,
will tomorrow be nothing, absolutely nothing.'
(Amadou Hampâté Bâ, Malian philosopher and writer)

The plane goes in for landing. Undulating sand dunes stretch as far as the eye can see, with some stringy bushes and a handful of low yellowish brown houses. Is that all? Is this the Great and Forbidden City Timbuktu, according to oral tradition mysterious, beautiful and rich? It looks mostly like a small overgrown village in the middle of nowhere. But it is Timbuktu. And on closer acquaintance it turns out to be far more than an ordinary village.

Timbuktu was founded by Tuareg tribespeople around AD 1100, at the point where the Sahara borders on the fertile Sahel and the Niger river makes a bend to the north before going south to the Gulf of Guinea. The town developed into a busy trading post for camel caravans crossing the desert from north to south and pirogues sailing from east to west on the river. Trade flourished: gold, salt, cloths, hardware, dates, fish, millet and rice, as well as cattle and slaves. People settled there, and built houses and mosques. Gradually, Timbuktu was established as an important religious, scientific and literary centre for the whole Niger river region and the Islamic world. In its heyday, around AD 1400–1500, the city probably had a population of about 100,000, including merchants, judges, priests and scholars, and seven mosques, two of them large.

As a result of conflicts, invasions and pillage the city gradually fell into decay. European explorers who managed to reach Timbuktu some centuries later had difficulty hiding their disappointment: 'The sight before me did not answer my expectations. I had formed a totally different idea of the grandeur and wealth of Timbuktu,' the French adventurer René Caillié wrote in 1828. All he could see was 'a mass of ill-looking houses built of earth. Everything had a dull appearance.'

At my school in Norway, a single sentence was devoted to Timbuktu in my history book: 'In the Middle Ages, Timbuktu was a centre for art and learning.' According to the atlas, it was situated in the middle of the desert – so how was it possible to develop art and learning? This was more than a young Norwegian girl could grasp. The dream of visiting Timbuktu one day took shape.

It was not easy. Several attempts failed for several reasons, including the armed conflict in northern Mali in the mid-1990s. But when I attended a meeting in Bamako, the capital of Mali, in May 1998, it was clear that it had to be now or never. The visit is a quick one, taking Air Mali 400 miles early Saturday morning and going back on the same plane just as early on Sunday. A bit crazy, and I don't spend many hours in the mystical city, either. A sandstorm delays my arrival for three hours, and sightseeing is impossible during the lunch hour and Saturday prayers. The visit can only start at 4:30 p.m. But I get a very knowledgeable guide: the head of the Office for Culture, Ali Ould Sidi. He arrives wearing a splendid light blue tunic and a white turban. On the way to the mosque, he explains that the turban is wound in such a way that it takes the shape of the first letter in Allah's name.

The grandeur of Timbuktu was a long time ago. The city now contains scarcely 15,000 souls. Still, the historic atmosphere and current challenges are fascinating. The town is a sprawl of low, flat-roofed mud-brick houses with nomad camps in between. The buildings face inwards to protect the inhabitants from the sun and the sand, and in previous years also from attacks. Occasional camel caravans pass by, swaying slowly at every stride, while small mules trot along pulling carts laden with water and wood. Everywhere it is dry and hot. Not a blade of grass; only sand with a few bushes and trees. The 'green belt' around the city, which is supposed to prevent sand drift, consists mostly of thin bunches of straw. The draught caused the river to recede. The harbour is still there, a little way from town, but it is completely dried out, without a ripple of water against the docks. The boats have been moved ten miles away, where the Niger river still flows quietly along. Drinking water is pumped up from deep wells using sun panels (supported by UNICEF), but its distribution has to be rationed.

The town seems to be slowly filling up with sand. The mosques don't tower above the houses as they once did. On some of the old drawings, the urban agglomeration is situated on a hill dominated by three sturdy minarets. Now you must go *down* several steps from the street level to enter the houses. The wind brings in sand, and during the rainy season, mud plastering on the buildings slides down into the narrow streets and alleyways. Every year, the façades are repaired with mud mixed with cow dung. Still, one gets the impression that the city is on the verge of collapse and will progressively disappear.

The Djinguereber mosque – the largest – is neither architecturally impressive nor in good repair, but it is very old. It was originally constructed around AD 1400, when Mansa Musa, king of Mali, ruled the town. Inside, there is little of the lofty vaults and rich sculpture that characterize French medieval cathedrals. There is no stone in the Sahel. The pillars supporting the construction are made of sun-dried mud-bricks attached with mortar. There have to be very many of them. Each pillar is so thick that the aisles in between are quite narrow. The roof is of wooden beams, covered by mud plastering. Light and air filter in only through the doorways. It is quite dark, and even with modern electrical fans, chokingly hot. During my visit the mosque is empty. But how would it be with thousands of worshippers, tightly packed? Ali notes that Timbuktu had one of the world's first universities. Theology, Islamic law, history, grammar, logic, rhetoric, ethics and astrology were taught and studied. At its height, there were as many as 150–180 schools, spread all over town, with up to 9,000 students – but not all went to the mosque at the same time!

The city is still full of mysteries, but different from my expectations. There are thousands of manuscripts, most in Arabic and some in Songhay, kept from ancient times in libraries and private homes. The majority are neither studied nor analysed, even if considerable efforts have been made to collect and preserve the texts. An important part of the history not only of West Africa, but of other parts of the Islamic world, is stored away here and has never been made public. What could be discovered about people, events and cultures that we know little about today? Here are challenges for historical research and cultural preservation. Ali becomes more and more eloquent, talking eagerly on the way to his courtyard, where we enjoy couscous with lamb surrounded by his children and cats.

The discussion continues under the starry sky on the sand dunes outside the city. Representatives from the local administration explain:

> We had difficult times with armed conflict between Tuaregs and the authorities, but now we have peace. Recently, we had a big 'fire of peace' in town. The president came and representatives from the UN and many countries, Norway among others. We destroyed 3,000 weapons. But now we must respond to the needs of the population. Otherwise, we will have problems. In the old days, Timbuktu was a centre. Today, we are at the periphery. Conditions are tough – a fact people in the capital easily forget.

The voices take on a reproachful tone. Suddenly, the tensions between the centre and periphery sound strangely familiar. They remind me of my stay in Tromsø, in the far north of Norway, where people complained that their needs were neglected by the decision-makers in the capital of Oslo.

Great Empires

Before AD 1000, West and Central Africa passed through many stages of civilization. From AD 600, larger empires began to replace smaller kingdoms, and from AD 1100 to the end of 1500 people in the region experienced a very dynamic period, a 'period of greatness' for black Africa. The region saw some of the mightiest empires in Africa. In the west, the empires of Ghana, Mali and Songhay succeeded one another, while the empire of Kanem-Bornu dominated the east. All the empires arose in the grasslands of the Sahel and were related to the trans-Saharan long-distance trade. Gold, ivory and slaves were brought from the south and exchanged for salt, silks and goods from North Africa. For the trade to succeed, people needed protection, peace and order. Strong centralized states developed, with powerful emperors who could guarantee the safety of markets and caravan routes. For many centuries, black rulers thus controlled areas the size of Europe. Exceptional wealth was accumulated at the same time as learning, art and crafts flourished. Islam spread gradually with the traders, above all to the elites in the grasslands.

The first empire was that of Ghana, or the 'gold country' (which has no relation to the modern state of Ghana). It was created in the region between the Niger and Senegal rivers, where different ethnic groups were engaged in agriculture and cattle breeding. Here gold grew like carrots, it was said, and the kingdom was established in connection with the gold mines and markets. From AD 900 it became a real empire. It was governed by a king, assisted by a large council of influential people. The king had a monopoly on gold and taxed the transportation of goods in and out. The wealth acquired made it possible to raise an army of warriors, including foot-soldiers, archers and horsemen, and to oblige lesser kings or chiefs to submit. The emperor was an animist, but accepted Islam with benevolent tolerance.

From AD 1000 the empire of Ghana broke up. Its place was taken by the empire of Mali, which became much larger. Gradually, it expanded from Gao and Timbuktu in the east to the Atlantic Ocean in the west. More complicated forms of government were developed. The king, Mansa, had a clan of noblemen and an army. The core area was divided into provinces, cantons and villages and was controlled directly. The conquered provinces were ruled indirectly, through representatives of the king and local leaders, who had to supply foodstuffs and weapons. Other states subordinated themselves and sent presents. A remarkable security and religious tolerance prevailed across the whole empire. For two centuries, Mali was the wealthiest state in West Africa. When the most powerful ruler, Mansa Musa, a Muslim, went on a pilgrimage to Mecca, he gave away so much gold that prices fell on the Cairo market.

It was difficult to keep such a great empire together. From about AD 1400 it ran into trouble. The Songhay people became the rulers of West Africa. They were a river people from Gao, whose leaders decided to re-establish law and order after the fall of the empire of Mali. Sonni Ali created an empire that by AD 1600 was the greatest in the region, extending from Agades to the Atlantic. He was a powerful ruler who led one army after another to conquer different ethnic groups. He was never defeated. He was also extremely brutal, and some ethnic groups were almost anni-hilated. Later, the Askia dynasty took over and built up an administration with a well-educated bureaucracy and a professional army. Islam was now made the supreme religion. Nobody in West Africa could escape the pressure from the empire of Songhay as long as it existed. But a new factor entered the picture. Soldiers from the Sultan of Morocco came looking for gold from the north with something completely new – namely firearms. Faced with this weapon, the Songhay were defeated in a major battle in 1591.

The empire of Kanem-Bornu around Lake Chad was as important to Central Africa as the other empires were to West Africa. Even if it was not as big, Kanem-Bornu lasted longer, as much as a thousand years from AD 700, varying in power and size. The political organization and admin-istration, a decentralized feudal monarchy, was reminiscent of the empires of Mali and Songhay. The noblemen soon converted to Islam. The army had highly trained troops, and law and order were established over a very long period, in spite of outbreaks of violence.

Government without Kings

Both during and after the great empires, a number of smaller kingdoms and alliances sprang up in the grasslands and forest regions of West and Central Africa. Through the ages, there has been a multitude of societies and civilizations, each differing from the others in regard to settlement and economic life, social organization and religion. Historical maps of Africa showing the ethnic groups and communities look like patchwork quilts. From one era to the next, the patches change in number, size and locations. Among important societies, one can mention the Wolof states, the Mossi kingdoms, the Hausa emirates, the Ashanti empire, the Fouta-Djalon theocracy, the Abomey kingdom, the Senufo villages, the Fulani empire, the Bamileke kingdoms, the Congo empire, the Luba and Landa kingdoms and the Fang people.

Besides centralized states, there were numerous decentralized non-state societies. It is estimated that about half of the population south of the Sahara lived in decentralized societies before the colonial era. In West and Central Africa, these were found both in the forest regions and the grasslands, and included farmers as well as cattle breeders. In the same region, there could be both centralized and decentralized societies. Best known are perhaps the government without rulers of the Igbo people and the autonomous cities of the Yoruba, of which Ife was the most important, in the forest areas around the lower part of the Niger river (today's Nigeria). In close relation to Ife, the Benin empire was developed (which is not in the modern state of Benin).

The Igbo were divided into several large groups that differed somewhat with regard to language, customs and systems of government. Most governed themselves and did not concede power to chiefs. Some developed a form of constitutional village monarchy. The Igbo lived in villages in the rainforest, cultivating vegetables, corn, cotton and tobacco. They did this with outstanding success. In addition, they were skilled craftsmen in weaving and metalworking, which provided a basis for local trade. The villages were governed by lineage heads on the basis of family and religious ties. Every family, or part of a family, ran its own affairs, but observed strict behavioural norms based on a common religion. People were organized by age and status into groups with special tasks, sometimes also in 'title societies' (of people who had acquired titles) and secret associations. The society was democratic, in the sense that matters of common interest were decided in village assemblies. Here, a consensus usually was reached. People were also encouraged to take the initiative and solve problems themselves. Such small societies were vulnerable to external attacks, but the decentralized structure made it difficult for others to control them over a long period of time.

The Yoruba people were forest farmers, like the Igbo, but lived in towns instead of villages. These towns were often quite large and served as important centres for crafts, with potters, weavers, metalworkers and carpenters, in addition to farmers. Every lineage head was responsible for his own quarter of the town, which governed itself. Each group also sent representatives to a council of chiefs, which exercised important political powers. It chose the *oba*, the traditional Yoruba ruler who had the task of executing political decisions. The *obas* were considered to be the descendants of the common Yoruba ancestor, Odoudouwa. The system was democratic at the local level. But important matters were decided by a small number of nobles. The central city states were linked together by agreements among the ruling families, under the political and spiritual leadership of the oldest Yoruba ruler, Oni in Ife. Thus peace was ensured at the same time as each town remained self-governing. Religion was very important for the Yoruba. They felt strong loyalty to Odoudouwa and the ancestors, and to the Oni of Ife who represented them. Sculptures were made in wood and bronze, burnt clay and ivory in honour of Yoruba beliefs and rulers. In Ife, an important school of sculpture evolved, producing heads, busts and statues of exceptional power and beauty.

The Benin empire was associated with Odoudouwa and with Ife as a holy city, but developed among the Edo, one of the neighbouring peoples. The empire reached its heyday around AD 1400, when the *oba* expanded the territory, built roads and embellished the capital. As in Ife, the artists were encouraged to honour the rulers. A special style of royal sculpture was developed. In addition to heads and figures, bronze plaques were designed and made to decorate the *oba*'s palace.

To fully enjoy the art of Ife and Benin, it is necessary to look outside Africa. Much of its art and treasures – more than two thousand objects – were removed during the colonial period and spread all over the world. The Metropolitan Museum in New York has an outstanding selection. The carved elephant tusks from Benin are a special attraction: 4.5 feet long, they present the history books of the *obas* and their merits in small reliefs around each tusk. The details are astonishing. Future generations can find here an account of the past, at a time when there was no written language. The heads of the *obas* and queen mothers are also distinctive. They are cast in brass and bronze using the 'lost wax method'. The models are made of wax. Each figure is covered with a thick coating of clay and then fired. The wax melts and the clay hardens, so that the form can be filled with molten metal. The heads are rather abstract, with impersonal faces denoting power and wealth. They are richly decorated. The hair is plaited with all kinds of symbols, and the neck is surrounded by opulent bead collars. The large, almond-shaped eyes have a moving beauty. The Ife sculptures are more portrait-like, with a sublime dignity.

The Slave Trade

While the period from AD 1100 to 1600 was one of dramatic greatness, following centuries were marked by transition and social change. The great empires in the grasslands broke up and were replaced by smaller kingdoms. People moved towards the rainforest areas. The trans-Saharan trade followed different routes. Travel by boat became more widespread. Contacts with European seafarers along the Atlantic coast increased, and the slave trade became more and more important.

Slavery was no new phenomenon in Africa when the Europeans started their slave trade around AD 1500. For centuries, the victors in local conflicts had acquired slaves. Slaves were taken northward across the Sahara by the trade caravans. But the transatlantic slave trade was different. The slaves were deported to another, distant continent. The trade was extremely comprehensive and longlasting (about four centuries). It is estimated that nearly 55,000 crossings were organized, mostly by the Portuguese. The British were close behind them, followed by the Spaniards and French. In addition, the slave trade was characterized by a pitiless brutality, both during the crossings and on the plantations in the New World, making it an extreme example of human barbarism and degradation.

Contacts with the Europeans along the Atlantic coast started about the mid-1400s, when the Portuguese began sailing to Africa. They were traders, and were welcomed by local chiefs. The goods were paid for in gold. Increasingly, the Europeans wanted slaves. They needed labour, particularly after the Portuguese and Spaniards established plantations in America. The Dutch, British and French followed. At first, criminals and prisoners of war were sold. Gradually, the Africans went to war to get slaves. A vicious circle was created. The Europeans had a decisive weapon – guns. The more guns an African chief had, the stronger he was in fighting his enemies. But to obtain guns, he had to sell slaves. If he didn't capture slaves, he and his people could be themselves captured. Recent research estimates that about twelve to fifteen million slaves were transported from Africa across the Atlantic in the course of four centuries.

Denmark and Norway participated actively in the slave trade. The government in present-day Ghana resides in a castle dating from the slave period, which has the typical Danish name of Christiansborg. In 1672 it was suggested that a triangular route be started from Denmark to Guinea and the West Indies. The ships would carry goods from Copenhagen to Guinea that could be exchanged for slaves. In the West Indies, the slaves could be exchanged for sugar, which could then be sold in Copenhagen. Thousands of slaves were transported by Danish and Norwegian ships across the ocean from Africa to the West Indies during 150 years or more. The Danish author, Torkild Hansen, has described this Scandinavian slave activity, and it was no less brutal than the rest of the trade.

Not many castles and forts remain in their original style. One of the most important is Elmina, which was built by the Portuguese in 1482 and later captured by the Dutch. While the coastline in the Ivory Coast consists only of sand and lagoons, that in Ghana has rocks and stones. The forts and castles were constructed so that they could dominate the sea, as well as the forest and surrounding villages. Local stone was used, in addition to bricks and cement transported from Europe. The structures were extremely solid. It was not easy to get in – and being locked in, it was even more difficult to escape.

Elmina is surrounded by a fishing village. Its bustling activity contrasts with the desolate castle. From the outside the castle looks impressive, with tall white walls and towers. Once you enter, the cruel past becomes evident. As many as a thousand slaves could be held in the dungeons, females separated from males. Several hundred women were packed in a single room. Two containers were placed at the various ends to serve as toilets. The food was extremely poor. After some weeks, the women were too weak to move. They lay on the floor in a mixture of urine, faeces and menstrual blood. The stench was almost unbearable. Many died. At times, all the female prisoners were ordered into the inner courtyard, so the governor could select one, who was washed and brought up to be raped. If she became pregnant, she was not sent away with the other slaves, but remained in Elmina. The men were in chains and branded with hot metal. They were packed in an underground tunnel without light, water or sanitation. If anybody dared to complain, the punishment was merciless, a slow torture until death came as a relief. The stone walls showed scratches from the nails of desperate prisoners.

Africans were not the only ones to die in Elmina. The coast of West Africa is called the white man's grave, because so many Europeans died from climate fever (a common name for diseases like malaria, dysentery, yellow fever and Guinea worm). Some survived only a few days. Others died after some weeks. Not many lived to return to Europe.

Today, the cannons are rusty. The boys are energetically playing football on the beach, where the boats previously landed to get captives. We enjoy a cold drink and listen to the wash of the waves against the cliffs, while darkness falls. There are no sailing ships on the horizon. But the past will not let go. There was a young Norwegian, born in Trondheim in 1690, who boarded one of the slave ships as an apprentice seaman aged only 16. According to the reports, it must have been a frightful trip, leaving painful memories. But later in his life, the young sailor never mentioned these experiences, although he spent his career at sea and became a famous hero in both Denmark and Norway, honoured by the name of Tordenskiold, or 'shield of thunder'.

African Slavery

The transatlantic slave trade was prohibited shortly after 1800. But Africa's domestic slavery continued. Towards the end of the nineteenth century, perhaps one-quarter of the population of West Africa – probably more in Central Africa – were slaves. Rich families could afford several hundred slaves. Labour was in short supply, and women as well as men represented a valuable resource. Slaves were acquired by conquest, taxation or purchase. They were employed in all areas of the economy: in agriculture and domestic service, as porters, craftsmen, businessmen and soldiers. Ethnic groups with high mortality rates wanted female slaves to maintain the population. Some accepted mixed marriages. There were different categories of slaves, but all were under their master's authority and had to work extremely hard. Nevertheless, compared to the European system, traditional slavery in Africa was a much milder affair. The African slaves were treated better. They could improve their status, become rich and work themselves into freedom. Sometimes they could obtain important positions in the administration or the military.

The female slaves were often domestic workers with similar tasks to the free women. They were more integrated into the families. In Central Africa, where there was an extensive slave trade in the 1800s, slave women could be sold and married several times in the course of a lifetime. A single woman could have as many as ten different masters and husbands. For some, the solution was to escape to the nearest town or missionary station.

The European colonial powers brought the transatlantic slave trade to a halt by about 1850. Slavery was also prohibited in the African colonies. But implementation of the abolition took time, because of the economic interests vested in the system by local chiefs, as well as by European colonial masters. It was not unusual for slaves to continue as vassals, 'debt prisoners' or forced labour after they were formally 'free'. Even today, the repercussions of slavery are noted in the weak economic and social position of many former slaves and their families.

Colonial Exploitation

When the transatlantic slave trade ended, an important and profitable, but 'shameful' business was replaced by a 'legal' one that was even more comprehensive and lucrative. Around 1830, the European mission was to bring trade, Christianity and civilization to Africa. The trade expanded rapidly, including palm oil, peanuts, wood, cotton, salt, alcohol and weapons. At the same time, developments within weapon and transport technology, together with the discovery of quinine as a preventive medicine against malaria, made it possible for Christian missionaries, explorers and traders to penetrate further into the continent. Soon the Europeans became more ambitious. They did not want only to trade. They sought to conquer and control the African communities. From 1880 to 1918, there was a scramble for Africa among different European powers trying to acquire as much as possible of the resource-rich continent. In the course of a few decades, practically all of Africa became a European possession. Only Ethiopia and Liberia maintained their independence (and Ethiopia was occupied at a later stage).

The colonial period can be divided into different phases. The first phase covers the conquest of the colonies. This took place mainly by coercive force, although in many cases a collaboration was established between the colonial power and traditional leaders. But a number of ethnic groups resisted the conquest and subsequent oppression, particularly the use of forced labour. In West and Central Africa, bloody clashes took place during colonization of the Islamic empires in the Sahel, and of the Asante and Dahomey kingdoms (now Ghana and Benin) along the Gulf of Guinea. Colonization of the decentralized societies in Nigeria also took time. In Central Africa, inhumane conditions in the use of forced labour on plantations and in railway construction led to a number of revolts. These met with strong international reaction, as recently as the period between the two World Wars. Generally, though, the situation in the colonies was relatively peaceful after the First World War, and various forms of modernization were accelerated.

To control the colonies and promote production and trade, the colonial powers developed a physical infrastructure and a state system according to the European model, with a bureaucratic administration backed up by laws and decrees and coercive powers to ensure peace and order. They concentrated on the development of productive capacity, construction of modern means of transportation and collection of taxes. In West and Central Africa, most of the countries were French colonies, but some were British. There were also Portuguese and German colonies, as well as Belgian and Spanish. Some countries experienced several colonial rulers. The colonial dominance varied from one country to another, and each ruling power introduced its language and institutions. The impact also differed among different groups of Africans. Life in rural areas was affected only to a limited extent, and continued very much as before in spite of changes in the methods of production. The position of local leaders varied, but they rarely disappeared, even if their power was reduced. The urban areas, on the other hand, underwent great change with the establishment of a commercial and industrial modern sector with new working methods and professions. The new, Western-educated African elite was of special importance.

Disaster or Blessing?

The colonization of Africa was extremely complicated and multifaceted. Looking back, the question arises of whether the overall impact of colonialism was a disaster or a blessing for the continent. It is not easy to say. Analyses have been based on varying assumptions. Differing views have been expressed. Some maintain that the whole business was a bloody affair that never should have taken place. Others, on the contrary, think that the positive aspects were more important than the negative. As it is impossible to provide a complete picture here, I present the summary made by the African professor of history at the University of Ghana, A. Adu Boahen, in the *UNESCO General History of Africa*. In my view it gives an accurate and nuanced evaluation while maintaining a clear perspective.

In the *political* field, Boahen underlines that a positive impact of colonialism, once it was consolidated, was a greater degree of peace and stability than before. In place of the hundreds of independent clan and lineage groups, city states, kingdoms and empires without clearly defined boundaries, were now established 50 well-defined states with new bureaucracies and new judicial systems. But the indigenous systems of government were weakened and, according to Boahen, the new states created many more problems than they solved. Their boundaries cut across pre-existing ethnic groups, states and kingdoms. Each nation state was made up of a medley of peoples with different cultures, myths of origin, tradition and language. The states were of different sizes, and were unequal in natural resources and economic potential. The government and all public property belonged not to the people, but to the colonial rulers. The view became widespread that people could take advantage of the state at the smallest opportunity. Full-time or standing armies were created, which were previously unknown in many parts of Africa. The armies were not disbanded after independence and became a very serious impediment for the peoples of the continent.

The most important negative impact of the colonial rule, according to Boahen, was the loss of African sovereignty and independence, and with them the right of Africans to shape their own destiny. A new type of African nationalism, and also of pan-Africanism, developed under colonialism. But the nationalism was not the result of a positive feeling of identity with or commitment to the new nation state. It was generated by a sense of anger and frustration caused by the oppressive and discriminatory measures introduced by the colonial rulers.

Africa obtained a share in the *economic* progress, some will say. Boahen agrees that colonialism had important economic consequences for the continent, although it was a mixed blessing. The infrastructure of roads, railways and telecommunications was positive. Mineral resources were exploited and the mining industry bloomed. The cultivation of cocoa, coffee, tobacco, groundnuts, sisal and rubber spread over large areas. Land was commercialized, and the growing of cash crops enabled individuals to acquire wealth. The demand for consumer goods and a higher standard of living increased. The introduction of a cash economy, currency and banking activities, and the tremendous expansion in the volume of trade between Africa and Europe, led to the integration of the African economy into that of the world in general and into the capitalist economies of the colonial powers in particular.

But most of the present-day developmental problems that African countries are facing can be traced to the colonial impact, according to Boahen. The colonial period was a time of ruthless economic exploitation, rather than economic development of the continent. Most roads and railways were constructed to transport resources out of the continent, not to facilitate intra-African contacts or to promote overall economic development. Local African and inter-African trade were discouraged, if not banned altogether. No attempts were made to diversify the agricultural economy or to encourage the processing of locally produced raw materials and industrialization. The production of a single, or at best two, cash crops in each country was the rule, like cocoa in the Gold Coast and groundnuts in Senegal and the Gambia. Such industries and crafts as existed in Africa in pre-colonial times were more or less destroyed. Under the colonial system, Africans were, in most cases, made to produce what they did not consume, and to consume what they did not produce. Expatriate banking, shipping and trading companies were established on the continent, and the huge profits that accrued from export and import activities went to them and not to Africans. The assets that were created in the colonies were usually not realized and invested in Africa, but re-

---

Box 11.1 Time of Martyrdom

The White killed my father
My father was proud
The White raped my mother
My mother was beautiful
The White bent my brother under the sun of the roads
My brother was strong
The White turned toward me
His hands red with black blood
And said in His Master's voice:
'Boy! An easy-chair, a towel, water!'

(By David Mandessi Diop, poet from Senegal/Cameroon. From *Coups de Pilon*, 1956. Translated by Simon Mpondo and Frank Jones)

mained inaccessible in the metropolitan capitals. Above all, the economic growth that was achieved during the colonial period implied a phenomenal and unjustifiable cost to Africans, in the form of forced labour and forced movement of population, compulsory seizure of land and compulsory cultivation of certain crops.

Boahen describes how the colonial period changed the *social* structure of the continent. After the first decades of colonial rule, there was a rapid population increase. The pace of urbanization was greatly accelerated by the creation and widening of the gap between urban centres and rural areas. The traditional social structure was radically altered. The urban dwellers became divided into the elite, or bourgeoisie, the non-elite and the urban proletariat. In many areas, a rural proletariat emerged in addition to the peasants. The status of African women generally deteriorated. Particularly in the urban areas, the quality of life was improved by increased employment and the provision of health and sanitary facilities. But urban slums expanded, and social services were grossly inadequate and unevenly distributed.

Both Islam and Christianity gained more ground under colonialism. Western education spread. Each country acquired a lingua franca, and education was based on European language and culture. African traditions, art and culture were degraded and condemned. There was contempt for manual labour and agricultural work. In the field of education, the emphasis was on primary schools. Secondary and higher education were not started until much later. Most Africans remained illiterate. Local languages were not developed, and the Western-educated African elite became an alienated group. Colonialism therefore led to stagnation, if not decline, of African culture. Many Africans felt a deep sense of uncertainty and inferiority.

In October 1999, I spent a long tropical evening with Boahen on his porch in Accra. He summed up his view of colonialism:

> It was neither an unmitigated disaster nor an unqualified blessing for Africa, in my opinion. There were both positive and negative aspects. Totally, the negative carries more weight than the positive, though. The element of economic exploitation was very far in excess of that of economic development. Constructive measures were implemented, but given the opportunities and resources, the power and influence of the colonial rulers at the time, they could and should have done far more than they did. Therefore, the colonial era will go down in history, on balance, as a period of growth without development – a period of lost opportunities and humiliation of the peoples of Africa.

I cannot express it better.

Lasting Impression

In the history of a continent, the colonial period lasted a relatively short time, less than one hundred years. Still, it was a very important period. It represented a watershed, changing the course of development from what it otherwise would have been. The period of independence has been even shorter. Most of the countries in West and Central Africa achieved their independence around 1960. Only Guinea Bissau, Cape Verde and Sao Tome and Principe had to wait till the 1970s, after a long liberation struggle against the Portuguese. Independence, therefore, has lasted slightly more than one generation. Many people of today bear testimony to the deep impressions from the colonial past.

The decolonization was extremely rapid. The Second World War created a completely new international situation. In the course of ten to fifteen years, the majority of the colonies became independent states. It was a revolution with great consequences. But in hindsight, less was changed than one might have expected. The African countries became independent politically, but Western influence and their economic dependence continued, even if the forms of it changed.

The relationship with the colonial power was different in the previous British and French colonies. With the exception of Guinea, all the French colonies joined the French-African '*communauté*' or community, which gave France considerable power in areas of defence and foreign policy, economic relations and monetary policy, in addition to language and cultural policy. Close personal contacts between African and French leaders ensured French influence over the African leadership, while the Africans obtained political and financial support. An example was given in 1996, when French troops intervened to control soldiers in the Central African Republic demonstrating in their capital, Bangui, because they did not receive their salaries. The president of the Central African Republic, Ange-Félix Patassé declared: 'But I am French! Just because I have become Central African, it does not mean that I have to give up France ... As an institution of the republic, the French army has to defend me!'

The British colonies became members of the Commonwealth. But this did not entail the same contractual obligations, and the relations with the previous colonial power were more varied from country to country.

TWELVE

Poor Amid the Riches: Hard Work with a Meagre Outcome

We thank the almighty God,
For giving us cassava.
We hail thee, cassava
The great cassava.

You grow in poor soils
You grow in rich soils
You grow in gardens,
You grow in farms.

You are easy to grow
Children can plant you
Women can plant you
Everybody can plant you.

We must sing for you
Great cassava, we must sing
We must not forget
Thee, the great one.

This tribute to cassava was written by Flora Nwapa in the 1980s. Nwapa was the first female novelist in Nigeria in modern times, and 'Cassava Song' is one of her few poems. The poem is based on an ancient female tradition in Igboland, where Flora Nwapa came from. Here the women sing while they work – or, more precisely, they *sing their work*. A woman who sings her work is assumed to be hardworking. At the same time, Nwapa's poem is a protest. Cassava is a tasty and nutritious root that has been a Nigerian staple food for a very long time. Under the influence of the white man, some Nigerians started to view the cassava as inferior to expensive, imported rice. Nwapa therefore defends the cassava and the women who grow it, who are also supposed to be inferior. In Igbo society, yam is considered 'king of the crops' and is above all cultivated by men, while women cultivate cassava. The tribute to cassava is at the same time a song of praise to womanhood, and particularly motherhood; to 'Great Mother Cassava', who loves children and who has sustained the people even when other crops failed, for example during the Biafran war at the end of the 1960s.

Men's and Women's Agriculture

Traditionally, there was no shortage of land in sub-Saharan Africa. But labour was needed to cultivate it. The wealth of a family or lineage was determined by the workforce at its disposal. The lineage formed the basis of society, and individuals were subordinate to the family. Both men and women were given land to cultivate, but it was controlled by the family. The lineage and the family could be organized in different ways. Usually, men had a dominant position, even if women could exert considerable influence. Descent, as well as the transfer of power and assets, often followed the male line, but could also follow the female line.

Society was organized according to the main economic activity – agriculture, cattle breeding or a combination. Within the same economic activity, labour could be divided in different ways. In some ethnic groups, men did most of the agricultural work, but more often women did. The division of labour could, in practice, be rather complicated with men and women taking turns to do what was needed. Often men cleared the ground and removed trees and roots, looked after the cattle, went hunting, conducted long-distance trade, engaged in warfare if necessary, and dealt with political matters. Women planted cereals and vegetables, weeded, harvested and stored the crops, provided firewood and water, gathered wild fruits and plants, traded locally and were responsible for the welfare of the household. Because of their efforts, women represented an important resource, and could have a certain economic autonomy.

The colonial period brought numerous economic and social changes. The right to land became increasingly personal and private, and was assigned to men as 'heads of the household'. Women became economically more dependent. Usually, they earned little money and did not have access to capital, which required property as collateral. Production became more varied. In addition to traditional crops, people started cultivating specialized products such as cocoa, palm oil and groundnuts to earn money. The most fertile land was used for cash crops. These were generally the responsibility of men. Able-bodied men were also engaged, voluntarily or by force, to work on the European plantations, in construction, mines and industry. Subsistence farming was left to women, who often had to operate on their own, using the least fertile land.

The pattern of women pursuing subsistence farming and men cash crops continued after independence. During the early decades, agriculture in general, and subsistence agriculture in particular, were to a great extent neglected by the authorities. This included the allocation of resources and measures to increase productivity, as well as to improve living conditions in rural areas. To the extent that assistance, training or support for technological innovations were provided, the focus was on cash crops, because these yielded export revenues. Subsistence farming was ignored, and women continued cultivating as they had done for centuries. A 'women's agriculture' was established, with women producing food for local consumption without modern tools and inputs, often using a hoe or digging stick, without access to credit, with low productivity and a meagre outcome. 'Men's agriculture' was characterized by men cultivating cash crops, in many cases using draught animals or a tractor with a plough, aided by fertilizer and modern chemicals, and earning a cash income. The neglect on the part of the authorities, combined with environmental degradation and population problems, led to a large-scale agricultural crisis in Africa during the whole postcolonial period. Not all countries were hit, but on the whole, the production of food no longer kept up with the population growth. The continent became less and less able to feed its inhabitants. Food had to be imported. Poverty in the rural areas increased. Gradually, the exports of agricultural products also stagnated.

Women's Triple Workload

The main food crops in West and Central Africa are sorghum and millet, corn and rice, yam, cassava and bananas. In addition, cowbells, groundnuts and squash, cucumber and tomatoes, as well as mangos and papaya are cultivated. In the grasslands, sorghum and millet dominate, because they require little water. Yam, cassava and bananas depend on the humidity of the forest areas. The tsetse fly prevents cattle breeding near the coast, but in the grasslands the farmers can supplement land cultivation with livestock farming. Some ethnic groups are traditionally nomadic and live by cattle breeding. People fish along the rivers and the coast. There are still a few tribes living by hunting and gathering in the rainforest (in the Central African Republic and the Democratic Republic of Congo).

Women's work is of special importance. In sub-Saharan Africa, women produce and process most of the family's food. The food crops demand extensive effort. First, the land must be slashed and burnt and the soil turned. Planting must take place before the rains come. Irrigation systems are rare in subsistence agriculture. Often planting takes several weeks, and weeding as well as harvesting may require months of labour. Possible

---

Box 12.1 The Weaker Sex?

The weaker sex, is it?
Is it a weaker breed who pounds the yam
Or bends all day to plant the millet
With a child strapped to her back?

(From the *Lion and the Jewel* by Wole Soyinka, Nigeria, 1962)

surplus for sale must be marketed, and this takes considerable time. Women in the village help one another, and older children also assist. In some cases, men may give a helping hand, especially when it is urgent to plant seeds or harvest crops.

People in West and Central Africa mostly eat a porridge of mashed cereals or roots with a tasty sauce. If there is little to eat, the porridge is served with only a few green leaves. Otherwise, the sauce can contain both meat, fish and vegetables. Cooking usually is very time-consuming. Eleven steps are required to make porridge from grains of maize. The process is extremely demanding for women with no modern aids. The grains first have to be taken off the cob and threshed. By sifting the grains in the wind, the shells blow away and the grains can be soaked in water. After some days, the grains are washed, dried and ground. The cornstarch is dried again before it is stored and used. Yam and cassava also require extensive cleaning, cutting, possibly grinding and cooking. Some types of cassava contain a toxic substance and it takes days of cooking, steaming and drying to eliminate it. It is estimated that African women in rural areas on the average spend four to five hours every day processing food for the family.

African families are large. Most women have five to six completed pregnancies, followed by long breastfeeding periods, as well as abortions and stillborn babies, so that there are few years when they are not directly involved in childbearing and child care. To manage all their tasks, women usually have to work and take care of children at the same time. You see them everywhere, bending in the fields with a child on their back, maybe one inside and another alongside. In other words, women combine economic activities and household duties with much more physically demanding work and many more children than we are used to in the West. In addition, they care for sick and elderly people.

Particularly in the grasslands, gathering firewood and collecting water can require great effort. Water is needed for people and animals to drink, and for cooking, washing and possibly vegetable gardening. If the village does not have a well or waterhole nearby, the walking distances can be very long, particularly in the dry season. A vessel of water can be heavy, weighing up to 40, 60, even 100 pounds, so that two people have to lift the vessel on top of the head of the bearer. Firewood can be difficult to find. Deforestation and degradation of the forest have created problems in many places.

Seventeen Hours a Day

Much of women's work in Africa's rural areas is heavy – heavier than men's work, where the man has access to modern equipment and tools.

The more primitive the tools are, the harder a person has to work. The allocation of time becomes a delicate issue. It is estimated that an ordinary African female farmer may have a working day of about 17 hours, as follows:

Rising, washing the children and herself, eating and feeding the children	4:45–5 a.m.
Going to the field	5–5:30 a.m.
Working in the field possibly with some of the children	5:30 a.m.–3 p.m.
Collecting firewood and going home	3–4 p.m.
Processing raw materials	4–5:30 p.m.
Fetching water	5:30–6:30 p.m.
Cooking for the family	6:30–7:30 p.m.
Eating and doing the dishes	7:30–8:30 p.m.
Washing the children and preparing for the night	8:30–9:30 p.m.
Sleeping	9:30 p.m.–4:45 a.m.

Usually, women work longer days than men, not least because of their household duties. It is estimated that women can work 12 to 13 hours more per week than men. There is reason to believe that women's working days have become longer in recent years. Increasing economic problems and poverty, depletion of the soil, heavy rains and drought may have contributed to this, together with a growing need for cash to buy necessities like sugar and salt, soap and kerosene, possibly medicine, and to pay school fees for the children.

The great majority of Africans live in rural areas. When women must work from early in the morning until late at night, seven days a week, to make ends meet, they often get caught in a vicious circle. They don't have time and energy to participate in activities that could improve their situation, and they lack money to buy time- and resource-saving devices. Thus, they are forced to continue the process with much exertion and low productivity. In many cases, the contribution of children is of vital importance. The pressure can be great, especially on the girls. In some places, men have lost tasks they had before in livestock farming, hunting and in regard to warfare. They may seek other employment, if necessary in other regions. If the husband is at home, he might take care of the children and do housework in special situations. But it appears to be generally unthinkable to change the traditional division of labour and obtain a more equitable distribution of the work among family members.

The Shared Man

Traditionally, African marriages were an economic, social and political matter decided by the eldest in the family. Younger members, particularly the women, usually had no say. The marriage pact entailed a transfer of different kinds of resources. The bride-price was the most important. Because women represented valuable fertility and labour, men paid a compensation to the wife's family. Some societies practised monogamy, but polygamy was very widespread. Depending on his financial and social status, a man could have from two to ten wives. Some chiefs took several hundred. Christianity is clearly against polygamy, but it is accepted by Islam, even if it is recommended that a man should limit himself to four wives and treat them equally. Marriages could be short-lived. In many ethnic groups, divorce was common. Islam did not reduce the number of divorces, because it is very easy for a Muslim man to reject a woman. The high mortality, together with the age difference between spouses, meant that many women became widows and remarried. In some ethnic groups, the custom was that the brother or another relative of the husband married the widow.

In modern times, the situation in the private sphere has become extremely complex. In addition to traditional practices and religious decrees, modern laws have been adopted. The various sets of rules are not always in agreement, and people may comply with different rules. In practice, established customs often carry more weight than modern laws, even in urban areas. Thus, formal statutory rights for women can in many cases have little effect on their real situation. Some countries in West and Central Africa have forbidden polygamy by law, while others permit it, in some cases with the permission of the wife. Nevertheless, different forms of polygamy are very frequent. For a man, many wives represent an important supply of labour. Wives as well as children are a sign of strength and virility. Marriage can be official and formal, but also traditional and informal. A man can have one formally accepted wife and several others. In addition, different kinds of cohabitation and extra-marital relations are practised by men.

Opinions vary with regard to polygamy, also among African women. It is said that the more wives a man has, the less important he is in the life of each woman. The mother–child unit becomes more central. Where the burden of work is great, it can be an advantage for women to be able to share the tasks, and a polygamous marriage entails more rights for a woman than the status of mistress. Traditionally, the position of first wife implied a certain authority. On the other hand, some say that polygamy gives a man power over more women. Households with several wives are often characterized by rivalry and friction. The youngest or last wife in particular may be bullied by the others. The husband may also neglect older wives in favour of younger ones.

Whether people adhere to modern legislation, religious decrees or traditional customs, the man is usually considered the head of the household and has property and inheritance rights, while the women are subordinate and dependent. As a rule, all African women participate in productive activities. But they mostly earn low wages, are limited to the informal sector and have little access to capital. Their revenue may be important when the husband doesn't earn much. But if he dies, the women's lack of inheritance rights can lead to quite desperate situations. Some ethnic groups practise 'separate purse', which means that each spouse manages his or her finances. The woman disposes of her own income and can obtain considerable economic autonomy. The contribution of the husband to his wife and children may be modest, however.

Urbanization has reduced the authority of the family. Romantic love has gained in importance. Particularly in urban centres, tensions may arise due to differences in the social and cultural backgrounds of spouses. In addition, patterns of residence have changed. A number of patterns can be found, from extended households where everybody lives together in the traditional way, to scattered residences where a man has several wives living in different dwellings in the town, or one wife in town and one in the village. The 'family' can for practical purposes be reduced to a woman with the sole responsibility for several children, who are quite often of different fathers. By the year 2000, about one-quarter of the households in sub-Saharan Africa had a female head of household. Divorce was frequent. But if a woman leaves her husband, the family can demand that he keep the property and the children, and that the bride-price be reimbursed. In some cases, the woman just leaves. In big cities like Abidjan, advertisements can be found in the newspapers where husbands seek wives who have disappeared.

Urban Explosion

Sub-Saharan Africa has the highest population growth in the world. After independence, the population increased around 3 per cent per year. It doubled in 25 to 30 years. The growth was fastest in the poorest countries and among the poorest segments of the population – where there was least ability to meet basic needs. Towards the end of the twentieth century growth was slowing down, and the AIDS pandemic will reinforce this tendency. But due to the high fertility, the population will probably continue to increase in most places until the year 2050. The countries hit hard by HIV/AIDS will have a slower growth than they would otherwise have had. Nevertheless, the efforts to improve living standards are a race against the expanding number of inhabitants.

At the same time, urbanization in this region is the fastest in the world. From 1960 to 2000, the urban population in sub-Saharan Africa more than doubled, from one-sixth to one-third of the total population. In West Africa, the number of cities increased more than five times. Rapid population growth, combined with economic and social problems in rural areas, contributed to the urban explosion. Both women and men moved to urban centres. Some also went abroad. During the 1990s, more than two million people from Burkina Faso and nearly one million from Mali were living in the Ivory Coast. In the cities and towns, more women than ever before managed to make a living on their own. Some got an education and were employed in the formal sector as teachers, midwives, nurses and secretaries. Others obtained jobs as domestic workers. The great majority worked in the informal sector, in petty trade and odd jobs. A few developed big businesses, but most were engaged in small-scale operations. Accompanied by small children, the women set up a table and a chair in the marketplace or on the pavement and sell spices, fruit and vegetables, prepare fast food, offer simple sewing, braid hair, take care of small children or whatever. Very many struggle hard to survive. Some resort to begging or prostitution.

Planners set the scene for a city like Abidjan to become a magnificent metropolis, a Paris in Africa. The city centre lies on a plateau facing the lagoon. The water reflects the highly functionalist buildings. It's like a mini-Manhattan, particularly in the evening, when thousands of lights sparkle and glitter. Then you don't see the decay of the last decades, the lack of maintenance and the garbage. Ever since the 1950s and 1960s the influx of people has been enormous. The city grew from about a hundred thousand people to more than three million. Traditional villages were replaced by 'popular' quarters, where immigrants lived, often under extremely poor conditions. Street children and beggars became permanent features of the degraded urban landscape.

Bori Bana is a stone's throw from the centre of town. The name signifies 'here the journey ends'. It is a slum area squeezed in between the freeway and the lagoon. Between ten and fifteen thousand people live in small square dwellings of cement and mud-brick blocks stuck together, separated only by narrow alleyways. Adults and children perform odd jobs, trade or beg to get money. Some have managed to steal a little water and electricity from the utility suppliers. There is no drainage or waste collection. Toilets exist only on some pillars out in the lagoon. There are people everywhere, mostly women and children. The odours from rotting garbage, urine and burnt fat prickle the nostrils. Children play in the sewer, sometimes fishing. Their entertainment is in a small shack, where speculators have installed a video machine screening violent and pornographic films. There are even toddlers among the audience. Quite a compensation for basic education! The slum is also a favourite place for criminals, because the police do not dare go in.

The UNICEF representative tried several times to get the authorities to visit Bori Bana and introduce social services. He failed. However, the authorities hired bulldozers and levelled several slum quarters to the ground, particularly the most visible, to make the commercial centre of the country look more attractive. Without rights, people could only take away whatever they could transport. They were offered 'reasonable' alternative housing. But this was far from the centre of town and cost more than most people could afford.

Unsustainable Development

Immediately after independence, Africa's new leaders were very optimistic. Now they were free and could develop their countries. It was a formidable task. The decolonization was poorly managed. The structures of economic production and trade inherited from the colonial powers were deeply distorted. There were only 1,200 people with a university education in the whole of sub-Saharan Africa.

Former French colonies differed from the British. Economic and social conditions varied from one country to another, as did the policies. Some chose a 'socialist' course, while others preferred 'capitalism', but it is still possible to distinguish some common features. In spite of everything, the economy in the new states performed relatively well during the first ten to fifteen years. Times were prosperous and primary commodity prices were high. Production and exports increased. Most notable was the massive expansion in health and education across the continent. In the course of two decades, child mortality was reduced by nearly one-third. Life expectancy increased. The number of children enrolled in primary school doubled. More adults became literate. As many as 70,000 students graduated yearly.

But the African economies remained, with few exceptions, as dependent, monocultural and vulnerable as before. Primary commodities, mostly agricultural, continued to be the main exports aimed at Western countries, while industrial products were imported from the West. When the new African leaders took over, they tried to develop economic activities on the existing foundations. Development plans were elaborated. Western countries provided technical and financial assistance. Many countries engaged in large-scale foreign borrowing. Regardless of political leanings, the prevailing view was that the state must be an engine for economic growth. The national administration was strengthened. As far as possible (there were differences between the countries belonging to the French *communauté* and others), currency and import controls, price regulations and subsidies were introduced. Mines, manufacturing industry, banks and credit institutions were nationalized and statal and parastatal enterprises created. But problems related to management and know-how, efficiency and profits were frequent.

Manufacturing industry was seen as the key to a modern society. Industrialization was to be promoted by the extraction of oil and minerals, the processing of agricultural products for export and the production of consumer goods for domestic markets. But progress was slow. African countries depended on support from the former colonial powers, and foreign capital and technology from multinational companies. Domestic markets were small, and the competition from imported goods was strong. Generally, productivity was low. After some decades, Africa was still the least industrialized continent. In agriculture, the cultivation of cash crops was expanded, but, most important, the marketing of agricultural products was controlled. Agricultural prices were kept down to subsidize urban consumers and provide export revenues for the state – a policy that contributed to the crisis in rural areas. Besides the economic activities controlled by the state, an informal black or parallel economy sprang up, with a considerable production of goods and services.

From the beginning of the 1970s, the developing countries tried to change the international macroeconomic conditions. A campaign was organized for a new international economic order. At the General Assembly of the United Nations in 1974, a plan of action for a new international order and a charter of economic duties and rights of states were presented. The documents required that states should have the right to dispose of their own resources, the international terms of trade should become more equitable and the access to the markets of industrialized countries should be improved. But powerful Western countries objected. They did not want substantial changes in the balance of power and resources in the world economy. Attempts at regulating primary commodity prices through international agreements also failed. A few agreements were concluded, but did not work in practice.

Generally, sub-Saharan Africa was poorly prepared for the series of powerful shocks that hit the world economy in the 1970s and 1980s. A deep recession in the West, increases in oil prices and an exceptionally high interest rate damaged poor, oil-importing and commodity-exporting African economies. At the same time, the prices of manufactured products increased, so it became impossible for many countries to maintain the level of imports. A great number also got into difficulties servicing their debt. Simultaneously, the inflows of foreign capital dropped. In the Sahel, the situation was aggravated by droughts, first in 1968–74, then in 1977–78 and 1983–85.

Crisis

The economic crisis was soon felt in many countries through its adverse effects on the balance of payments, the budget deficit and inflation. Production, the supply of goods and real incomes sank. In many countries, the debt burden became unmanageable. The International Monetary Fund (IMF), and the World Bank became strongly involved – so much so that many countries had to cede economic sovereignty, and in fact came under international administration. Economic reform packages and structural adjustment programmes were elaborated to stabilize the economy, improve the resource allocation and promote economic growth. The measures were extremely controversial. It was generally accepted that countries had to change their economic policies. But some took the view that the solution ought to be a lesser, not greater, integration into the world economy. There were different opinions regarding the weakening of the state, liberalization and privatization of the economy. The effectiveness of the different measures in an African context was doubted, and the negative social consequences were criticized. UNICEF demanded 'adjustment with a human face'.

In the course of the 1980s and 1990s, most of the countries in West and Central Africa reformed their economic policies – often several times. Public expenditures were reduced and macroeconomic stability improved in many countries. Market forces and private sector activity were given free rein and the terms of trade for agricultural production liberalized. The results were highly uneven across countries, but overall the economic performance was weak, and the per capita income declined. The structural problems were deep-seated and the international macroeconomic conditions remained unfavourable. Primary commodity prices were generally low, and Western protectionism against imports from developing countries was upheld. The flow of foreign capital to African countries was small and the debt burden crippling. Simultaneously, there were significant reductions in development aid.

There is no quick fix. The crisis is deep and complex and at the beginning of the twenty-first century, it is not over by far. The reforms have not solved the fundamental economic problems of the African states. In addition, the continent has been economically weakened. From the early 1970s, Africa lost trade equal to about 20 per cent of its gross domestic product. By 2002, two-thirds of the governments in West and Central Africa were seriously indebted. While middle-income countries in Latin America had their debt problems solved in the 1980s, this was not the case with Africa. After 15 to 20 years, despite several debt initiatives, reschedulings and write-offs, the highly indebted poor African countries still had not received substantial debt relief. For many, the situation was untenable. The debt equalled or exceeded countries' gross domestic product (GDP), and the burden had profound effects. A considerable proportion of the scarce budget resources of poor countries was utilized for debt servicing, instead of for developmental efforts, and conditions for debt relief were tough.

Average growth improved in West and Central Africa around the end of the century, but after two decades of decline many countries were back at the level they had been in the 1960s. Infrastructure was run down. Production was generally low and the share of world trade minimal. Many countries experienced severe brain drain and capital flight. The dependency on aid to implement development activities was marked. Countries differed. In 2001, Cape Verde and Gabon were better off as middle-income countries, while all the others had low income – on average, nearly US$350 annually per inhabitant, or around 1 per cent of the income of a country like Norway. Statistics from developing countries are often unreliable, and the income per capita is difficult to assess in countries with a widespread subsistence economy and a large informal sector. Possibly, people's living standards were not quite as bad as the numbers seem to indicate. But even if this is taken into account, the income level was in most cases very low. Sub-Saharan Africa was the poorest region in the world. If South Africa is excluded, the total income of the region was not much more than Denmark's. Among 47 countries, each had an economy about the size of a medium municipality in a rich country. Worst off were the warring countries in the Sahel.

Within each country, the distribution of resources was usually very skewed. Poverty was extremely widespread. In 2001, about half of the population in West and Central Africa lived below the poverty line of US$1 a day, with one-quarter being extremely poor. Vulnerable groups, such as women and children, were hit the hardest. The situation was clearly illustrated in the city markets. The smallest portions that the poor could buy were reduced to a tablespoon of tomato purée, 15 small pieces of macaroni, two tablespoons of oil or two quarters of an onion – each for about four or five cents.

Resources That Don't Do Much Good

Sub-Saharan Africa does not lack resources. In addition to a talented population, the continent has a rich fauna and flora of great biological variety. There is fertile soil, water and important natural resources like oil and gas, strategic minerals and precious metals. Countries in West and Central Africa export substantial amounts of oil, iron ore, phosphate, bauxite, uranium, manganese, copper, cobalt, diamonds, wood, cotton, coffee, cocoa and groundnuts. In many cases the resources have been exploited – and are still being exploited – at an alarming speed. In a well-forested country like the Ivory Coast, there are practically no hardwood trees left, because all have been cut down.

Why, then, is the continent ravaged by poverty? To cut a long story short: Africa benefits little from the exploitation of resources. And what the continent gets contributes only to a small extent to development purposes and improvement in the living conditions of the great majority of the population. In addition, resources like oil, minerals and diamonds play an important role in the armed conflicts that have devastated the region in recent years (in Liberia and Sierra Leone, Congo Brazzaville and the Democratic Republic of Congo).

Many external and internal factors influence what happens in African countries. Nevertheless, a basic condition is the dependence of the continent on the rest of the world, a fact that is maintained and exploited both by Western interests and African leaders, and that has increased during the economic crisis. Globalization is old news in sub-Saharan Africa. The colonial period brought the continent into the Western economy, and the ties were to a great extent preserved after the African countries became independent. Today, the former colonial powers are still Africa's most important trading partners. Western (European) countries are the greatest consumers of African resources. Western companies control the production, processing and marketing of most of the oil and mineral resources, as well as of the agricultural products. The companies – sometimes assisted by former colonial powers – have considerable influence over which resources are exploited (or not exploited) and how the utilization takes place. The African economies are small and weak in relation to Western countries and companies. This imbalance is illustrated by the fact that a single multinational oil company has an annual turnover of about the same size as the GDP of 30 African countries put together.

If the West has a main responsibility for the development (or the lack of development) of sub-Saharan Africa in the course of the last century, this does not mean that the Africans themselves are without responsibility. Many African leaders have carried out policies that have contributed to a great extent to the present situation. Collaboration with Western governments and economic interests was considered to be advantageous technically, as well as economically. Exploitation of the country's resources gave the authorities revenue and influence. Development aid entailed a straight financial grant. But the African leaders did not always promote development. Some observers are even of the view that their policy to a large extent was 'anti-development', in the Western sense of the term. Few efforts were directed towards long-term productive activities and the promotion of a diversified economy. On the contrary, large amounts of money were spent for short-term gain, consumption and prestige projects. In many cases, small groups of the population benefited, while the rest were neglected or exploited.

THIRTEEN
Democracy in Khaki: Western Models and African Realities

> The powerful man is always right, even when he is wrong.
> (Proverb from the Bambara people)

He doesn't look like a general. He is small and slender-limbed with laughing eyes in the middle of a ball-shaped face. Nevertheless, he is a general in the Malian army. That is, he was, but resigned. The man's name is Amadou Toumani Touré. He led a military coup in 1991 and deposed the president at that time, General Moussa Traoré. Traoré had been in power in Mali for more than twenty years. By the end of the 1980s, unrest had grown. There were armed clashes with Tuaregs in the north. In the capital, Bamako, strikes and demonstrations were organized and thousands of people poured into the streets demanding democracy. In March 1991, violent confrontations took place with the police and security forces. 'Les évènements', or the 'events' as they are called, lasted for three days. One hundred and fifty people were killed and a thousand wounded. This made the army react. General Amadou Toumani Touré intervened. Moussa Traoré was arrested. The government was dissolved and the constitution annulled. Fifty-nine were killed in the night-time coup.

Touré, or ATT as he is called, immediately nominated a National Council of Reconciliation with the task of introducing democracy. A National Conference was convened, a new constitution adopted, and in June 1992 multiparty elections were held. Immediately afterwards, ATT resigned and handed over power to the newly elected president. It may seem very simple for citizens in the West. But in Africa it is rare to see a military officer take over power by means of a *coup d'état* – and then resign. Others have said they would withdraw, but have nevertheless remained in office.

In 1992, ATT, at the age of fifty-one years, all of a sudden realized that he was a retired president and jobless. 'I made a mistake,' he notes with a smile. 'I should have created an employment agency for former presidents before I left!' But ATT did not remain unemployed for long. He was appointed the leader of the Malian committee against Guinea worm, which entailed a close collaboration with UNICEF. ATT's involvement was strong. 'I would like to take vengeance,' he says. 'My mother was infected by Guinea worm as a girl. When she got sick, she was expelled from school.' ATT mobilized support on a broad basis, not only in Mali, but in eleven infected countries in West and Central Africa, and he contributed to important progress.

He did more. He established a foundation for destitute children, a children's hospital, health centres in rural areas, centres for street children and a workshop to produce artificial limbs for handicapped youths. At the regional level, he was active in protecting children in armed conflict, and African presidents called on him to solve political crises. The most important role he played was in the Central African Republic (CAR). In 1996, there was a military mutiny. 'We are treated like slaves,' the mutineers explained. 'We only get 50 dollars a month, and the last three months we have not been paid at all.' Local attempts to solve the problems failed. There were more mutinies. The civilian population fled under a hail of bullets in the capital, Bangui. Finally, four African presidents went there to mediate, and ATT was sent to monitor the agreement. He stayed in the CAR for 18 months. A Conference of Reconciliation was followed by a national government, and then legislative and presidential elections in 1999 led to a fragile peace. ATT was appointed a citizen of the CAR and France made him a Grand Officer of the Legion of Honour.

But the basic political and economic problems remained unsolved. The elections confirmed the president in office, and the tensions between the government and the opposition continued unabated. An unprecedented fuel crisis, considerable unpaid arrears in the wages of civil servants and an influx of refugees from the war in the Democratic Republic of Congo (DRC) aggravated a precarious economic and social situation. Soon, the streets of Bangui erupted in violence again. There were strikes and a failed coup, and by mid-2001, ATT was back in the CAR, this time as the UN Secretary General's Special Envoy.

ATT is unusual, even if some military leaders later followed his example and voluntarily stepped down in favour of elected presidents. When ATT is asked why African heads of state rarely resign, he answers:

As long as there is no acceptable retreat, the presidents will cling to the office. They are afraid people will resort to reprisals if they resign. In my case, the army did not want to remain in power. And I am from Macina. I am educated in the Peul culture. For us the 'House of our Fathers', or our native country, is the most important. It was natural for me to give my word and then keep it.

This was in 1999, and ATT did not know that he would be elected president of Mali in 2002 and get a new chance to put his approach into practice.

The dilemmas were clearly illustrated when the president of Burkina Faso in March 2001 made the original move to institute a National Day of Pardon, asking the population to forgive the 'torture, crimes and injustices committed by citizens of Burkina against other citizens in the name of the state'. Between 25,000 and 28,000 people filled the Ouagadougou stadium in the presence of three previous heads of state and people known for their moral authority. But the families of some of the most famous victims were absent, demanding to know the truth before they were willing to grant their pardon.

More than Fifty Military Coups

To understand how unusual ATT's resignation as president was, it is necessary to go back into history. When the African countries became independent in the 1960s, the rulers went from white to black. The new black leaders took over the whole colonial set-up: nation states with artificial borders, armies with modern weapons, European education and legal systems and bureaucracies designed to put down rebellions and accumulate wealth. Traditional African leadership continued, but in an altered and weakened form. Towards the end of the colonial period, National Assemblies and multiparty systems were introduced in all the colonies except the Portuguese. It was a 'lightning democracy', created under pressure and according to Western models. Many of the established political parties became actively involved in the struggle for national sovereignty.

The new African leaders carried on with the existing structures in their own way. The Western parliamentary institutions did not work very well. Because people were used to authoritarian colonial rule, it was not easy all of a sudden to make a multiparty democracy function properly. Besides, a centralized government with a single-party system seemed more suited to ensuring a firm leadership of the country (leftist or conservative), consolidating the nation state and keeping ethnic/regional, cultural and religious antagonisms in check. The state administration was strengthened, with more emphasis on coercive control and economic exploitation than on public services. Opposition parties were undermined or abolished.

Strong leaders sprang up in many countries during the liberation process. Allocating enormous power to a single person was in accordance with the chief system established during the colonial rule. Traditionally, African leaders acted as part of a collective decision-making process. The elders in the village sat under the palaver tree talking until they agreed. But the colonial system had no arrangements to ensure a balance of power, accountability or popular participation. Most of the new African regimes were soon characterized by personal autocracy. The president ruled the country like a chief ruled his village. The head of state and his supporters controlled riches and resources. Nepotism and corruption spread. Abuses of power, violence and breaches of human rights became frequent. As long as the Cold War lasted, this was tolerated to a great extent by foreign powers with political and economic interests in the region.

Not long after independence, the military actively intervened in the politics of several countries. It had a well-organized machinery. The distance between the barracks and the presidential palace was short. Some officers and soldiers were dissatisfied with their conditions, or were influenced by events in other countries. Most often, the military claimed that misrule and corruption among politicians caused them to take over, so as to ensure order and effective government – a fact that did not prevent military heads of state from abusing power in much the same way as civilian leaders. By 2002, there had been more than fifty military coups in West and Central Africa.

The giant of the region, Nigeria, holds the record. By the end of the century, the country had been ruled by military regimes during 29 of its 40 years of independence. Of eleven presidents, nine were military. The president who took over in 1999 also came from the military, but was elected by democratic elections. Senegal is at the other end of the scale with decades of multiparty democracy and regular elections. There had only been two presidents, when the opposition won the elections in 2000. Between these extremes are many variants. With one exception, however, all heads of state have been men.

'Thin' New Democracies

Towards the end of the 1980s and the beginning of the 1990s, a movement was created in most African countries demanding multiparty democracy, open elections and respect for human rights. Many people were disappointed because their leaders did not promote development and freedom, social justice and national unity. On the contrary, the situation was characterized by authoritarian rule, economic austerity measures and increasing poverty. Democratization was now supported by the donor community as well.

In some countries, the popular demands led to turbulent processes of change. In Niger, between 1992–98, a total of twelve referendums were held at a price of US$20 million. From the National Conference in 1991 until the military took over in 1996, the country had no fewer than five governments and four prime ministers, one transitional regime, two parliamentary elections, two military mutinies, civil disobedience organized by the losing parties and armed rebellion in the north. More and more, impatient voices were heard requesting that democratization soon should end and the living conditions of people be improved instead. The officer responsible for the coup in 1996 was later elected president, but in 1999 he was murdered. A new head of state was elected, who was still in office in 2002. The situation in Niger has perhaps been extreme. But it was not the only country with unrest and changes of regime.

Since 1990, multiparty elections have been held in all countries in West and Central Africa, with the exception of the DRC; presidential and legislative elections one or more times, and also local elections. In a number of cases, the elections were organized in a proper manner that was considered to conform to generally accepted rules. In other cases, democratization was more in name than reality.

A number of rulers did all they could to ensure their own re-election. The president in Congo Brazzaville became known for his remark that 'one does not organize elections to lose'. There was no lack of ingenuity – of a kind that exceeded anything a Western outsider could imagine. Electoral laws were amended so as to limit the right to vote and to be elected. Central and local representatives of the authorities were changed, civil servants were awarded pay rises and wavering supporters given access to public services. The media were censored. Parties, meetings and demonstrations were forbidden and political opponents arrested. There were erroneous registration lists with 'ghost' entries, failure to register eligible voters and manipulation of electoral districts. At the polling stations, military and local leaders were extremely active, and ballot boxes disappeared during the vote counting. Not all irregularities were the result of deliberate manipulation. In many places, essential equipment was missing and people were unfamiliar with election procedures. But not infrequently, the interventions of the ruling elite were so comprehensive that the opposition boycotted the elections, wondering if the democratization was an illusion. It was all the more grotesque when well-intentioned, but naïve Western observers arrived on election day and declared the process 'free and fair', simply because people could put voting slips unobstructed in the ballot boxes.

Organizing political parties according to a Western model was problematic in an African context. Class and conflict dimensions are not the same as in European societies, and social and political dividing lines are more fluid. Ethnic/regional affiliation carries greater importance. In addition, traditional village democracy was aimed at consensus, avoiding confrontation between a majority and a minority. In the 1970s and 1980s, the governing party in many single-party states tried to represent the nation as a whole. But democratization changed the rules of the game: to win an election a majority was sufficient, so parties needed only limited geographical support. Many came first of all to represent certain ethnic/regional groupings. Elaboration of alternative party programmes was no simple affair either, in situations described as 'a democracy without choices', due to the prevailing economic constraints and structural adjustment policies. In some countries, a multitude of small parties was created – 30, 40 or 50. Often, they had a personal, not ideological, basis and were focused around a male politician who no longer belonged to the ruling elite. Characteristically, the opposition parties lacked material, economic and human resources to work effectively under the difficult conditions imposed by authoritarian regimes.

Most often, the elections did not entail a change of regime. Of the 50 presidential elections that were held from 1990 to 2002 in West and Central Africa, a little more than 60 per cent confirmed the existing president in office, while less than 40 per cent brought a new person into power. In many cases, the newcomers were not really new. They came from the ruling groups and had occupied important posts in the past. At times, the military did not accept the result of the elections and staged a coup. In 2002, two-thirds of the region's presidents had a military background, either legitimized by elections or not. The question was raised, are we, in reality, dealing with a khaki democracy?

Black-and-white Cocktail

Politics in the new African states was characterized by a strange mixture of European and African. The national institutions conform to a Western model, usually British or French. The countries have constitutions with legislative, judiciary and executive powers. Laws and regulations are strongly inspired by the West, even if their content may be adjusted to local conditions. Among the ruling elites, there is broad acceptance of Western concepts of justice and human rights ideals. The African leaders know the European systems well. For most of them, a modernization of the society implies that they follow a European way.

All the colonial powers wanted to 'civilize' the Africans. The British, as well as the French, established schools for black children using their own curriculum as a model. In English-speaking countries, the children learnt about Shakespeare and in the French-speaking about 'nos ancêtres les Gaulois' (our ancestors, the Gauls). Western education was not only the admission ticket to the modern sector of society. It created an *educated elite*, strongly influenced by the culture of the colonial power and more or less alienated in relation to African heritage.

The French placed greatest emphasis on 'cultural assimilation'. In the French-speaking countries, many educated Africans have a strong attachment to the former colonial power. They travel to France as often as possible, cultivate friends and contacts, enjoy French art and health services and buy French goods. They make a great effort to educate their children in France. The top leaders regularly meet the French political elite. When the old president in the Ivory Coast, Félix Houphouët-Boigny, died in 1993, no fewer than six former French prime ministers, in addition to the former and the current French presidents, attended the funeral. The French have also preserved a noticeable presence in the French *communauté* – stronger than the British in the *Commonwealth*. France has military bases in several places in West and Central Africa. Many African governments have French advisers. The French business communities are considerable, even if the economic crisis has reduced their numbers during recent years. All over the region, there are French research and cultural centres. Thousands of French development assistants work as teachers.

European influence does not mean that Africans become French or British. They may have different and partly conflicting attitudes. A clear example is Senegal's first president, Léopold Sédar Senghor. He was a poet and became known between the two World Wars in the négritude movement, which tried to create greater appreciation of black identity. This did not prevent him from becoming, at a later stage, the leader of 'La Francophonie', the organization promoting French language and culture. After he retired as president, he took up residence in France. Senghor openly admitted that he fell in love with the country that colonized his own. He expressed a mixture of devotion and admiration on one hand, and revolt and bitterness on the other in relation to the French. Other leaders are more nationalistic. All shades of ambivalence can be noted among present-day well-educated Africans. It is often impossible for an outsider to understand when they are being most European or most African, or sometimes both at the same time.

Politics in African countries has a clear African character. Besides Western-inspired policy papers, development plans and budgets, the political activities centre to a great extent on family, local and regional relations. Traditionally, African chiefs expected personal loyalty from their subjects, and in return gave them protection and help. A system of mutual gifts and services was developed. The clientele got welfare, while the leaders got power. This system continued after independence. A *network, clientelistic or patrimonial state* was created, according to political scientists. Personal relations between family and friends, political allies and supporters are of basic importance, and the connections go informally in all directions, from the highest echelons of society to the village level. It is expected that those who gain control over the state will reward their followers and relatives. Actually, many African top leaders are more heads of clans than heads of state: they pursue the interests of a limited network, instead of developing a state that serves the common good.

In such a clientelistic system, it is difficult to implement objective rules in the allocation of benefits and rights. But the system can promote loyalty and support for the rulers. It may also function as a kind of social security arrangement, where the well-to-do distribute resources to those who have less. However, the networks have obvious limitations. They are often based on family, ethnic/regional or religious affiliations and may be opposed to rival networks or cliques. In some places, political life is dominated by competing strongmen and their allies. In countries like Liberia, Sierra Leone and the DRC this has degenerated into warlord politics. By favouring their own, the networks can create great disparities between those who belong and those who don't, particularly when the leaders have access to state power and resources. No matter how such networks have worked in different countries, they have in course of recent decades been unable to prevent a marked increase in the number of poor people.

In the draft constitution for Nigeria in 1976, political power was defined as 'the possibility to acquire riches and prestige and be able to share benefits in the form of jobs, contracts, gifts of money etc to relatives and political allies'. Such an approach may be found in many parts of the world. Among Africans, it is very widespread, and few mechanisms are established to counteract it. Wealthy people have high status. At the same time, it is necessary to share one's wealth and influence with others, to maintain a good name and reputation, strengthen the network and combat rival groups. Short-term gains are easily given preference, to the detriment of long-term investments. At elections, it is usual practice that the winner takes all – riches, power, privileges and prestige. In a situation of political uncertainty and scarcity of resources, the accumulation of riches can become all the more intensive. It can take place at all levels. At the top, it has more a character of uninhibited greed than at lower levels, where people run a real risk of being in need. When the differences are blurred between collective and private interest, formal and informal activities, then methods that are half legal and half illegal may easily be utilized. In this way, corruption and the abuse of power spread. Public enterprises are robbed and personal profits acquired by private individuals and businesses. The enormous fortunes that some African leaders have laid up abroad speak for themselves.

As in the West, African countries established governments and National Assemblies to promote a distribution of power and control. Even with 'democratization', the influence of these bodies was often limited.

Presidents created their own secretariats and informal 'shadow cabinets' made up of centrally placed persons in the network, which could yield considerable power. The formal cabinet usually included a number of ministers. They might be well qualified and actively engaged in their work, but in practice their role could be relatively insignificant or limited. In many countries, ministers changed very frequently. Chad, an extreme example, had 200 in the course of six years, but it was not unusual that the length of office of technical ministers (the portfolios of health, education, women's affairs, etc.) in West and Central Africa was only six months to one year. It seemed that the building of alliances was a more important facet of the appointment of ministers than the programmes the politicians were supposed to be implementing.

Most of the time, National Assemblies played a modest role. Electoral systems varied. Each had its advantages, but majority elections in single-member constituencies made the representation of different groups difficult, while proportional representation encouraged the proliferation of parties. Usually, the president's party dominated. The National Assemblies had scant resources, and few documents were presented that could provide a solid basis for discussion of national policies. The function became mostly a formal acceptance of different proposals. In a few cases, the opposition won a majority in the Assembly. Then, the members could become an active force, and there were lengthy debates and clear attempts at putting a brake on the presidential politics.

Weak States

In many African countries, the state became overextended and marred by inefficiency, abuse of power and plundering of national resources. Among donors, the view became widespread that it was necessary to pare down the size and responsibilities of the state and to reorient its activities. The slogan was: 'Less and better government'. Personally, I accepted this view before I moved to Africa. But it was not long before I changed my mind. Generally, African states were much weaker than I thought, and less government did not necessarily lead to better government. Sometimes it led to worse. If a number of state businesses could profitably be reorganized, public services usually needed to be strengthened.

Different countries pursued different strategies in regard to the economic crisis and the demands for structural adjustment, but frequently the scope of state activities was rolled back by closing or privatizing statal and parastatal enterprises. These were transferred to local commercial networks or, in many cases, to foreign entrepreneurs. State bureaucracies were scaled down and public expenditure cut, sometimes dramatically.

The possibilities for the authorities to implement measures aimed at improving people's living standards, or even to support followers and relatives, became extremely limited – even though the privatization of state assets could yield a short-term windfall. Generally, the capacity to govern was undermined.

In many cases, states got into difficulties maintaining core public functions such as health services and education, water supply and sanitation, law and order, taxation and construction of basic infrastructure. The salaries of public employees fell by up to 50 per cent in the course of 15 years, to partly under the poverty line – if they were paid at all. Some public services continued with praiseworthy efforts, but absenteeism, lack of motivation, poor quality, private user fees and corruption became more and more frequent. There were strikes and demonstrations, and sometimes military mutinies. In the privileged part of Abidjan where we lived, the collection of waste stopped all of a sudden, because the local administration was short of funds. Mail was withheld, because the employees did not receive 'gifts', and we had to pay the same telephone bill several times over to prevent the line from being cut off. Generally in sub-Saharan Africa, it is estimated that the access per inhabitant to public services – including social services – was reduced by 50 per cent between 1980 and the mid-1990s.

In aid-dependent countries, the administration faced special problems. External donors contributed valuable technical and financial resources. But the poorer the country and the greater the need for the money, the less capacity the bureaucracy usually had to deal with the allocations in the expected way. The donors had numerous and strict requirements. Ministers and civil servants spent enormous amounts of time on contacts with donors, project plans, applications and reports. It is estimated that an African country with considerable donor aid could receive a thousand delegations and send nearly ten thousand reports every year.

Vicious circles are easily created. When the public administration can't deliver, it becomes steadily more discredited and weakened. Often donors contributed to a worsening of the situation by bypassing the bureaucracy or topping-up the salaries of state employees. In many countries, tasks that should be public were taken over by others. Social services were privatized, at times with the support of external donors. In some places, private customs services and police, private militias and armed groups were established.

The state revenues are a particularly delicate issue. Usually, African countries lack a functioning system of taxation of private citizens. Income tax forms are unknown. Experiences both during and after the colonial period have led people to associate the state more with coercion and exploitation than with support and help. They do not believe that they will obtain benefits if they pay taxes or make contributions to the social security system. The money will only disappear. Imports and exports have traditionally been taxed, but the liberalization of trade has reduced this income. It is complicated to collect indirect taxes, and most countries have a very large informal sector which is not taxed. In addition, many people are exempted from taxes and duties for political reasons. Prominent politicians may disregard their own laws, participate in illegal or semi-legal economic activities and fail to meet their obligations. 'They send a dangerous signal saying that laws exist to be circumvented,' one of my Ivorian friends sighed. It was common knowledge that some senior leaders were involved in dubious financial transactions. Nevertheless, they could, without a blush, arrange an ostentatious celebration when their personal fortune amounted to one billion CFA francs.

The auditing of state finances and the administration of justice are insufficiently developed in many countries and are marked by political intervention. Police enforcement is arbitrary and legal protection poor. Using bribes, well-to-do citizens can escape control and prosecution. In many cases, the police themselves set up roadblocks to collect illegal duties. As they cannot live by their salaries, they need money for survival. At the same time, they contribute to considerable insecurity among ordinary people, who live from day to day under a law of arbitrariness and never know what is going to happen.

African Independence Number Two?

A democratization of society is far more than the organization of elections. In the course of the 1990s, changes were taking place in many areas. Some people go so far as to talk about an 'African independence number two'. State control of the political activities of citizens was reduced. Debate became more open, and the media were given greater latitude. Voluntary organizations were created, and a political opposition. The accountability of politicians was emphasized more than before.

These changes clearly had a positive impact. But by the end of the century, most countries were still far from the kind of popular participation and transparency in public administration that we are used to in Western countries. The civil society we refer to is something completely different in Africa from that found in the West. Some countries have very few voluntary organizations, apart from those representing the ruling elite. In other places, a large number of associations has been created during recent years, but they are very heterogeneous. Many are small and weak, often operated by a single individual hoping to obtain support for social or other activities. Interest groups in the Western sense exist mostly in urban areas among the well educated. Some associations have close ties to the power elites. The president's wife often comes first with her own humanitarian organization. In popular districts and rural areas, there are mostly self-help and local community groups.

The press, radio and television have greater freedom and scope for action than before. Private press, radio and television stations have been established. But it is not easy to spread information in a region where literacy is low, communications are defective and the media have few resources. Sub-Saharan Africa has the world's poorest infrastructure for information and communication. In the 1990s, there was on the average one telephone line for every 70 inhabitants. Nearly thirty times as many newspapers were printed per inhabitant in Europe as in sub-Saharan Africa, and Europeans had twelve times as many TVs. The greatest gap was related to the Internet, where there were 70 times as many users in Europe and 260 times more in the USA than in Africa. For many illiterate Africans, the radio represents a lifeline, especially in rural areas, and in recent years the number of community broadcasters has soared.

The ruling elites in most African countries regard journalists with suspicion and their activities are highly circumscribed. Imported newsprint and advertisements may be cut off, editorial offices closed down and reporters harassed or jailed for offences such as 'endangering state security', 'criminal defamation' or 'falsehoods'. Journalists are most exposed in situations of armed conflict, but election times also have an adverse effect on the media. It is particularly risky to report on the activities of the opposition. Even during normally calm periods, a journalist was arrested when he wrote that the national football team lost a match because the president was in the stand (implying that his presence brought misfortune), or reported that the president allegedly had health problems.

Universities and institutions of higher learning can play an important role not only in educating leaders, but also by producing information about and analyses of society. In spite of the spectacular increase in the number of university students immediately after independence, sub-Saharan Africa had relatively fewer students and people with higher education in the 1990s than other regions. The economic crisis had a very negative impact on the access to scientific literature, the quality of teaching and the conditions for research. The development of technical competence was seriously res-trained. Tens of thousands of well-qualified technicians left the continent every year. At many universities, student unrest was a common occurrence. Teaching was interrupted and the universities were closed for long periods. This was due to reduced resources, frustration caused by the studies and dissatisfaction with national policies, as well as by repressive sanctions from the authorities against criticism and demonstrations. However, the students played an important role in the democratization of political institutions in different countries.

Insecure Stability

The political stability was quite fragile in a number of African countries. Environmental degradation, economic stagnation, mass poverty and a skewed distribution of resources were endemic. If the government was in addition strongly centralized and ineffective, with extensive abuse of power and corruption, the dissatisfaction could become very noticeable. Civil wars were often associated with the emergence of famines.

In the course of the 1980s and 1990s, stability became more fragile than before. The deterioration in people's living standards heightened social tensions. At the same time, the room for political action was curtailed and the state apparatus weakened. The power and legitimacy of many governments were reduced. Established forms of government did not function well, while new forms were not properly established. Ethnic, religious and regional identities were revived. External as well as internal interests were engaged in a competition for resources – oil, strategic metals and precious stones. Several times this developed into armed conflict. In Sierra Leone, people have a saying: When the Lord created Sierra Leone, the angels protested, saying it was not fair to place all the riches of the world in one single country. Wait until you see who will govern the country, the Lord replied.

Instead of reducing ethnic/regional differences within various districts, the colonial power exploited them in many cases. This continued after independence. Often certain ethnic groups occupied the ruling positions, while other groups – sometimes the majority – were excluded or marginalized. Frequently the capital city or southern districts had more than their share in relation to the north, and this fuelled hostilities in many countries. Generally, the democratization processes in the 1990s did not broaden popular participation or representation in the decision-making processes. In some countries, it helped to reduce internal conflict. But in others, particularly deeply divided societies, it aggravated existing antagonisms. When previously excluded groups assumed power by means of the ballot box, this led to struggles between the new and the old power elites, at times using armed force.

In 1995, we in the regional office of UNICEF held the view that ten of the 23 countries in West and Central Africa were either in a crisis situation or were extremely vulnerable, while six were exposed to a medium risk. The criteria were a weak economy, difficult social conditions, poor governance and internal conflicts. By the end of the century, eight countries had experienced extensive armed conflict. In others, there were local confrontations. In some cases, the crises were longlasting, with the state more or less collapsing (for example, Liberia, Sierra Leone and the DRC).

There are no effective mechanisms for conflict resolution in the region, even if African countries have constantly been more engaged in more pressing problem areas. Nevertheless the Organization for African Unity (OAU) and the Economic Community of West African States (ECOWAS) have been active together with the UN. Several countries have contributed to peacekeeping operations. Some disputes have been resolved. With a few notable exceptions, Western countries have been reserved and ambiguous in their approach. The decision-making processes are often cumbersome and the resources insufficient. In many cases, the peacekeepers lack knowledge of local conditions as well as the capacity to make use of traditional methods for conflict resolution. At times, the situation is complicated by some African countries supporting the warfare of one or the other party at the same time as peacemaking efforts are taking place.

When the leader of the OAU in 1998, the president of Burkina Faso, was asked what he would prefer, if he had to choose between democracy, human rights and stability, he spontaneously replied: 'If we have peace, we can have both democracy and human rights. Without peace, we will not have anything.' Preferably, we should have everything. But the answer stresses the importance of stability in present-day Africa, however fragile.

African Democracy?

Both internationally and nationally, it has been emphasized during recent years that sub-Saharan Africa has to become 'democratic'. But what does this actually imply? Western countries point out the value of their own political systems. When it comes to the crunch, it seems to be essential that African countries organize multiparty elections according to the Western model. Then everything is apparently all right, however manipulated and fictitious the elections might be.

Democracy or rule of the people is no simple concept. It involves a certain tension between individual freedoms and collective decisions. The solution cannot be a simple formula, independent of time and place. By the end of the century, there was broad agreement that good governance should include the rule of law, effective state institutions, transparency and accountability in the handling of public affairs, respect for human rights and participation of all citizens in decisions concerning their lives. How this should be practically implemented must depend on the local conditions.

It has been said that the task of creating an African democracy remains unsolved. It is probably possible to develop political arrangements that can function better than those imported from the West. These can be based on local structures and traditional forms of government. Some ethnic groups have, for example, inclusive systems where women play a far more important role then we are accustomed to in the West. It is in the nature of things that the Africans have to resolve their governance problems themselves. Each country must create its own institutions related to its own history and traditions, progress and defeats, hopes and fears. Political leaders must be conscious of their responsibility and take the lead. National considerations must count for more than personal and family interests. There is little that is more destructive and demoralizing than uninhibited use of force and seizure of public resources by the ruling elite. Intellectuals and artists, media people and traditional leaders, voluntary associations and women's groups have important contributions to make. In addition, the majority of people must get involved, express their views and wishes and make the leaders accountable. Elections are a decisive means of doing this. But they can be organized in different ways, and must be part of a long-term strengthening of national institutions and building up of democratic processes.

It takes time to transform long-established authoritarian practices and deep-rooted clientelistic relations into a more open and democratic political culture. The changes are complex and require determined efforts over a long period of time. Some African leaders have taken the task seriously and started to break fresh ground. At the beginning of the twenty-first century, several countries experienced a change of regime in a constitutional manner. But the social disparities, poverty and illiteracy make political transformations arduous. If the demands for democracy in sub-Saharan Africa are going to be more than empty rhetoric, the outside world must be willing to follow up: to insist that good governance is important, contribute to the strengthening of legal institutions and public services – and respect national sovereignty. This means slackening the external directiveness and accepting other forms of decision-making than those that conform to a Western model.

FOURTEEN

Queen Mothers and Market Women: Modernization with Regard to Discrimination against Women

A woman is smarter than a king.
(Proverb from the Hausa people)

The small statuette has been with me for more than twenty years. Wherever I have travelled, it has been on my desk as a source of inspiration. The reason is not its artistic value. The statue is rather insignificant – a mass product for tourists, I think, made of grey soapstone. It represents an African woman, not very young, wearing a headscarf and a necklace ornamented by a large jewel. Her expression is calm and serene. The statuette is from the capital of Sierra Leone, Freetown, and carries the inscription: 'Hotel Mammy Yoko, June 1980'. The hotel is named after one of the most prominent female chiefs in the country, 'Madam Yoko', as I discover when I finally find an article about her. As a child, she was given the name Soma, but her adult name was Yoko. She married three times, becoming the wife of Gongoima, Gbenja and Gbanya. Following the death of Gbanya, she was recognized not only as 'principal lady', but also 'Queen' of Sennehoo. However, I have never met her. She was born in 1849 and died in 1906.

Why should a Norwegian woman keep a mass-produced bust of Mammy Yoko on her desk? A dear African friend gave me the statuette. But there is more to it. Madam Yoko was a prominent female chief in Sierra Leone who lived just a short while ago – yet I had never heard of her. We learn so little about women in other cultures. And a country in West Africa had a female chief, an event we in the West would consider impossible, in view of the usual roles of men and women on the continent and beyond, and the dominant position of men. It was extraordinary. If women could become political leaders in Sierra Leone, they should be able to occupy high positions also in other countries, under favourable conditions. (This was a short time after the first World Conference on Women, and women leaders around the world were even fewer in number than they later became.) For a young Norwegian woman, struggling hard to break out of traditional gender roles, acquire a higher education (far from usual for Norwegian girls in the 1950s and 1960s) and participate in political life (where very few women were able to penetrate in the 1970s), this was quite a revelation – and an encouragement.

So Mammy Yoko became an example, illustrating that it was possible to do things differently from what was usual in traditionally male-dominated societies. At the same time, the bust raised an unanswered question: How could it be that the lady became a chief? The search was long, but one day I found an essay about Mammy Yoko in an American book. An anthropologist (typically a woman), Carol P. Hoffer, visited Sierra Leone and wrote about 'Madam Yoko: Ruler of the Kpa Mende Confederacy'. She relates how women of the Mende people have for centuries enjoyed high office as lineage heads, heads of secret societies and chiefs. A 1914 listing of paramount chiefs indicated that 15 per cent of the Mende chiefdoms were ruled by women (in 1970 it was 9 per cent). Among the Mende, inheritance follows the male line. Women produce offspring for their husbands' patrilineages. This is a scarce resource, and in an area with high child mortality their nurturing role is greatly valued. Mothers are looked upon as strong and supportive. As paramount chiefs, they are seen as mothers writ large.

Mende women are initiated at puberty and become members of the women's secret society, Sande, that protects women's rights. Here they can acquire religious influence. Women can also accumulate economic power as wives, especially if they are head wives in large polygamous households. The head wife organizes co-wives, children, clients, wards, and in the past, also slaves, and she markets economic surplus. In particular, if they are born of chiefly lineage, women can achieve significant political power.

Mammy Yoko came from a chiefly lineage. Her father was a warrior, and she married three warriors. She first married a man whom she left. Her second husband died shortly after the wedding. Her third husband was a mighty warrior who became the chief leader of the Bumpe area. He dealt extensively with the British colonial administration. The relationship was characterized by collaboration as well as conflict. Yoko was once obliged to get her husband out of British detention. This she did so skilfully that Gbanya elevated her to the status of head wife, encouraged her to strengthen her political position and sent her on diplomatic missions over a wide area of the interior and to Freetown. Before Gbanya died in 1878, he designated Yoko as his successor. She was then 29 years old and childless – she remained barren all her life.

Yoko was a most attractive woman, intelligent and dignified. She was very determined and had considerable diplomatic skills. She was particularly clever at building alliances, using her affiliation to the Sande society in an effective way. She also developed her contacts with the British with considerable wisdom. These were turbulent times, but Yoko followed a steady course, enhancing her own power with each adjustment in the political structure. She was recognized as a paramount chief by the British in 1884, succeeding her husband in office. But she extended the area under her hegemony far beyond that controlled by her warrior-chief husband, until she was paramount over all the Kpa Mende. A British official wrote of her:

> By sheer ability and force of character this resolute little woman has built up in the formative years of the country the biggest chiefdom in the whole Protectorate. Madame Yoko was not only a sagacious chief, but a woman of a mentality unusual in members of a primitive race.

After her death, her chiefdom broke down into 14 separate chiefdoms. According to accounts, she may have committed suicide, because she could not stand the shame of losing an important border dispute, or from the effect of a poison in a mistakenly concocted native medicine. A younger brother succeeded her, as she did not have her own descendants.

Box 14.1 The Queen Mother

The end of the year came round again, bringing the season of festivals. For the gathering in of corn, yams and cocoa there were harvest celebrations. There were bride-meetings too. And it came to the time when the Asafo companies should hold their festival. The village was full of manly sounds, loud musketry and swelling choruses.

The path-finding, path-clearing ceremony came to an end. The Asafo marched on toward the Queen Mother's house, the women fussing around them, prancing round them, spreading their cloths in their way ...

There was excitement outside the Queen Mother's courtyard gate.

'Gently, gently,' warned the Asafo leader. 'Here comes the Queen Mother.

Spread skins of the gentle sheep in her way.

Lightly, lightly walks our Mother Queen.

Shower her with silver.

Queens and Female Chiefs

How extraordinary was Mammy Yoko? We don't know exactly. Information is extremely sparse. Only fragments are available. As far as we know, female leadership has long roots in different parts of Africa, even if conditions vary from one area to another. In ancient Egypt, women enjoyed very high status for several thousand years. Female goddesses played an important role, and there was a succession of ruling queens. The names of around one hundred and fifty Egyptian queens are recorded before Indo-European and Semitic nomads penetrated the area in about 2000 BC, bringing a weakening of the position of women.

Many ethnic groups in West and Central Africa have had female chiefs, queens or queen mothers, but women are rarely mentioned by name in historical accounts. One was Queen Amina of Hausaland in present-day Nigeria. She was a great warrior and famous ruler during the sixteenth century. According to tradition, the area where seven Hausa states were established around AD 1050 was previously ruled by a dynasty of 17 queens. Amina, or Aminatu, which was her full name, was born in the state of Zazzau (later named Zaria after her sister), the daughter of an active warrior queen. She was 16 when her mother became queen. Many

---

Shower her with silver for she is peace.'

And the Queen Mother stood there, tall, beautiful, before the men and there was silence.

'What news, what news do you bring?' she quietly asked.

'We come with dusty brows from our path-finding, Mother. We come with tired, thorn-pricked feet. We come to bathe in the coolness of your peaceful stream. We come to offer our manliness to new life.'

The Queen Mother stood there, tall and beautiful and quiet. Her fanbearers stood by her and all the women clustered near. One by one the men laid their guns at her feet and then she said:

'It is well. The gun is laid aside. The gun's rage is silenced in the stream. Let your weapons from now on be your minds and your hands' toil.

'Come, maidens, women all, join the men in the dance for they offer themselves to new life.'

(Extract from *New Life in Kyerefaso* by Efua Sutherland, author from Ghana, 1958)

suitors gave her expensive gifts. But she did not want to be tied to one man. Many legends exist about Amina. Some state that she ruled from 1536 to 1573, while others maintain that she became queen only in 1576. In any case, she conquered the other Hausa states and numerous cities during a period of 34 years, helped by her sister and heading an army of 20,000 men. The ruins of several old fortifications bear her name. Expanding her kingdom provided a basis for growth in trade. The state of Zaria played a role both for the north–south and east–west trade. Amina herself presumably imported previously unknown luxuries such as 40 eunuchs and 10,000 kola nuts. After her death, Zaria lost its status. But the Hausa remained independent manufacturers and travelling pedlars. There is a song honouring the queen: 'Amina daughter of Nikatau, a woman as capable as a man.'

Queen Pokou lived during the eighteenth century and is considered the founder of the Baoulé kingdom. She was born early in the century in Kumasi (presently Ghana) and was the niece of the Ashanti king. The Ashanti dynasty inheritance followed the female line. The queen mother designated the king among the sons of her daughter or the sons of her daughter's daughter. She could herself rule if the king was dead or dethroned. Pokou was queen mother, grand priestess and the second highest person in the kingdom. She was beautiful, a woman of intellect and very dynamic. Married at the age of 14, she bore only one child, Kouakou. In the wake of deadly quarrels about succession, Pokou and her followers chose to move west. Pursued by the king's army, they reached a river they were unable to cross, because the river god demanded that the people make him a sacrifice of whatever they had that was the purest and the best, the person they loved the most. Pokou's parents, uncles and others refused to sacrifice any of their numerous children. Pokou dressed her only son regally, covering him from head to foot in gold, and then threw him into the river. Instantly, the trees lining the shore, the boulders and the hippopotamuses formed a bridge, which the queen and her faithful followers crossed and found themselves on new land. They formed a new people in present-day Ivory Coast, which was called Baoulé. It means 'the child is dead'. Pokou remained the venerated queen until she died in 1760.

During the British conquest of parts of West Africa, few tribes resisted as strongly as the Ashanti in present-day Ghana. Over nearly a hundred years, the British attempted to break their power. Finally, when all seemed lost, the Ashanti put themselves under the command of a woman, Queen Yaa Asantewa, who led them in their last desperate attempt to keep the foreigners at bay.

Yaa Asantewa was born somewhere between 1840 and 1860 and may have been 40 years old when she was enthroned as queen mother. A British official described her as 'a thin, brown, leathery lady, with fierce blazing eyes'. A photo of her in full uniform shows her as a bit roguish with a twinkle in her eye. She hated the British. When the Ashanti King Primpeh I and his mother were exiled to the Seychelles Islands, the position of leading the resistance against the British fell to her. The British governor came to Kumasi in 1900. She surrounded the city with her troops and kept it under siege for two months. The British sent reinforcements. When they arrived with new weapons, their force was superior. But Yaa Asantewa did not give in, and the battle lasted several weeks. When she was finally captured, it is said that she spat in the face of the British officer. Now it was her turn to be exiled to the Seychelles Islands. Here she lived for 20 years and presumably died in 1921. The rebellion made the British more cautious in dealing with the Ashanti. Africans still sing: 'Yaa Asantewa, the warrior woman who carries a gun and a sword of state in battle.'

It was not only the Hausa and Ashanti women who went to war, although the tradition was hardly widespread. In Dahomey (now Benin) a group of women warriors became famous as the 'Amazones'. They were probably unique in West African history. The group may have begun in the seventeenth century as a company of elephant hunters. Towards the end of the eighteenth century, they were called into service to reinforce the army. In the first half of the nineteenth century, the women became a regular elite unit. In the beginning, the recruits were women who could not adjust, were convicted of adultery, or were delinquent or war captives. Later, volunteering was encouraged, or members were selected by drawing lots. The Amazones were professional warriors. They did not bear children, but they were not warriors for life. After about twenty years, they returned to their village.

The Amazones were renowned for their zeal and ferocity. The most fearsome were armed with rifles. There were also archers, hunters and spies. They exercised regularly to be physically and mentally fit for combat. They sang: 'Men, men, stay! May the men stay! May they raise corn and grow palm trees ... We go to war.' When not in combat, they guarded the royal palaces in Abomey and grew fruit and vegetables. They could also go out and take captives to sell as slaves. At most, there were 14,000 members of the troop (in 1845). But this number was reduced towards the end of the century, and finally the regiments ceased to exist. The last were probably killed in combat with the French.

African Womanpower

Women chiefs, queens or queen mothers – does this imply that there has been matriarchy or female rule in Africa? Most of those who have studied the status of women in different African societies (mostly Western scientists), will answer 'No'. There is no example of a society where women have unambiguously had *more* power than men. As far as we know, women at the highest levels of leadership in sub-Saharan Africa have traditionally been more the exception than the rule. In many cases, queens and women chiefs have wielded real power. But men have usually had a dominant position in society as a whole. Ideologies expressing male superiority have been extremely widespread. Men have generally made the laws and rules of society. Families have on the whole been patriarchal in the sense that men have dominated women, and the elderly have dominated younger people. This does not mean that relationships have been similar to those in the Western world, and they have shown great variation. Women have been extremely oppressed in some ethnic groups, while they have had considerable independence and power in others, and with more power in relation to men than has been common in the West.

The debate continues. African researchers, in particular, underline that use of the concept of 'matriarchy' should not be limited to societies with female rule. Other aspects of women's status and culture should be considered, such as mother-right, matricentrism, female leadership and female transmission of property and descent. On such a basis, it can be argued that 'matriarchy' has been a fundamental characteristic of traditional African societies.

The female social scientist, Ifi Amadiume, from Nigeria believes that Western anthropologists have had difficulties understanding aspects of the traditional societies they encountered in Africa. In particular, they have found it very difficult to accept the invisible, transitory or distant role of men as fathers, and the strong position of women on the basis of their economic activity and role as mothers. In African thinking, motherhood has a central role. The mother is believed to be sacred. Her authority is unlimited, and motherhood has been worshipped as an integral part of goddess religion. According to Amadiume, the scientists were misled by their ethnocentric bias: they failed to see these aspects of the organization of local communities, and therefore 'masculinized' reality.

In traditional African societies, women were agriculturists, while men were hunters. In Amadiume's view, a mother and her children constituted a separate economic and social unit – the smallest unit within the family structure and productive activity. The matricentric unit produced food for itself, had its own compound and brought together in one household those who ate from one central cooking pot or plate. The members of the unit experienced a strong solidarity, bound in a common spirit of motherhood with a strong emphasis on love. A family included one or more matricentric units. The head of the family represented fatherhood, law and justice and the ancestral patriarchal ideology emphasizing violence and power. The family head was normally a man. But in some ethnic groups it could be either a man or a woman. Such groups had a flexible gender system, which could include both 'male daughters' and 'female husbands'. This implied that women could assume the legal and social duties usually allocated to men, after a special ceremony.

As the matricentric unit represented a viable, and to a great extent autonomous, female-controlled system, Amadiume considers it as a 'matriarchal' construct. On this basis, African women had an autonomy that was unknown to women in the Western world. On the foundation of the matricentric unit, women could contribute to the family as a whole, involve themselves in trade, establish networks and build up influence, wealth and status. Women had important roles as daughters, wives and mothers. They participated in the organization of economic, social, cultural and political activities in the community. Most African societies had formal or informal women's organizations that controlled or organized agricultural production, trade and markets, in addition to the culture and ideology of women. In some societies, these organizations were very strong.

In traditional African thinking, society was perceived as an organic unit, able to develop only through harmonious interaction between members, all of whom were important and efficient. Arrangements were set in place to ensure that everybody could participate in an appropriate way. A system of control maintained the balance between different groups. Forms of government with two 'co-rulers', a man and a woman, were an example of this. They sprang out of 'dual-sex' political systems, contrasting with the 'single-sex' system that obtains in most of the Western world. In the 'dual-sex' systems, each gender managed its own affairs. The interests of women, as well as of men, were represented at all levels. How the power was divided concretely between women and men varied from one ethnic group to another. For women, the essential aspect was autonomy, not dominance over men. The leadership roles of women varied. In particular, they took on a different character in centralized and decentralized societies. Amadiume wonders if the African women should be most proud of their feudal or market queen mothers?

Dual-sex Politics

The dual-sex political systems are first of all described among ethnic groups around the outer delta of the Niger river, particularly the Igbo and the Yoruba. The systems varied from one ethnic group to the next. Inheritance and descent usually followed the male line, but women as well as men participated in lineage institutions, age grades and other associations.

Among the Igbo societies with a monarchy, there were two monarchs. The male *obi* was in theory the head of the whole community, but in practice was concerned more with the male section. The female *omu* was the mother of the community, but dealt mainly with the female section. She did not derive her status from a relationship to the king. Both the *obi* and the *omu* were crowned and acknowledged heads. The purpose of the system was to establish a division of labour which could ensure that the needs of both sexes would receive adequate attention.

While the function of *obi* was inherited by the eldest son, the *omu* was chosen from among the members of certain lineages. The selection was usually done by female friends and kin. The *omu* was generally an elderly woman known for her wealth, intelligence and character. She headed the women's group in the village. As *omu*, she chose her councillors and assistants and gave them titles corresponding to those of men. Both the *obi* and the *omu* had a council of dignitaries, and the two cabinets supplemented each other. The Igbo women were active traders. The *omu* oversaw the local markets, determining their rules and regulations, fixing the prices and solving conflicts. Some *omus* could become very influential.

Among the Yoruba, the men were also head of the lineage. The women were represented by an *iyalode* or queen, who was a chief in her own right. She participated in the government, spoke on behalf of the women and warned the men not to interfere with women's affairs. Like the *omu*, she had her own council and coordinated the women's activities. As the Oyo state grew in size and importance, a hierarchy of priests, lineage heads, military chiefs and judges surrounded the king. Here the 'palace women' played an important role. They included priestesses and dignitaries who guarded the state treasury and the royal regalia, took care of the king's spiritual well-being and were responsible for part of the capital. In Benin, the king appointed his mother as a kind of co-ruler. She participated in the council meetings with the four most important advisers.

Enterprising Market Women

Traditionally, female trade activities were a characteristic of the people living along the African west coast. The women were involved in trade both on the local market and across longer distances. Some women established relationships with Portuguese, French, British and Dutch traders and obtained trade rights, capital and expertise. They became the privileged 'Signares' in Senegal, 'Señora' in the Gambia, 'Nhara' in Portuguese Guinea and 'Créoles' in present-day Ghana and Benin. They could play an important role. One of the most famous was Bibiana Vaz, who married a Portuguese captain in the eighteenth century and traded along the whole Guinea coast, particularly between the Gambia and Senegal rivers. She owned one big and several small ships, and during a short period she created a kind of 'republic for people of mixed descent'.

The most frequent were different kinds of petty trade within limited areas. This took place first of all along the coast of the Gulf of Guinea, even if some cases have been recorded also in the interior. Some of the wives of the rich merchants in Timbuktu and Djenné engaged in a discreet trade with luxury products at an early stage, while others took part in caravan expeditions. The market women in the Yoruba city states were well known. In addition to their agricultural work, they spent considerable time trading foodstuffs and producing various handicrafts: palm oil and soap, millet beer, baskets, pottery and, above all, cotton and indigo-dyed cloth. Women also traded salt. The women were organized in guilds, and the profits could be considerable. In Dahomey (present-day Benin) the women traded in palm oil, and in the Ivory Coast and Ghana in kola nuts. In coastal communities among others in Senegal and Sierra Leone, women bought the fish caught by the men, dried and marketed it. In connection with their trade, women could handle their own income to a great extent and involve themselves in economic transactions of considerable importance. They could move outside of the household and the local community, build up networks with women elsewhere and establish contacts with influential men.

During the colonial period, the women's networks were used to protect the rights of women. Little is known of resistance by women against the colonial powers, but the commercially active women reacted when their position and livelihood were threatened. Their determination, courage and organization brought results. The most famous resistance was the 'women's war' (the Igbo name) or the 'Aba riots' (the term used by the colonial powers) in Nigeria in 1929. But women organized protest movements before and after this in other cities along the coast, from Nigeria to the Ivory Coast. In Nigeria, there were protests up to 1966, when the military regime stopped all such activities, but these resumed when the regime became more tolerant. In 2001–02, women in the Niger Delta demonstrated against exploitation by multinational oil companies..

The background to the women's war in 1929 was a rumour that women were going to be taxed. This had not been done before, and Igbo and Yoruba women became very angry. They had been dissatisfied for a long time, because of the weakening of their economic and political position under colonial rule. They thought the chiefs appointed by the British were dishonest and exploitative. In addition, the prices for palm oil products fell at the same time as the duties on alcohol, tobacco and textiles were increased.

The women held meetings to discuss the situation. The outcome was that they attacked the native district offices and courts of the colonial administration. They released prisoners and looted the shops of white traders. Large numbers of women participated in the rallies, from a couple of hundred to more than ten thousand. In a mass demonstration against the colonial power, they stripped naked or dressed in sacks with green vines in their hair. They called the soldiers 'pigs'. Some carried big machetes. In the course of three weeks, the rebellion spread across the whole province of Owerri. The trade women contacted their colleagues, and the protest continued to the province of Calabar. On two occasions, British district officers called in police and troops, who fired on the women, leaving 50 dead and as many wounded. No one on the British side was seriously injured.

The British administration established a commission of enquiry to investigate the events, but it was not understood why the women revolted. Considerable force of arms was utilized to prevent the repetition of such incidents. The events nevertheless led to the inclusion of women in the native courts, positions that had previously been reserved for men. It was not until the 1950s that new attempts were made to tax the income of commercially active women. Although limited, these proposals led to outcries. More than a thousand trade women demonstrated, and the proposals were modified.

In spite of the priority given to men both during colonialism and after independence, women retained an important part of their traditional market trade. New groups joined in. With modern means of communication, particularly train and bus, women's trade became regional, even international, with salt, fish, kola and coconuts, bassia- or karité-butter (a plant fat used medically and for cosmetics), textiles and gold.

During the late twentieth century, women along the West African coast more or less dominated the trade in foodstuffs and part of the trade in textiles. In handicrafts, they dealt primarily with pottery, while metal products were a male domain. Since women usually had little cash to invest, they mostly traded in everyday necessities on the local markets. Even when they could count, their ability to read and write was often limited. Businesses demanding greater investment and contact with more distant markets were usually handled by men. But there were notable exceptions, among them the Ghanaian, Togolese and Yoruba matrons who sold cloth wholesale, the Wolof women gold traders connected to the Mecca pilgrimage network and the women trading in contraband diamonds from Sierra Leone and DRC. The best-known market women are the 'Mamies traders' in Ghana, the 'business-women' (commerçantes) in Benin, the 'Nanas Benz' in Togo and the 'Nagos' in Lagos. On the basis of traditional rights, many of the women operate in a separate economy. Some acquire considerable wealth, buy houses and vehicles and invest in economic enterprises.

In Central Africa, the women traders were late getting going. They gradually established themselves in big cities like Brazzaville and Kinshasa, selling fish and vegetables in particular. In the DRC, these businesses became widespread after the violent riots in the 1960s, because many women became sole heads of household. A galloping inflation also forced women to contribute more to maintenance of the family.

The Hausa women in northern Nigeria are a special case. They live in Muslim isolation, 'purdah'. Nevertheless, they developed extensive trade. As long as they respect the purdah, they are permitted to have a separate economy and a certain autonomy. They started with sewing, embroidery, hairdressing and even money-lending. The money they earned was used for themselves, or for trousseaus for their daughters and the bride-price for their sons. In spite of Muslim law, the trousseaus remained the property of the women and could serve as an insurance in case they became widows or were repudiated. Thus the women had a certain room for manoeuvre in spite of their subordinate position.

Women with extensive trade were the exception, generally speaking. Urban African women are found mostly in the slums and poorer areas of cities. Most of the activities are small scale and scarcely ensure survival. The women's trade activities have not given them a strong position in the financial and commercial enterprises of modern capitalism. Here men dominate – as they do in the West, where the firms originate. Women are employed only in lower positions, if they get any work at all.

Male Dominance

The male dominance that existed in traditional African societies was changed and reinforced by the introduction first of Islam, then of Christianity and finally by European colonial rule. The developments entailed some improvements, especially for the most vulnerable women, but generally the status of women was weakened. This was particularly noticeable in societies where women had previously been in a strong position. Despite the differences between Islam and Christianity, both religions emphasize the subordination of women in relation to men. The colonial masters, usually men, came from Western societies characterized by strong male dominance, and supported this approach in educational systems and in government. It was neither understood nor accepted that women could have political influence or play important economic roles. Their place was in the home. They were supposed to be subservient and passive in relation to men.

During colonial rule, the political and economic activities of women were either neglected or opposed. Traditional religions were banned. The status and autonomy of women were reduced. Their control of the markets was abolished, and they had to pay fees. The activity of women's organizations was restricted. In some cases, women leaders were arrested. At the same time, women were excluded from development activities introduced by the colonial powers, such as Western education, agricultural training and cash cropping. In decentralized communities, new male leaders were imposed on the population. In centralized communities, female leaders were disregarded. The British acknowledged only the male *obi*, for example, and not the female *omu*. The tasks of the *omu* were taken over by the colonial administration and the Christian church.

After independence, traditional women leaders were given greater opportunity to function at local level, although conditions varied. The *iyalode* still plays a role, formally and informally, which is not the case with the *omu*. In the new echelons of national power, however, women were absent, at least in visible and formal roles. One country in West and Central Africa – Guinea – tried during the early years to ensure the representation of women in political bodies. But this was an exception, in spite of the organized female resistance to colonial rule and the political activism of individual women. Even Guinean women were far from political equality. In general, in the new African states men occupied the leading economic and political positions, and women were left out in the cold. Modern industry, business, trade and administration continued with strong male dominance after independence, as it had during colonialism and as was the case in Western countries. Women were generally marginalized, and their interests given low priority. The economic crises of recent decades also hit women particularly hard, and there was a notable feminization of poverty.

Different political developments during the last part of the twentieth century led to wide variation in the activities of women's associations and interest groups in different African countries. There was also a great diversity of organizations, from traditional women's societies and community-oriented groups in rural districts, to more elitist professional, social and political organizations in towns and cities. After equality became an international issue – and especially following the democratization processes in sub-Saharan Africa in the 1990s – women's organizations, including women's rights organizations, became more active, above all in urban settings. There was also a flourishing of female creativity within the arts and written literature, providing a new focus on the experiences and lives of women.

Women's activism had an impact, but it was limited. At the beginning of the twenty-first century, gender equality in African states was still a distant ideal. Questions related to the status of women were given increasing attention, and some reforms were implemented. In several countries, laws were revised to improve women's salaries and strengthen their rights, in particular on issues of pregnancy and birth, and property ownership in marriage. Ministries and secretariats were established to deal with women's affairs, but usually they had low status and few resources. Most governments included at least one woman, but rarely more than two or three, and they mostly dealt with women's questions or social sectors. Few women held high positions in administration. In the social areas, where women are traditionally very active, only a handful were appointed. In the National Assemblies in sub-Saharan Africa, women made up an average of 14 per cent in 2002, compared with a world average of 15 per cent. But there were marked differences between countries.

A Mother President

A milestone was reached when Ruth Sando Perry became head of state in Liberia. She was the first – and until mid-2002 the only – African woman to hold such an office in modern times. A handful of women have been appointed prime ministers: in the Central African Republic in the 1970s, in Rwanda and Burundi in 1993–94, in Senegal in 2001 and in São Tomé e Principe in 2002, but none was head of state. Ruth Perry became chairman of the Council of the State of Liberia in 1996 and held this position until 1997. It was a completely male-dominated government, including several leaders of warring factions, and was supposed to negotiate a peace in the course of nine months and to organize elections for a new president. Perry's position as a leader was extremely demanding, as she relates.

> The civil war had lasted for many years, and conditions were terrible. In 1996, peace finally seemed to be possible. But they had to change the chairman of the State Council to get a neutral person. Many were proposed, but there was always one faction who objected. At last I was accepted. I am

a teacher and a mother of seven children. I helped my husband when he was involved in politics. After his death, I was elected senator. But I did not get involved in politics after the war broke out. I did not support any faction. It came as a complete surprise when I was asked to be president. The faction leaders pressed me: As a mother, take us as your children, they said, and we will collaborate.

'It was very difficult,' she explains:

I was often frustrated, humiliated. There were secret attacks. There was a shoot-out in the executive mansion. I continued working, though it looked awful with blood everywhere. I went out on national radio and asked for discipline and peace. I gathered the women and called upon them for help. The security and peace process had to be maintained. The warring factions had to disarm. People had to be able to resume their daily lives. Internally displaced people and refugees had to get out of the camps, and presidential elections had to be organized. I travelled extensively in the country, asked the young boys to give up their arms and got water and crackers and portable radios from the business community for those who demobilized. Voluntary organizations engaged in the rehabilitation. I went to the US and got clothes, medicines and educational materials. We got 70 per cent disarmament, and the electoral process was correct. I succeeded because I focused on the task of creating peace. I did not lobby to become more influential. I projected myself as a true mother and a stabilizer, using faith, discipline, courage, patience and tolerance.

It is typical that an unusual situation had to arise, that put centrally placed men out of action, before a woman could become the political leader. Liberia had a significant number of educated professional women, and many served in political positions and were activists for peace and change during the war. When no men were acceptable, a woman could become head of state – but only temporarily, managing an interim government. The basis was not political experience alone, but Perry's traditional role as a mother. She also exploited traditional female values and mobilized women to solve the difficult tasks confronting the country. In this way, she succeeded in her role in a way that was probably not possible for a man. According to the peace agreement, Perry could not stand for election as president. But another well-qualified woman did. She won only a few votes, however. The situation was back to 'normal'.

FIFTEEN

Where the Masks Speak: Under-valued Traditional Culture

The real only acquires its depth and only becomes true when it
is extended to the flexible dimensions of the supernatural.
(Léopold Senghor, Senegalese poet)

'Masks threaten people', was the headline on the front page of newspapers
in Abidjan on 5 January 1996. The article was from *Man* and continued:
'The Glaes masks in the West of the Ivory Coast threaten to ban the
country and set fire to villages and towns in a mysterious manner, because
they are being exploited by people to make a profit.'

Traditional circles considered the situation to be very serious. The
Ivorian Tourist Office had planned – without consulting the organizers
of the Glaes festival beforehand – to bring a number of tourists to the
festival where the masks of the Wè people are brought out of the sacred
woods. Not only that. The Tourist Office had advertised that the festival
was the most important of the year, had divulged the date and the route
of the masks, and had publicized pictures from secret ceremonies. For a
price of 3,000 CFA francs, tourists could make audiotape recordings. For
5,000 francs they could take pictures. But such sacred ceremonies are not
for sale, and the proposals were described as blasphemous. Among the
Wè people, the most important mask has a religious function and prays
to the gods of the universe. By its magical power, the mask can also
influence people and society.

As a result of the Tourist Office's behaviour, the date of the Glaes
festival was hastily changed. Tourists got to see only a few secular masks,
and the Tourist Office had to offer an apology to the Glaes (the mask
society representing the spirits).

A Myriad of Religions

The masks were an unknown aspect of the culture in West and Central
Africa, and one that is both fascinating and disquieting. Not all ethnic

groups have masking traditions, and they are mostly found in the rainforest and wooded grasslands. In the Ivory Coast about one-third of the ethnic groups use masks.

According to how they are defined, the number of different ethnic groups in sub-Saharan Africa varies between 500 and 2,000. There are large groups with several million people and small groups of only a few thousand. In the Ivory Coast, there are four large ethnolinguistic groups, but it is estimated that the total is more than sixty. In a country like Nigeria, there are perhaps four hundred. These ethnic groups differ greatly. Each has its own history, social structure and traditions, language and culture, even if many are little known outside a restricted circle. There are groups that enjoyed a highly developed civilization before the Greek and Roman era. Others have come into being during recent centuries. Their economic activities vary from agriculture, cattle breeding and fishing to handicrafts and trade. Some ethnic groups have a complex and rigid social stratification, with castes and classes of royalty, nobility, commoners, workers and bondspeople (often former slaves). Others have a flat, flexible structure of village, family, household, age and status groups. Often profession and position are linked, so that religious leaders, warriors, shepherds, traders and craftsmen have a special status. Everywhere, the family is central. It may be an extended family or core family, comprised of loosely connected descent lines or of clearly delimited clans.

Sub-Saharan Africa is characterized by great religious multiplicity. There are innumerable variations of traditional religions, possibly as many as there are ethnic groups or even villages. There are different gods, sacred symbols, religious customs and decrees. Islam has spread from the north in the course of nearly a thousand years. Christianity came much later and penetrated slowly from the south. The traditional religions are open and tolerant in character. Even when attempts were made, particularly from Christian organizations, to combat them, they continued to exist, often alongside or woven into the new religions, as these spread. African elements entered into Christian and Muslim rituals. Many participated in both traditional as well as Christian or Muslim religious practices.

During colonial times, both Islam and Christianity received an increased response. The conquest by colonial powers made many Africans associate their own traditions with an Africa that had failed. The colonial rulers favoured world religions, as opposed to the indigenous African belief systems. Western education, promoted to a great extent by Christian missionaries, opened new vistas of knowledge and technology. At the same time, it contributed to a downgrading of traditional religion and culture.

By the end of the century, it was estimated that around half the population in West Africa was Muslim, and it was concentrated mainly in the

Sahel. Islam is a state religion of Mauretania. The population of countries like Senegal, the Gambia, Mali, Niger and Nigeria was more than 50 per cent Muslim. Christianity had its stronghold along the Gulf of Guinea and in Central Africa. In many places, traditional religions remained the most important. Perhaps a more accurate picture is given by saying that a country like the Ivory Coast has 30 per cent Christians, 40 per cent Muslims and 100 per cent Animists.

Worshipping the Ancestors

Concepts like 'civilization', 'culture' and 'religion' are rare words in UNICEF, as in other international development organizations. Activities are first of all related to economic and social conditions. The thinking is that the international community is spreading universally accepted benefits (development and welfare) on a basis that is accepted by all, and is therefore culturally neutral. This is correct – to a certain extent. But many of the world's peoples have no access to the international arena, and often the activities take place in countries with very different communities. When cultural dimensions are not taken into account, development efforts may have unintended negative consequences. Aid can become less effective, and recipients may experience tensions between traditional and new.

The people I met often expressed indifference or disdain for traditional African culture. Experts from other continents usually knew little or nothing about customs in sub-Saharan Africa. Well-educated people from the region believed that their cultural heritage was without significance for modernization of society, or they perceived it more as a problem than a resource. Some took a different approach. Several of my African colleagues struggled to bring cultural perspectives into development efforts. They regarded African traditions as a source of social stability and creative innovation, a force that could strengthen or hinder attempts to improve the conditions of women and children.

Africans are generally characterized as profoundly religious people. Religion is both a belief and a mode of living, and forms the basis for culture, identity and morals. You don't have to stay long in Africa before it becomes clear that traditional religion and culture are intrinsic to the lives of most Africans, whether they live in a village or a town, are believers or mostly follow established customs. The culture influences attitudes, ways of thinking and behaviour. In particular, religion forms the setting at the crossroads of life. Africans do not talk much about their traditions to a Western visitor. Perhaps the customs are taken for granted, or are not something to be shared with outsiders. It might also be that Africans fear negative reactions.

Box 15.1 Breaths

Listen more often
To Things than to Beings
The Voice of the Fire can be heard,
Listen to the Voice of the Water.
Listen in the Wind
To the Bushes sobbing:
It's the Breath of the Ancestors.

Those who have died never left:
They are in the lightening Shadow
And in the darkening Shadow.
The Dead are not under the Earth:
They are in the rustling Tree,
They are in the moaning Woods,
They are in the running Water,
They are in the still Water,
They are in the Hut, they are in the Crowd,
The Dead are not dead.

Listen more often
To Things than to Beings
The Voice of the Fire can be heard,
Listen to the Voice of the Water.
Listen in the Wind
To the Bushes sobbing:
It's the Breath of the dead Ancestors,
Who have not left,
Who are not under the Earth,
Who are not dead.

Those who have died never left:
They are in the Woman's Breast,
They are in the wailing Child
And in the Wood catching fire.
The Dead are not under the Earth:
They are in the Fire that is going out,
They are in the weeping Grass,
They are in the moaning Rock,
They are in the Woods, they are in the Home,
The Dead are not dead.

Listen more often
To Things than to Beings,

Many Western people consider traditional religions to be strange and primitive. The belief systems may seem odd to people who are unfamiliar with them. But in my experience, the African religious pictures of the world lack neither richness nor depth. They are based on complex symbolic structures and contain important humanistic and spiritual values. Tradi-

> The Voice of the Fire can be heard,
> Listen to the Voice of the Water.
> Listen in the Wind
> To the Bushes sobbing,
> It's the Breath of the Ancestors.

Every day the Pact is repeated,
The great Pact that ties,
That ties our Destiny to the Law,
The Destiny of our Dead who are not dead
To the Acts of the stronger Breaths,
The heavy Pact that ties us to Life.
The heavy Law that ties us to the Acts
Of the Breaths that are dying out
In the bed and along the banks of the River,
The Breaths that move
In the moaning Rock and the weeping Grass.

The Breaths that stay
In the lightening and the darkening Shadow,
In the rustling Tree, in the moaning Woods,
And in the running Water and the still Water,
Stronger Breaths who have taken
The Breath of the Dead who are not dead,
The Dead who have not left,
The Dead who are no longer under the Earth.

> Listen more often
> To Things than to Beings
> The Voice of the Fire can be heard
> Listen to the Voice of the Water
> Listen in the Wind
> To the Bushes sobbing,
> It's the Breath of the Ancestors.

(By the Senegalese poet Birago Diop. From *Leurres et lueurs*, Présence Africaine, Paris, 1960. Translated by Torild Skard)

tional culture has also provided favourable soil for the remarkable practical and intellectual skills and rich artistic creativity of African peoples.

It is difficult to describe traditional religions. Ideas and principles differ from one group to the other. Written sources are lacking. Nevertheless, attempts have been made to outline some common characteristics of belief systems in West Africa. The term 'animism' is not appropriate. The religions have elements of animism, but they include other ideas. Frequently, people believe in a sky god or god in the heavens, and in addition have other gods, like the earth goddess. 'Animism' also suggests that we are dealing with a uniform religion on a level with the great world religions, and this is not the case.

According to traditional African religions, a human being is a religious creature in a religious universe. Existence embraces a hierarchy of spiritual forces from God, via different deities, to human beings, animals, plants and minerals. The spirits can be masculine or feminine. They can protect and heal, or bring disease and insanity. The meaning of life is not to be found after death or in an existence hereafter. It is found in the earthly existence itself, above all in the living interdependence of human beings. Everything turns on this, and not on the destiny of individuals. The family group is at the centre, and the forces of the universe are directed towards it. The myths explain the nature and action of the forces. Rituals and decrees are able to protect the community and exploit spiritual forces for the common good. Humans are closely associated with nature, not to cultivate it, but because they are an integrated part of it. Nature is not to be subjugated. An alliance is created, and human beings learn how to handle the natural forces. In such a context, missionary activities, conversion and intolerance are without meaning.

The religions assume that there is a Creator. This being exists far above humans, who have to relate to less important deities. The ancestors play a special role. When a person dies, the body is exhausted, but not the soul. It simply moves from one dimension to another. There is no clear distinction between the living and the dead. All live in the same world. From their dimension, the ancestors can follow what is happening and watch over the family on earth. Worshipping the ancestors is very widespread. The ancestors can return through newborn infants. A human being consists of a body and two spiritual elements that give it life: the life force coming from the heavenly god, and an element from the ancestors. The present, past and future, the living, the dead and the deities are thus all connected.

Traditional African religions have not inspired the creation of temples or holy scriptures. Customs and beliefs are transmitted orally. The spoken word is a living force. Morals do not determine what is sinful, good or evil. There is an order that must be upheld and respected. The universe is full of the life force. Deities, the family ancestors and the human beings can influence its distribution and effects. Magic can capture and manipulate it. Magic uses different techniques: spells, amulets, fetishes and rites. The healer or naturopath is feared, but also highly respected. The soothsayer contributes to the understanding of the forces, not least their harmful manifestations, in the form of witchcraft and sorcery, and how to deal with them. As a rule, male heads of lines of descent are responsible for the religious rituals. Women may be proficient in herbal knowledge and acquire leading positions as soothsayers, among others.

Concepts like health and healing are given very broad meaning in traditional Africa. They not only comprise well-being in everyday life, but also success at work, good health for children and happiness in marriage. A disease or suffering is not only a sign of poor health. It may originate from an evil force brought about by misdeeds or a bad relationship with neighbours, ancestors or others. The healer tries to identify this and repair the damage by means of prayers and sacrifices. Herbal medicine and exorcism can sometimes cure the disease. Traditional African societies have developed a whole range of methods to treat different kinds of ailments and illnesses. They have extensive knowledge about various herbs and their effects. No matter how 'modern' Africans are, they still preserve a respect for, combined with fear of, magic, witchcraft and traditional medicine. Protective amulets (*grigri*) are very widespread, among Christians and Muslims as well. Even health workers with knowledge of modern medicine seek help in the village when they fall ill, after they have been to the Western-educated doctor.

Living Masks

Masks and statuettes are used in religious cults and ceremonies. They have nothing to do with theatre, nor are they related to witchcraft. They constitute a social institution that strengthens solidarity and the governance of society. A mask consists of four parts: the wooden object that is usually called a 'mask', the person carrying it, the ritual clothes the person is wearing and the spirit that animates the person and makes his or her own personality disappear. The mask is a sacred object used by the spirit to appear. The person carrying the mask often speaks a special language. The voice has an unusual tone. An interpreter translates and communicates the messages. A mask is not an artistic object, but an image of the spirit, which is supposed to evoke feelings of respect, fear, courage and joy. The masks cover a wide range from grotesque gaping dragons and elegant antelopes to human faces with frightening eyes or soft sweet smiles. For Africans, the masks are alive. Those in the museum are dead, like the butterflies of a collector. The living masks radiate metaphysical energy, intervene in the lives of human beings, speak and dance and perform impressive physical feats, supported by singers and musicians in an atmosphere of mysticism, passion and happiness. The audience are not passive listeners, but active participants.

The masks have a religious function, because the spirit is sent by God. They are often called upon in difficult times of disease or catastrophe, and are used during important rituals related to creation and history, fertility and birth, initiation and death. The masks also have a social and in some cases a political function. They increase the harmony between people, act as the guardians of society and maintain law and order.

Every mask has a specific role. The variation is practically endless. The Wè people in the Ivory Coast have sacred masks, warrior masks, song and dance masks, beggar masks and *griot* masks (*griot* is a traditional poet and storyteller). The masks have different status and authority. When a mask of authority has spoken, nobody can object: the decision is final. Some masks are only for entertainment, and are the secular masks that are among those shown to tourists and foreigners.

The sacred masks of the Wè people have an awe-inspiring face, topped by a spectactular hat of eagles' feathers and animal's skin and surrounded by a wide skirt of straw. The singers get the masks from the woods. They walk slowly to the public space, surrounded by *griot* masks, servants, friends and members of the mask family. Because of their sacred masks, the Wè people are contented and prolific, enjoy good harvests and victory in battle. To prevent misfortune and to call on the goodwill of the ancestors and forces of nature, the masks make ritual sacrifices of sheep and oxen. A great feast is organized in the village. If the ceremonies are not performed, people in the village feel insecure. The village risks crop failure, epidemic or invasion. Therefore, everybody rejoices when the masks appear.

The masks are utilized in connection with the passing from child to adult. The initiation rituals for boys are best known. Most of those who have described such processes have been men. But there are also ceremonies for girls or both boys and girls. For both sexes, the young are separated from their families, are taught the tasks of adults and learn about sexuality and married life, traditions and customs. They may be put to various tests, be cut or scarred to indicate the status of adult. Often the initiation is organized by secret brotherhoods or sisterhoods. Secrecy is important to prevent the magic forces from going astray and being turned to witchcraft. Statues and masks are used as aids during instruction and ceremonies. The initiation processes vary in duration, and among some ethnic groups may last for many years.

Display of the masks is a very sensitive matter – as with sacred religious symbols in all cultures. Usually they are shown only on special occasions or to the appropriately initiated. The identity of those who carry the masks is hidden. There are mask cults that are exclusively female (like the Sande cult in Sierra Leone) or include both sexes. Most cults are exclusively male, even if women are allowed to participate during the performance. Men belong to the 'mask society', representing the power elite in the village. In the mask society, the most important matters are discussed and common decisions taken. Here, the secret knowledge and languages are conveyed from one generation to the next. A human being is mortal, but the masks are immortal. Through the mask cults, men can not only maintain social power and control, but also promote a masculine view of society and strengthen their dominance over women. On the other hand, the cults of both sexes promote cooperation. The women's cults often contribute to confirming the identity and strength of women.

As an outsider and an uninitiated person, a Western regional director obtained access only to masquerades organized for tourists. But I could buy masks in the market. Sometimes Africans also gave me masks as a present, although most said they did not understand the point of acquiring such objects, as they did not carry great value. Possibly this was because the objects were made for tourists, but often it seemed as if the masking traditions were not appreciated in themselves. Among Western colleagues, there were some collectors. For them it was important if the masks were 'genuine' or not. They could be new, but utilized; old, but unused; good copies of old; old, but poorly preserved; old copies; utilized, but not nice; nice, but not utilized; new and unused – it was impossible to make out. At the end, I took what I liked. If it was not 'genuine', then at least I was not contributing to the impoverishment of an irreplaceable African cultural heritage. It was particularly before Christmas and when school started that masks of good quality appeared on the market, as people sold them to get cash.

History without Writing

There is a stunning wealth of myths and legends, epics and accounts, poems and tales, proverbs and songs in African oral tradition. Many places, poets and storytellers preserved events and learning from the past. Special societies transmitted religion, knowledge, history and social relations from the elders to the young people. Gradually, missionaries and other travellers wrote down material they picked up, but far from all the oral heritage is preserved in this way. It is said that 'when an old person dies in Africa, it is a whole library that burns down'.

It has been underlined that Africans do not have their own writing. This is only partly correct. In Muslim societies, the educated elite wrote their own language in Arabic letters. There are literary, religious and historical works in Peul and Hausa. Christians also wrote their local language with Latin letters. Original written languages have also been invented, of which historians have documented five, including the hieroglyphs from ancient Egypt. In West and Central Africa, the Bamoum people in Cameroon and the Vaï people in Liberia and Sierra Leone had their own writing. But these scripts were not very widespread. Many ethnic groups utilized other aids to preserve literature and history. They depicted events on physical objects, like the exploits of the kings of ancient Benin carved on elephants' tusks. The kings in Abomey (in present-day Benin) each had an animal symbol, which was represented by appliqués on large tapestries. The Dogon people in Mali carved figures of their ancestors on wooden doors and window shutters. Most ingenious were probably the Luba people in the southeastern part of the DRC.

The Luba empire was one of the most important kingdoms in Central Africa from the seventeenth to the nineteenth centuries. A number of art objects were produced to stimulate and record the remembrance of history. Men of memory were trained. Their most important device was the '*lukasa* memory board'. This is a hand-sized, flat wooden object studded with beads and pins of different colours, sizes and constellations. Every symbol can have several meanings. Coloured beads depict heroes and leading figures, while rows of beads show routes and travels. The board is divided into a male and a female part and provides information about lineages, kings and the history of the state. The historians used the memory board when they presented legends about the heroes of the Luba people, their migrations and government. While the memory boards conveyed the official history of the Luba state, ornamented staffs were used to remember the history of local clans. The owner 'read' the staff whenever his authority was questioned.

Thrones and stools often represented female figures, to remind the Luba of influential historical or spiritual women. Luba women played important roles as ambassadors, priestesses and political advisers. Only women's bodies were considered strong enough to contain the powerful spirits and sacred knowledge associated with kings. Every Luba king was reincarnated after death by a woman called *mwadi*. She inherited the deceased king's emblems, titles and residence. The *mwadi* became a source of spiritual capital and memory, which was expressed by means of memory boards, headrests and staffs. Intricate scarrings and elaborate coiffures were utilized to remember a woman's place in society and history.

From Creation to Death

In relation to myths and religious performances, statuettes and figures were – and still are – carved in local materials. According to the myths of some ethnic groups in the Ivory Coast, the universe was originally created by a woman. When a male deity later took control, the divine mother retained responsibility for the cultivation of the land and the fertility of all living beings. She is the mother figure to whom people pray and sacrifice. Among other ethnic groups, the first woman appeared together with a man, both springing out of the will of the Almighty Creator. In these groups, numerous mother-and-child statuettes are made, which are marked by their harmony and vitality. It is not a specific mother who is represented, but a symbol of motherhood, of the life force and creation. The face is stylized and the expression both near and distant. The child lies on her lap, but not always close to the mother. The most conspicuous features are the mother's breasts, bursting with nourishment and strength. They are the divine source of human life. Sometimes the child actively grasps a breast to suck.

Among other ethnic groups, animals play an important role. The Bambara farmers dance to obtain an abundant harvest. They carry two carved antelope headdresses, one male, and one female with a baby antelope. According to the myths, antelopes in the past taught the human beings how to cultivate the land. Antelope horns symbolize the growth of millet. The straightness and suppleness of the figures portray ideal qualities for a farmer. At the same time, the male antelope represents the sun, the female the earth and the baby the human beings. The fibre garments worn by the mask carrier represent the water needed for a rich crop.

The Senufo people in Burkina Faso, the Ivory Coast, Ghana and Mali believe that the world once was an enormous room filled with clay, darkness and strange beings. Here, there was a big bird, the hornbill. This bird became a symbol of fertility and is consecrated to the great goddess in the Senufo universe, Katieleo. It is often represented standing up with a large, bulging stomach and spread-out wings. The long beak is turned down towards the stomach as a symbol of the male element, while the stomach promises future offspring. The wings are covered with signs that are reminders of the inevitable transition between life and death.

Myths and rituals are not only related to life's beginning, but to its ending. For many ethnic groups in Gabon, the cult of the ancestors is aimed at ensuring close contact between the spirits and the living. When a chief died, the initiated took relics from his body, decorated them, smeared them with a magic powder and kept them in special baskets. On the top of these baskets they placed stylized figures, and the baskets were utilized during various ceremonies. The figures have a puzzling attraction. Some are like an upside-down spade, with the blade covered by thin horizontal copper threads. In the middle, there are two large, staring eyes and a slender nose. The face is beautifully composed, but disturbing. There is no mouth. Is this a being that can see, but not speak?

In the Abidjan market, I could get hold of masks and statuettes. But it was in the USA and Europe that I first learnt more about the history and traditions of African peoples. Some of the museums in West and Central Africa exhibit interesting artefacts. But more often the selections are small and poor. During the economic crisis, several collections have fallen into decay or been looted. There are neither funds nor conservators, not to mention investigations or exploratory activities. African governments rarely manage to give such matters priority. Western donors show little interest. How can new generations of Africans get to know their history and appreciate their culture?

Hand-made Dolls and Cars

The creativity of Africans is not limited to the religious and spiritual realms. In everyday life, one is constantly struck by people's ingenuity and shrewdness. '*Pas de problème!* No problem!' they assure you, smiling broadly, when everything goes wrong and we all-knowing expatriates are completely at a loss. It may take time. But they do not give up. Often they find a solution, even if it is not quite what we had expected. A proverb says that need teaches a naked woman to spin. The lack of money, tools and equipment may have stimulated people's inventive talent and resourcefulness. But to exploit the opportunities, imagination and flexibility are needed. This is shown by the varied informal economic activities that people are engaged in, the manifold associations and groupings in urban and rural areas and the experiments people are carrying out within health and education.

Westerners have a tendency to believe that illiterate people are stupid and ignorant. One of the first things I had to learn in Africa was that people who could not read and write could nevertheless be wizards at reasoning and maths – as many market women demonstrate. Without writing, Africans often developed a phenomenal memory. They can observe all details relating to people and the environment and reproduce them many years later. The storyteller, Amadou Hampâté Bâ, gives a accurate report from his childhood memories of conversations his grandparents had long before he was born.

Many Africans have an astonishing language capacity. When you ask which languages they speak, they most often think only of international languages (the ones that carry prestige) and might not know many of these. But if you specify that you are interested in African languages, they in many cases speak two, three, four, five or even more. It is not unusual to meet young people from Abidjan who speak Baoulé, Diula and Wolof at home and express themselves fluently in English and French in school. It is tragic that the abundance of African languages is often perceived more as a problem than a resource. The UN Educational, Scientific and Cultural Organization (UNESCO) started a large project in the 1960s to preserve oral traditions and promote local languages in Africa. Many specialists both in and outside the continent were involved. But lack of resources hindered the work. In the age of the Internet, the question becomes even more pressing: what will happen with the irreplaceable cultural heritage represented by the African oral languages and traditions?

African children are often masters of creativity and manual skills. Ready-made toys are rare in most places in Africa. Children have to use what they find around them. With nostalgic delight I often recognized toys from my own childhood, of the kind that are about to disappear in the Western world. African children still build farms full of animals, using stones, shells and clay figures. They make spinning toys out of cans and strings. Slingshots exist in numerous forms, and in Africa they are carved with expressive faces and figures. The boys' elegant acrobatics on home-made stilts is a real pleasure.

You may come across a white, blonde, manufactured doll in Africa. But most girl children have to make their own dolls. They do so with elaborate style. No two are alike, and they have an unmistakably local charm. The body may consist of a simple bamboo cane or corn cob. A colourful piece of cloth becomes a dress. The bead necklaces may be sumptuous, with several rows of nuts, glass beads and seeds. The head is covered with curls, ponytails and braids. She may have a headscarf or turban. The face is usually neatly painted or embroidered with big eyes and a mouth. As is the case everywhere, the dolls are loved and caressed, cared for and lulled to sleep. Then, they are fastened to the back with a piece of cloth, as the adult women do with their babies.

Small African boys have developed their own expertise. Everywhere on the streets and roads you see them driving cars. These are not large vehicles, only 8–12 inches in length, made of wire. The boys steer them rapidly along with a long stick. The cars are often real works of art, perfect in all details. They have wheels and a body, steering wheel and windows, bumpers and lanterns, fenders and decorations – and there is no doubt about the make of car!

In some places the boys have a complicated organization for producing the cars. It is reported from the 'garages' in Brazzaville in Congo before the war in the 1990s, that the groups of boys were led by a 'master producer' of twelve or thirteen years old, who could make several types of cars. He was assisted by a younger 'producer' who was not quite as competent, but was still capable of producing a whole car. A 'producer finisher' put the pieces together, built the compartment and fastened the wheels. An 'assistant producer' made the seats, the doors and wheels. A 'master straightener' had a group of 'straighteners' who unwound and prepared the wire. The boys often went to the rubbish heaps early in the morning or late at night when no adults were watching, to find wire, pieces of grating, cans or corks. In addition to cars, they could produce bicycles and mopeds, wheelchairs and locomotives, planes and helicopters. Sometimes the works of art were sold to raise cash. At other times, exhibitions or car races were organized.

The Fascination of the Millefiori

Adult Africans are no less creative. The Cocody market in Abidjan is a real adventure, even if it is not well known outside the Ivory Coast. Passers-by cannot guess what is hidden behind the high concrete walls. You have to search for a hidden staircase at the back to get up to the second floor, where all the handicraft products are sold. In return, the stalls are crammed full of objects. They are on all the walls, in the roof, spread over the counters and on the floor – it is practically impossible to move around. Here is a true Eldorado of wooden sculptures and masks, statuettes of bronze and green malachite, gold collars and silver jewellery, glass beads and amber, leather pillows and wooden furniture, pots of clay and calabashes, drums, *koras* and *balafons* (musical instruments), woven cloths, batik textiles and *boubous*. Indeed, here is – whatever you want! It is said half-jokingly that East Africa is nature, while West Africa is culture. There is some truth in this. The ethnic groups in this part of Africa have been, and still are, incredibly creative with regard to art. In comprehensive overviews of art in Africa, West and Central Africa usually get most of the attention.

In the multitude of art forms I first became fascinated by the beads. When people started talking about *perles*, I thought of the small white balls I knew from Europe. But this was much more than pearls. In Africa, people make beads of all kinds of material and they have many colours and shapes. There are ancient beads made of shell, ostrich eggs, bone and stone, medieval beads forged with costly metals and precious stones, and in modern times, beads made of semi-precious stones, amber and ivory, silver, ebony and bronze, coral and china. Everything is used that can inspire the imagination. The beads pop up everywhere as jewellery, valuables, mascots, offerings and charms. Each bead has its history, has wandered around, been passed from hand to hand, bought or exchanged.

The glass beads are special. From the twelfth century, Venice was the capital of glassmaking. From there, artistic glasswork spread to many parts of the world. Even today the Venetian 'millefiori' – a thousand flowers – with their delicate mosaic of tiny colourful blossoms, are considered the most desirable. Linked with gold and plain-coloured stones, they become striking necklaces. Previously, the Ashanti people made beads of powdered glass that were considered to have supernatural powers, but the shaping was rougher. Gradually, African craftsmen started using bottles and jars from the Europeans as raw material.

Few can dress up with such lavish pomp as West African women when they wish to be elegant. In spite of the economic crisis, it is still possible to come across women who are completely covered with jewellery. They have beads and coins in their hair, headbands and earrings. The neck is covered with layers and layers of beads, silver and gold and, in addition, they wear bracelets, waistbands and anklets. There is no limit to these fabulous creations. The most overwhelming I have seen are the earrings of the Fulani people. They are as big as teacups and made of 14-carat gold.

Seen with Nordic eyes, Africans should scarcely need clothes at all in the tropical heat. But dressing up is a real passion, and textiles are a refined art for many people. The street scenes in Abidjan are a visual feast. Particularly among Muslims, decency is a virtue. But colours and texture express a sensual joy. The women from Senegal are supposed to be the vainest. Their clothing is often magnificent, with intense colour and elaborate embroidery. The neck opening may reveal a shoulder and a scarf may be tied roguishly around the head. Nevertheless, in my view they are outclassed by the men from Sahel, whose long and loose-fitting *boubous* undulate around the body when they walk. The clean white or light blue colour reflects the sunlight. I have been told that some may wear as many as two or three pairs of trousers and ten coats, one outside the other, and finish with a veil, a skullcap and a cloak!

People in the region have traditionally made textiles out of cotton, wool and silk, goat's hair, raffia and other plant fibres. They have used various colours: black or brown from river clay, red from the angola tree, yellow from sulphur bark and, not least, blue from the indigo plant. Little by little, synthetic textiles and colours have been introduced. Still, much of the traditional character is preserved. Personally, I was most thrilled by the *kente* or *kita* textiles from the Ivory Coast and Ghana and the *bogolan* textiles from Mali. The *kente* textiles are woven in many different colours, with vertical and horizontal rectangles in strong yellow, gold and orange contrasted with green or brown. The colours glow. Originally, the textiles were used by political and religious leaders, and men tossed the fabric over their shoulder like a Roman toga. The patterns should not only please the eye, but convey a message or have symbolic value. Gradually, other people began using the textiles and the patterns are now printed instead of woven.

The *bogolan* textiles are actually 'mud cloths'. Yellow or white linen cloths are covered with mud and a caustic liquid is used to make light drawings on the dark background. The process is extremely complex. The patterns have to be soaked and rinsed several times. The drawings are geometrical, inspired by local animals, forcefully and clearly shaped. In recent years, a commercial textile industry has made modern versions of the old patterns. The regional director acquired a suit, and it was touching to see how proud Africans were when I dressed in African clothes. I have rarely been so elegant!

If weaving was most often a male occupation in sub-Saharan Africa, pottery was female and as such was usually overlooked and underestimated. Pottery is, however, a handicraft in the real sense of the term and requires advanced skills. The potter is described as a 'miner' when she is digging the clay, a craftswoman when she is shaping the pots and an artist when she is decorating them. She works scientifically, mixing clay, drying, firing and hot-bathing pots. As a trader, she buys and sells the wares. The potter worships the goddess of pottery and asks her to protect herself and her work so that she succeeds. Every ethnic group gives the pots and jars their own character. Often they have a special beauty in their simplicity and functional form. Many are carried on the top of the head, besides being used for cooking and household tasks. In addition, clay is utilized to make furniture, musical instruments and dolls, games, coffins and grave monuments, even beehives and rat traps. No wonder clay is called the 'plastic of Africa'.

The earth is often perceived as female in Africa. The potter is associated with fertility and creativity when she shapes the soft clay and transforms it by means of fire. Pots are made for weddings and are smashed later when the people die. Like the human body, pots and jars can provide locations for spiritual forces – ancestors, nature spirits, deities, diseases or human abilities. In several ethnic groups, women play an important role as mediators between human beings and the supernatural world of spirits and deities.

SIXTEEN

Between Village and Metropolis: Mixture of Traditional and Modern

When a child has learned to wash his hands properly, he may have dinner with his parents.
(Proverb from Ghana)

In a poor country in Africa, there is a Catholic cathedral which is bigger than St Peter's basilica in Rome. The place is Yamoussoukro, the birthplace of the late president of the Ivory Coast, Félix Houphouët-Boigny. It was a small village when he was born, but became the political capital of the Ivory Coast, even if there is not a single government ministry there. It takes two-and-a-half hours to get to Yamoussoukro from Abidjan. There is a splendid motorway. Suddenly, it widens like an airfield. On the horizon, a massive concrete block towers like an overgrown mushroom. The Hôtel President has everything that is required for a modern luxury hotel: marble, mirrors, swimming pool (although it does not always have water) and a multi-starred restaurant at the top.

The view is magnificent across the plain, with its rows and rows of palm oil and coffee plantations. The town sprawls, spider-like, and broad avenues reach out in all directions. Most stop in the middle of the bush. Cars are few and far between. Flocks of sheep wander at a leisurely pace, looking for wisps of grass. The centre of town consists of a few clusters of houses, a mosque and some white modernistic buildings surrounded by green gardens. Several colleges are located in Yamoussoukro. Houphouët-Boigny also built party headquarters and a cultural centre there. Close by is an 18-hole golf course with 15 different types of trees – and nobody is to be seen. The presidential palace is hidden behind a huge white wall, along with crocodile ponds and the gem of Yamoussoukro, the basilica.

I have visited the cathedral many times. To begin with, I was appalled. With a steeple of nearly 520 feet it is taller than St Peter's, even if it is not much. It resembles the Rome cathedral, built in the same neo-classical style with an enormous cupola resting on majestic rows of pillars. There are supposed to be 368 pillars in all, according to the travel guide. But where St Peter's is full of ornate and imaginative decorations, Our Lady of Peace has only long, clean-cut lines. There are no paintings, tapestries or carvings, and few statues. The building is grand, but barren.

The basilica was raised at startling speed, in only three years, using all modern technology. (It took more than a hundred years to build St Peter's.) The construction started in 1986 and was finished in 1989. A crazy project with exorbitant costs. The bill is said to have been about US$300 million – in a very poor country, even if it is not of the poorest. The design was aimed at world recognition, using marble, gold, costly tropical hardwoods and stained-glass windows. 'This is the greatest sonorized room in the world,' the guide says. 'There are 2,428 light projectors and super modern air conditioning. Seven thousand people can sit and 11,000 can stand in the nave simultaneously.' I wonder out loud: 'Why did the president build it?' An Ivorian colleague is accompanying us around, and he smiles:

> Houphouët-Boigny wanted to create something immortal, to honour God and contribute to peace. He was a strong believer and a great statesman. And he wanted to give the Ivory Coast something we could be proud of, and we are! A hundred thousand pilgrims and tourists come here every year.

'But so much money – where did it come from?' 'He paid it himself. He also gave the basilica 150 hectares of coconut plantations.' As far as I know, Houphouët-Boigny was not a rich man when he started his political career in the 1940s. But additional queries about where he got his money are not understood. My colleague only shakes his head: 'We can appreciate that he spent the money here in the Ivory Coast instead of salting it down in a bank abroad!'

The Project of the President

The Caribbean writer V. S. Naipaul visited Yamoussoukro some years ago. The cathedral reminded him most of all of the pyramids in Egypt. The purpose of both buildings is magnificence, he points out. The splendour is an aim in itself, to serve the divinity and be a benefaction to the people. It shows the ruler's greatness and generosity, is proof of his right to rule and the justness of his rule. The image that Houphouët-Boigny wanted to present of himself is illustrated by the portrait that exists in the church. The president is depicted on one of the stained-glass windows, the only black person in the crowd paying tribute to Christ on Palm Sunday. He is kneeling humbly at the Saviour's feet.

My Ivorian colleague stressed that the cathedral was consecrated by the Pope. It can be perceived as a bulwark in the middle of Black Africa against an advancing Islam. The head of the Catholic Church came to Yamoussoukro twice: first to place the foundation stone, then to bless the final creation. It is said that the Pope was not entirely happy about the cathedral and demanded that a hospital for the needy should also be built. But by the end of the century, this had not happened.

The basilica was offered to the Vatican as a present, and the Holy See takes care of operations and maintenance – a practical way of solving the problem of running costs. The annual cost for cleaning and maintenance of the church, its adjacent buildings and garden, amounts to around US$1.5 million. And there are no more than one million Catholics in the entire country. The Pope is represented by five Polish priests and monks who live in one of the buildings. The other building is for the Pope when he is visiting. 'So it is mostly empty?' I ask. The guide corrects me immediately: 'God lives there, of course!'

Some consider the whole reconstruction of Yamoussoukro as part of the late president's attempts to modernize Ivorian society. The old village was torn down and replaced by modern concrete houses. It is striking how un-African not only the cathedral, but all the monumental buildings are. They are resplendent, but completely Western in their functionalist style. They could be anywhere on earth. The architect was an Ivorian-Lebanese. Several international firms participated in the construction. The stained-glass windows and furniture were produced in Europe. All the persons depicted on the stained-glass pictures are white, except for the president, in a modern variant of European baroque.

Houphouët-Boigny shows that the Ivorians are capable, but capable of *what*? A kind of modernism, but what might it mean and how sustainable might it be? After the economic crisis and the death of the old president, Yamoussoukro has, predictably, had problems developing his country. Certainly, the number of inhabitants has tripled. But some institutions have been obliged to shut down, and there are signs of decay in those that keep functioning.

Little by little, as I saw it being used, I came to care more about Our Lady for Peace. During mass on Christmas Eve, the cathedral attracted more than 7,000 people. The enormous space was packed. When the organ struck up and the drums added an unmistakable African touch, the church came alive. In front of me, a group of teenage girls stood swinging and singing in exuberant rapture – except for one who lay under the bench, sleeping steadily throughout the service. It was dark outside. The basilica was illuminated only from the inside with a dim yellow light. The day after, the sun was shining. The intense red, blue and yellow colours in the immense glass windows were breathtaking. Those who have a sense of numbers say the 36 glass windows contain 5,000 shades of colour. They reminded me of the great Gothic cathedrals in France.

The crocodiles preoccupied V. S. Naipaul more than the cathedral. The essay he wrote after his visit bears the title 'The Crocodiles of Yamoussoukro'. There were no crocodiles there before. But the old president dug moats and filled them with animals. They are fed every day, and people can come and see them. When I was there, it was a rather uninteresting event. The crocodiles lay close together on the slope of a naked rock, sluggish and practically motionless with their jaws open. They did not even stir when a piece of meat fell nearby. Naipaul notes that live hens were sacrificed earlier.

Why Houphouët-Boigny wanted crocodiles has created considerable speculation. Presumably the president's family has the crocodile as a totemic animal. But is this a reason to place a few dozen animals in an artificial pond and feed them with live hens? The crocodiles are very much feared. They are perceived as evil and dangerous. Some say they are supposed to inspire awe. The ritual with hens creates an impression of mystical, magic force. Thus the supernaturally ordained position of the president and his power as a ruler are confirmed. The fact that nobody really knows why the president put the animals there does not make it any less mystical.

The World of the Day and the World of the Night

Based on his impressions and experiences, Naipaul wonders if the Africans actually live in two worlds: 'the world of the day', which is the white world, and 'the world of the night', which is the African world. The first is a realm of knowledge, machines and modernization, the second, of spirits, magic and true gods. Whatever people say, it is the second world that really counts. Here, the real forces are in action, natural and supernatural, concerning life and death, disease and health. Here is mysticism and witchcraft. People, animals and plants can be transformed and become quite different from the world of the day. Naipaul quotes an African intellectual who states that: 'The world of the white is real. But we black Africans, we have everything in the world of the night, the world of darkness.' Whether one conceptualizes in the form of a 'world of the day' and a 'world of the night' or a 'black-black' and a 'black-and-white' Africa, it is striking how different the worlds are that exist side by side in African countries. We white people generally know only the world of the day, or the black-and-white reality.

In Western societies, people may be associated with milieus which have different norms and modes of living. In sub-Saharan Africa, the differences are more complex and cover a wider span. Together with glaring differences in technology, material circumstances and social conditions, there are very distinct philosophies of life, values and cultures. There is the Africa of the past and of the present, the traditional and the modern, the original and the colonial. There is Islam, Christianity and traditional religions. There is the individual and the community, dependence and self-reliance, justice and welfare. There is female and male, old and young. In this conglomeration, the village and the town represent two central but opposite poles.

In Western countries, the processes of transformation from the old agricultural society to the modern industrial, and then post-industrial information society have been gradual and not too rapid. They have extended over several generations (and some people still think the changes have been too fast). In Africa, modern Western means of production and forms of society were imposed from the outside. Wide gulfs existed between the new and the old. Towards the end of the twentieth century, parts of African society had undergone profound changes in an unprecedentedly short span of time. Other parts were left behind. Many people live in an oscillation, not only physical, but also mental, between different worlds which differ dramatically in several ways. They live both in the traditional and the modern spheres. It is not automatic that the modern takes precedence, as is often the case in the West. Naipaul's images of 'world of the day' and 'world of the night' create the impression that there are two separate worlds. This is not necessarily the case. Living in both worlds at the same time may be experienced as both natural and expedient. Traditional and modern are woven together in varying patterns. At times, though, the complexity and tensions may be difficult to handle.

In the West, individualism is firmly established. Every human being is perceived as an independent entity. Choices relating to life and career are primarily made on the basis of private circumstances and wishes. Birthplace and family are important, but not necessarily decisive. In sub-Saharan Africa, people do not feel detached from the social groupings they belong to. They are solidly integrated into the family and the local community they come from. The identity of the individual, and his or her norms and values, are formed by the community (family, clan, ethnic group). For many, the village is the core of the community. Africans may travel far and take up residence in the town. Still, the village remains both their native soil and their source of attachment to traditional culture. Because the ancestors are buried there, it becomes a religious centre with considerable impact on the conduct of everyday life.

Modern society is based on a rational, scientific way of thinking, which is in sharp contrast to the approaches of traditional African religions, and to some extent those of Islam and Christianity as well, but here the differences are less. The rational, scientific way of thinking is non-religious in character. It is distinguished by an objective analysis of causal relationships and forces in the material world. This has led to revolutionary improvements in the human condition. This way of thinking has also developed an over-intellectualized approach to the human being, that downgrades emotions and the irrational. It implies an arrogance in relation to the basis of our existence that leads to a neglect of the laws of nature and a transgression of the boundaries of human intervention. Traditional religions, on the other hand, are deeply subjective in their attitudes towards natural as well as supernatural forces. They view existence and human life as a whole, and are based on a profound respect for nature. The irrational

---

Box 16.1 The Rivers Speak

May the bushes cover my body,
my feet, my face,
so nobody watches
when I silently listen to the water
of the rivers speaking to me.

The sound of the pebbles
brushing against the water
are the kisses of the evening and the moon
and the kisses of the sunrise.

One day somebody told me
that the rivers do not speak,
that they simply follow their course
and slip away without a word.

How sad I was the day
I heard those words,
I ran down to the river
so it could explain to me
why I hear it so clearly
and others do not hear it at all.

(By Raquel Ilonde, poet from Equatorial Guinea. From *Antologia de la literatura guineana*, 1984. Translated from Spanish by Graciela Villanueva and then from French by Torild Skard)

is considered an important element. Continuity in the passing of generations is emphasized in a way that is being lost in Western societies.

A Thin Membrane of Modernism

Modern society is very attractive to many people in sub-Saharan Africa.
People with Western education are often entranced by technological
advances and strongly wish to emulate the West. Nobody blames them for
this. They may live longer and lead a less strenuous life. But few seem to
give much thought to what is required to achieve a successful modernization. What conditions must be fulfilled and what consequences will it
have? Proposals to introduce 'appropriate technology' or low-cost solutions
rapidly lead to objections. Are we not going to get the best? And if
problems related to modern methods of production are presented, such
as pollution or ruthless exploitation of resources, an aggressive question
is soon asked: Don't you want to give it to us? Further discussion becomes
difficult.

The modernization that attracts many Africans is first of all focused on
modern consumer goods and amenities, like running water, electricity,
telephone, radio and television, washing machines and refrigerators, roads
and cars, hospitals and schools. There has been considerable development
of modern infrastructure in West and Central Africa since independence.
But it has taken place in an unsystematic and fragmented way – a few
airports and harbours here and there, a couple of power plants and
factories and then some roads. A thin membrane of modernism has been
drawn around a society that basically functions in an entirely different
way. The spirit of modernism has not penetrated. Many enterprises are
extremely vulnerable, because basic conditions are lacking, completely or
partly. Every now and again, the membrane tears.

A key problem has to do with repairs and maintenance. The number
of dilapidated health and school buildings and water pumps filled with
sand that I have seen around in the region is not small. Maintenance is
also a recurring problem in large enterprises, like power plants and telephone companies. Funds, spare parts and skill to fix the new devices may
all be lacking. In many cases, Western partners do not wish to transfer
their technological know-how to Africans, or they overlooked the need
for future repair work when the buildings and plants were constructed.
Ownership of the enterprise may also be unclear – is the local population
responsible for maintenance, or are others? But if people wait long
enough, perhaps somebody will come and fix it all. Apparently, local staff
have only partly acquired the necessary industrial work discipline.

I experienced the most dramatic failure in modern technology in Benin and Togo, when the production of electricity from the big Akosombo dam in Ghana suddenly fell to half. The prevailing drought was only part of the explanation. Insufficient maintenance of the turbines contributed to the failure. The power quotas were rapidly reduced to six hours per day in Ghana's neighbouring countries importing electricity. In urban areas, people had many problems. Electrical equipment stopped in buildings without generators. It became scorchingly hot when air conditioners and fans no longer worked. Candles had to be used for lighting and gas or coal for cooking. In many places, there was a shortage of water and petrol, because the pumps depended on electricity. Sanitary installations stopped functioning. Food started rotting in freezers and refrigerators. When the electric current came back after a break, it was at times so powerful that connected equipment broke down. Supermarkets and shops, small businesses and offices, police stations and banks – all got into difficulties. Restaurants had to shut down, except for the few that had a generator. Public administration worked on a fraction of its capacity. In fact, the rural population managed the best, because they did not depend on electricity. In the countryside, the cold chain for vaccines continued using petrol or gas. The central storehouse in Lomé, however, was in a critical situation before a generator was procured.

Cultural Confrontation

UNICEF's regional office in Abidjan was a meeting place between Western and African, old and new. Before I came to Abidjan, I thought it could be difficult to create a good team with people from 20 different nations. There were experts from all over the world working in the areas of social science, communication and administration. The majority of staff were from the Ivory Coast and neighbouring countries, mostly assistants, secretaries and drivers. Yet the collaboration among the international professionals went amazingly well. We had all been through a protracted Western/international education and had experience with modern management and working methods. But tensions arose in relation to the local staff, who in many cases held divergent views on organization and performance.

My predecessor, an African, did an important job mobilizing support for women and children among the ruling elites in the region. It became important to involve supporters in the organization. As a consequence, some people were employed in the UNICEF offices more on the basis of personal relations than technical competence. The instructions I received from UNICEF's headquarters were clear: I had to tidy up, raise the technical standards and improve the efficiency of the work. This was no simple task, as I realized the first time I terminated the contract of one of the Ivorian employees in the regional office. A delegation of six local staff came to protest. They were all mature women with families and children. Several belonged to influential families in Ivorian society. The oldest spoke with authority and commitment: 'We come as mothers. You must temper justice with mercy. Robert has a large family and think of the children! They are small and go to school. You cannot lay him off!'

In management, we had not taken the matter lightly. On the contrary, we were very thorough and conscientious. When I came to Abidjan, Robert had been working in the office for several years. He was employed in spite of the fact that there were doubts about his qualifications, and his performance was not in accordance with his job description. But my predecessor did not take action – probably because Robert was closely related to centrally placed politicians in the Ivory Coast. But for a Western regional director, such arguments did not carry the same weight.

I did not take action immediately. Robert was given another year and a schedule of performance discussions, guidance and evaluations. With no result. Perhaps he did not take us seriously. His powerful patrons would make sure that he was not dismissed. There was quite a fuss when people started suspecting that I might make my threat good. The leader of the staff association and the ombudsperson in the office came to see me, both local staff. The appointment and placement committee, in which different groups of staff participate, recommended that the contract should be prolonged by another year. And the mothers lined up – the most senior and respected staff members of the office.

For a Western head of office the reasoning sounded strange. Robert could not do the job. Everybody admitted this. Still, they wanted him to stay – because he belonged to the 'family'! My deputy, a man from Kenya with long experience in UNICEF, could not hold his tongue:

> I am also a father. If he had taken his responsibility seriously, he would have put all his strength into improving his performance long ago. What about the distressed children in the region? It does not benefit them if we waste UNICEF's resources!

After the meeting, Robert complained to the Ivorian Ministry of Foreign Affairs. The chief of protocol was very polite. But he had received a report about unfair treatment of an Ivorian citizen. I explained our procedures. When the chief of protocol heard how seriously UNICEF deals with personnel matters (with a thoroughness and objectivity that is probably unknown in many Ivorian workplaces) and how many Ivorians we had employed in the office, he did not have much to say.

African Time

Industrial production makes different demands on planning, punctuality and exactness than subsistence agriculture does. An industrial discipline has little by little permeated the whole of modern society. But in sub-Saharan Africa, these transformation processes have not gone that far.

The tensions between old and new were evident in the approach that many Africans had to time. As technology developed, we in the West adapted to constantly tougher time schedules. Everybody has a watch. More and more people observe and obey the passage of time. The watches have become more and more accurate, showing not only hours and minutes, but also seconds and even tenths of seconds. Most Africans do not have a watch. The days follow the sun. In the lives of farmers in the rural areas, a few minutes or hours more or less rarely have great importance. In urban areas, the time requirements are different. Effective time management becomes a virtue. But getting it under one's skin is not done in the twinkling of an eye. Often, unexpected events create delays. In 'African time', we Westerners noted and laughed in a resigned fashion, when Africans were late, nothing was urgent and dates were postponed indefinitely. Not even the authority of the regional director was sufficient to start meetings in the office on time.

In many cases, the performance of local staff was not up to the expectations of management. Staff members were reserved and did not wish to take responsibility. Experiences from an authoritarian colonial or post-colonial administration seemed to play a part. When tasks were discussed, some underlined that 'the boss is responsible, we do what we are told'. If they did not receive instructions, they did not do anything. When they were encouraged to take initiatives, several refused, 'so we don't do anything wrong'. If they did do something wrong, then they would get a scolding, they said. Once when we put on pressure, a staff member burst out: 'OK, I'll take initiatives, just tell me what to do!' If staff were criticized for errors, they could feel embarrassed. But they could just as well give a disarming smile: 'It's human to make mistakes, isn't it?' They seemed far from the inexorable, achievement-oriented, competitive society.

A Painful Reorganization

The tensions related to performance were particularly tangible when we had to reorganize the regional office. An order came from headquarters to save money. Local staff were extremely apprehensive. How would they manage? How many would lose their jobs? In the management we emphasized transparency. Different proposals for reorganization were elaborated with staff representatives. Afterwards, we organized staff meetings. But many did not believe I was serious when I said I would listen to people. The boss decided. And the reorganization was in reality not a requirement from UNICEF headquarters, they thought, but something I had invented for personal reasons. When some started to understand that they could in fact propose alternative solutions, it was too late. In the placement process that followed, we introduced standardized tests, in order to be fair. This created general panic. Many were unfamiliar with this type of procedure, and were convinced that they would fail.

Suddenly, there were anonymous telephone calls with death threats to our home in Abidjan. I was on mission. My husband was told in broken English that madame would be killed, because she hurt people. What this was about, was not explained. Emergency orders were issued immediately. When I landed at the airport, I was met by four masked, armed guards who escorted me home in an unfamiliar car along strange out-of-the-way roads. Our poor dog. She was so alarmed when they all suddenly marched into the living room that it took weeks for her to recover. Extra guards were placed around the house day and night. Police patrolled in the neighbourhood. We were told to stay at home as much as possible. Several colleagues in the office also received threats.

The threats were discussed with the Ivorian Ministry of Foreign Affairs, the UN Resident Coordinator and UNICEF headquarters. Fear lurked in the bottom of my belly. Be killed in Africa? That was not exactly the intention. We were supposed to assist women and children! Should we leave? But perhaps those who called actually did not want to kill us, only to scare us so we would do what they wanted. We had to keep cool. The Ivorian authorities did not believe that the threats were serious. It was not unusual in the Ivory Coast to make such warnings. But we had to take all precautions. It was unclear what this implied. But I got a mobile telephone, and my driver drove me back and forth to the office along a different route every day. A bodyguard would be too exaggerated, I thought.

My husband believed we should engage in psychological warfare. We should organize a big garden party to show that we were not afraid. No sooner said than done. Nearly a hundred people were invited for a celebration. The guards were very concerned and believed this was not advisable. We explained that in our home country we always organized a big social gathering when we were in mortal danger. Then we were sure we could participate in the funeral feast. Everybody laughed – and the party was on.

We invited the criminal police to the office to interrogate those who received telephone calls. A representative from the Ministry of Foreign Affairs participated in a staff meeting. He pointed out that the threats conflicted with the traditional hospitality of the country and could not be accepted. 'And we know who is doing this!' he stated and stared intensely at the staff. The audience gave a sudden start. Afterwards, 15 staff members came to see him to ask for advice. He explained that they had to distinguish between person and institution. The reorganization was no personal impulse on my part, but a global instruction from UNICEF in New York. It was no use trying to punish the regional director in Abidjan.

After this, there were no more telephone calls. When the process was over, only one local staff member had lost her job. On the other hand, several left voluntarily to get the compensation for removal of their positions.

'Aimé was a Little Boy'

Some Africans with Western education try to reduce the tensions between modern and traditional by differentiating between various arenas. On the one hand, the workplace with Western requirements and norms, on the other, the private sphere where African culture dominates. They behave differently in the two arenas. With such a distinction, people of different status in traditional society (different classes or castes) could nevertheless work together on a basis of equality in a modern working environment. But private meetings were out of the question, not to mention marriages or close friendships across the dividing lines. This approach solved some problems. But it was not always easy. Once when the director general of UNESCO, Amadou M'Bow from Senegal, was on a mission, his suitcase was left out on the airfield. The person who was supposed to handle it was M'Bow's assistant. He was also Senegalese and of distinguished birth, which M'Bow was not. The assistant could collaborate with M'Bow on the job. But he considered it beneath his dignity to do him a personal favour like carrying his suitcase, even if M'Bow was the director general and head of the organization.

A watertight division between job and private life was impossible to maintain in relation to salaries and social benefits, in particular. African families are generally large, particularly in polygamous households. In addition to biological links, assigned roles can entail family ties. The majority have an abundance of 'brothers' and 'sisters'. Only some of them are biologically related. At the same time, strict rules demand mutual support and distribution. If you have been lucky enough to acquire something, family and relations have a claim to it. Such family solidarity is useful under adverse material conditions, in societies where most people have neither social security nor pensions. But it is not easy to combine with Western wages and modes of payment.

The local staff in UNICEF generally had a good salary in relation to their countrymen and -women. But the family allowances were not adjusted to African family traditions. Family responsibilities could therefore be hard to handle. Relatives took it for granted that the local UNICEF staff were very well off and just moved in with them. It was impossible to say no. There could be as many as 15, 20, even 30 people to support. Sometimes staff asked for a special confirmation of what they earned, to show to family and relatives who thought they earned much more than they actually did. In such situations, the temptation could become pressing for some to try to increase their income by not quite legal means.

However urbanized and modern present-day Africans might be, the ties to the family and the village took on great importance at the decisive moments in life: birth, marriage and death. In the case of death, traditional rituals were essential. It could be a very delicate task to combine the demands for a traditional funeral with a Muslim or Christian one. The customs differ: should the funeral take place at once or is it advisable to wait for weeks and months? Should the funeral take place in the village or the town? What kinds of rituals should be performed? Should the deceased have clothes and equipment for the journey to the hereafter? One of the local staff once asked for leave to go to the village and organize the funeral of a close relative. He nearly wept when he explained how the elders in the village on one hand and the priest in town on the other made demands that were nigh impossible to combine. 'They will kill me if I don't do what they say,' he said. I do not think he was talking nonsense. It was said that the village had great power. People who did not behave as they should might be put to death.

The practical solution in many cases was to organize several ceremonies before the deceased was buried. When an Ivorian staff member in the regional office, Aimé Konian, died, everybody in the office dressed in a kind of uniform. It must not be too sad, because Aimé was Baoulé. According to tradition, one should not be deeply grieved at the death of the first three children in a family. God has provided and then taken them back again. Only when the fourth child dies should there be real mourning. Tradition dictated that the coffin with Aimé's body should be transported to Yamoussoukro, to be entombed in all simplicity. But Aimé's father was Christian. So first there was a vigil with prayers in Aimé's house and a requiem mass in the Catholic church in Abidjan, before the funeral procession left for Yamoussoukro. Here, there was a stop at the family house, where a traditional ceremony was performed. The children walked around the coffin to protect themselves from evil spirits or spells. Then, the cortège went to the family grave chamber. After another Catholic service, the coffin was lowered into the earth.

In the office, the question arose as to what we should do. In an international and religiously neutral organization, we could not organize a 'memorial service'. The Baoulé tradition would probably not consider a 'mourning ceremony' to be appropriate. The solution was a 'commemoration'. Aimé's family thought it was unnecessary to make too much of the death. Nevertheless, three family members participated. It was a touching ceremony, where staff members spoke about Aimé. Messages of condolence from UNICEF friends not only from the region, but from all over the world were read aloud. Aimé's uncle thanked us on behalf of the family. He was very moved. He uttered a few simple sentences: 'For us Aimé was a little boy. We saw him grow up and now he is gone. Today we understand that he is not gone, after all, because he lives in what he has been for you. Thank you so much. *Merci.*'

Part III
Conclusion

SEVENTEEN

Our Beloved Africa: Is a Renaissance Possible?

'Creativity is the highest civilizing faculty. Africa breathes stories.'
(Ben Okri, Nigerian author, 1997)

At the beginning of the twenty-first century, sub-Saharan Africa is in widespread and profound crisis. 'Hopeless Africa', the British journal *The Economist* stated on its front page in May 2000. The text continued: 'The crisis in Sierra Leone is only the latest in a catalogue of horrors. The continent is plagued with floods and famine, poverty, disease and state-sponsored thuggery.'

It may be tempting to adopt an afro-pessimistic view. But such an approach is both biased and dangerous. It is true that Africa is struggling with a number of serious problems. But characterizing the continent as 'hopeless' is an unwarranted simplification. The continent is too complex to be described by a single word. Such a negative cliché disregards all positive aspects and precludes a further analysis of difficulties and possibilities. In addition, a condemnatory description might turn into a self-fulfilling prophecy. How many English-speaking business people who use *The Economist* as their reference would be inspired to invest in Africa after such a declaration?

The one-sidedness of *The Economist* headline is illustrated by *Le Monde Diplomatique* on the other side of the channel. This newspaper printed a special edition on Africa at about the same time as *The Economist* did. Here the title was 'A Continent of the Future'. *Le Monde Diplomatique* notes that foreign investments in Africa are more profitable than in other places, even if the volume is not great. Sectors like transport, energy, mining, communication and tourism are expanding, and local managers are being recruited in large numbers by multinational companies. The magazine continues with a review of 'Afrique en Renaissance' – renewal in Africa.

The Economist received so much criticism of its May article that it wrote a new one in February 2001, called 'Africa's elusive dawn', presenting a more balanced view.

From 1990 to 2000, sub-Saharan Africa did not make much progress in achieving the goals of the World Summit for Children. But the perspective can be turned around. It is possible to note what *has* been attained instead of what has *not*. Even if the goals were not reached, the situation of women and children was improved during the decade – in spite of difficult climatic conditions, widespread economic crises and considerable political problems. There was progress, even if it was not very great. Determined politicians and enthusiastic civil servants, hardworking health workers and teachers, active leaders and eager local groups carried on against all odds and obtained results with the support of the international community.

It is easy to forget the positive steps forward. But they must be included alongside the failures. The point is not to be either very pessimistic or very optimistic on Africa's behalf. The description of the situation should be as realistic as possible, so as to form a basis for action. It is also important to evaluate developments from a long-term perspective. The present must be seen in light of the past, and it must be recognized that there are no quick fixes. Some measures are urgent, but policies must be long-term.

Unfinished Liberation

The Economist is not alone. Among Western donors as well, voices have been heard during recent years demanding a reduced involvement in Africa. The continent should 'manage on its own'. This is unacceptable. Western countries, particularly the former colonial powers, have their fingers planted deep in the African soil in different ways. To a large extent, they are party to and share the responsibility for what has happened and what still happens – or does not happen – on the continent. It is not possible to disclaim responsibility and turn one's back.

The African countries have been politically independent since the 1960s, but the decolonization is far from complete. Political freedom of action is clearly restricted. Developments have not led to economic independence. The greatest responsibility for the future of the continent rests with Africans themselves. But the future does not depend solely on them. The international community, in particular the International Monetary Fund (IMF) and World Bank, Western financial interests and governments of the rich countries play an important role. They make decisions of crucial importance for African countries.

In the spring of 1998, UN Secretary General Kofi Annan presented a report on peace and sustainable development in sub-Saharan Africa. He maintains that African leaders as well as the international community have failed the African people. They have not done enough to address the causes of conflict, to ensure a lasting peace and to create conditions for sustainable development. According to Annan, Africa must rely on political rather than military responses to problems. Africa must take good governance seriously, ensure respect for human rights and the rule of law, strengthen democratization and promote transparency and capability in public administration. The African countries must implement economic reforms to promote growth and pursue policies that alleviate poverty.

On the other hand, Annan stresses, the international community must support Africa, intervene where it can have an impact, and invest where resources are needed. New sources of funding are required, and existing resources must be better used. Finally, trade and debt relief measures must be implemented to enable Africa to generate and to reinvest its own resources better.

The UN Secretary General tries to present a unifying view, and it is possible to agree with most of it. Annan has been criticized, though, for being too sympathetic to multinational companies and to the economic reform programmes of the IMF and World Bank. Personally, I find it difficult to see how Africa's problems can be solved when decolonization and national liberation are excluded from the political agenda. African leaders must be able to determine their own national policies and be accountable primarily to their own citizens, not to the IMF or World Bank and donor countries. The state should be strengthened, but also changed, so that it serves the common interest instead of exploiting people and resources. The economy must be developed so that countries get more out of their own resources, become more self-reliant and less exposed to international macroeconomic fluctuations.

Living in sub-Saharan Africa, one is frequently struck by the after-effects of the colonial period, in fact, the whole period from the slave trade up to the present time. Many Africans experience this as several centuries of continuous oppression and exploitation. Africa was drained of human and material resources. Attitudes of superiority and inferiority were formed that still persist today in varying degrees. The colonial contempt for African civilization affected both white and black, so that traditional culture and knowledge are generally considered to be inferior. Not only the white man's modern technology, but his whole civilization is perceived as superior. Africans lost self-esteem and self-confidence. The economic crises and dependence on aid during recent decades have not improved the situation. A cultural liberation is therefore needed, not least in French-speaking African countries, where the ties to the former colonial power appear to be the strongest.

There are groups and movements working to increase the appreciation of African civilization and to find constructive ways of integrating traditional and modern. They are often scattered and lack resources. As the point of departure, a strengthening of African identity must be a matter for Africans themselves. But the UN itself, and UN organizations like UNESCO and the UN Development Programme, where African countries are broadly represented, as well as countries without colonial and great power interests, can play a supportive role, along with voluntary organizations and milieus in different parts of the world. The outside world can help Africans to preserve their cultural heritage, oral as well as material, to analyse history, languages and culture, carry out artistic and cultural activities and develop African models for society. Intellectuals, scientists and artists can play a central role here. Further, cultural dimensions should be included in various development efforts. In extending basic education, for example, the focus should not only be on access to schooling and the quality of teaching, but also on the cultural basis of the education. Should the children be alienated from traditional culture, or manage to combine African and Western in a fruitful way? In the area of health, there are

---

Box 17.1 Tell Me

Tell Me
What The Griot[1] Says
Who Sings about Africa
From Time Immemorial
He Tells About
The Patient Kings
On the Summits of Silence
And the Beauty of the Old
With Fading Smiles
My Past Came Back
From The Bottom of my Memory
Like a Totemic Snake
Tied to my Ankles
My Loneliness
And my Shattered Hopes
What Should I Bring
To my Children
If I Lost their Soul?

1. Traditional poet and storyteller

(By Véronique Tadjo, poet from the Ivory Coast. From 'Latérite', 1983. Translated by Torild Skard)

untapped possibilities of bringing modern and traditional medicine closer together that may be significant, not least in the struggle against HIV/AIDS.

Consensus and Cubism

Strengthening African culture is essential for people outside Africa as well. The continent has much to contribute to the international community. The African consensus principle has helped the UN solve international conflicts. In the debate on human rights, Africans have focused on collective and traditional rights (of the ancestors) and the rights of future generations. They have emphasized the importance for social development of solidarity within the extended family. The unconscious and spiritual, myths and dreams, have not been repressed in the same way in Africa as in the West. European artists, like the Cubists in modern painting, have been inspired. The intense emotions often expressed by Africans, in joy as well as in sorrow, come as a relief to the more inhibited Nordics.

It is hard to evaluate one's own culture properly. Undoubtedly, Western civilization has produced astonishing technological advances and a material living standard that people in the past could not have dreamed of. It has also promoted individual rights and development. But at the same time, its culture is one of the most aggressive and greedy on earth. The white man has conquered large swathes of the world, has wiped out peoples partly or completely and is now, through globalization, about to dominate the whole world economically. At the same time, air, soil and water are being polluted and resources exploited in a way that is threatening the very existence of our planet. There are dramatic disparities between rich and poor. Not only in poor countries, but also in rich, considerable segments of the population experience misery and distress, isolation and lack of meaning. Is it surprising that many wonder if this really is the good life? In such a perspective, African cultures can enrich humanity.

Western societies are often criticized by African analysts because they are too individualistic, are characterized by economic disparities and destroy social ties and the environment. Models of society have been promoted in recent years emphasizing 'self-reliant growth', achieved through participation of people acting in their own interests and under their own control. In this connection, it is often pointed out that Africa should be more self-sufficient, particularly with regard to food. Further, there should be 'people-centred development', of a kind that satisfies the basic needs of all people in both the long and short terms. This implies that poor people get employment and access to the means of production, that there is a different distribution of benefits and resources and an ecological balance is upheld. A third core concept is 'democratic govern-ance', with its supporting freedoms of speech and organization, and a system of justice that protects all citizens from injustice and abuse. A decentralization of the colonial state may open the way for local self-government based on Africa's historic conditions, and it is also proposed to introduce states of a more federal character.

The Debt Carries the Face of a Child

At the Millennium Assembly of the United Nations in September 2000, globalization was a main theme. World leaders asserted that the central challenge was to ensure that globalization becomes a positive force for all the world's peoples and that more than a billion men, women and children are freed from the abject and dehumanizing conditions of extreme poverty. To achieve this, good governance is needed within each country and at the international level, with an open, equitable, rule-based, predictable and non-discriminatory multilateral trading and financial system.

Globalization facilitates international financial transactions. But private resource flows are not usually directed to poor, unstable African countries. An exception is the extraction of oil and minerals. For the rest, countries south of the Sahara enjoy little of the increased volume of global transfers. During the 1990s, most did not even receive enough investment to com-pensate for the reduction in development aid.

The new information and communications technology has created great hopes for accelerated development in sub-Saharan Africa. For a continent with a dispersed population, little access to modern knowledge and poor communications, this could have great importance. But it will require extensive investment to make the new advances accessible beyond the well-to-do in urban areas. And what can be done in districts where most of the population is illiterate?

In relation to the liberalization of international trade, the question arises of who will benefit from it? Sub-Saharan Africa faces a number of obstacles. Its countries must develop so that they have more products to export. They have to influence the rules of the game so that African interests are taken care of in international trade intercourse, and African products must gain access to international markets. It is of special impor-tance to open up Western markets for agricultural products. By the end of the century, the protectionism of the rich countries cost developing countries more than twice as much per year as they received in aid. The subsidies of the Organisation for Economic Co-operation and Develop-ment (OECD) to its own farmers equalled Africa's total GDP.

Simultaneously, African countries must manage to control the exploitation of their resources so that this serves the common interest and that of the local population. With corrupt leaders and a badly weakened state, cynical business leaders can, without hindrance, make a good profit and disregard the health of employees and consumers, the depletion of resources and destruction of the environment. This applies to the exploitation of oil and minerals as well as to agricultural production. A completely different attitude on the part of the authorities is necessary, in addition to an active monitoring on the part of local and international organizations.

At times, it is asserted that the development assistance to sub-Saharan Africa has been of no avail. The continent is sinking into poverty in spite of the considerable amounts that have been transferred to it. Such a statement is as wrong as it is simplified. It shows how the attention is directed towards development aid, instead of to more important macro-economic conditions. It is true that Africa has received a good deal of aid over a number of years. But the amounts have not been enormous. In relation to the needs, they have been grossly insufficient, and in the course of the 1990s they were heavily reduced. In 2000, sub-Saharan Africa on average received about US$20 per inhabitant – a reduction from $36 in 1990. The reduction created bitterness among many Africans. African countries have implemented extensive economic reforms under pressure from the international community, but they have not got the increased aid as expected. Lost trade in the course of recent decades has counted for more than the aid that has been provided.

In all, there has been – and still is – a draining, not a strengthening of Africa's resources. Countries differ. But the majority on the continent are caught in a sinking spiral of poverty, bringing a deterioration of living conditions for most people and a weakening of the capacities of the state. Outside finance is necessary to break the vicious circle. If sub-Saharan Africa is to achieve the goal of reducing the incidence of poverty by half by 2015, the flows of external resources must be more than doubled. Without support, problems will become worse. It will not be possible to stop the AIDS pandemic, combat other deadly and crippling diseases and ensure basic education for all. The stability of many countries will be undermined, and poorer governments may be tempted to engage in black market activities like the smuggling of precious stones, illegal woodcutting and trafficking in drugs and weapons to get badly needed funds.

The debt burden contributes to a strangling of many poor countries. Debt carries the face of a child, it is said, because it hits the weakest and deprives children of health and educational services. In 2000, the African countries were paying for debt servicing at a level five times the size of funds required to control the HIV/AIDS epidemic. Without substantial debt relief, these countries will have few chances for a positive development. Debt relief, on the other hand, would impose only a modest strain on rich countries, because the African economies are so small.

Up to the year 2002, the issue of debt relief was moving at a snail's pace on the international agenda. A number of initatives were launched, but the relief provided was in practice generally too little, too late and too slow. When African countries requested greater transfer of resources, Western countries would demand more democracy and human rights. Serious efforts are needed to improve governance in many African countries and the external world definitely has a role to play. But the approach must be one of sagacity and targeted support. Withholding funds and making democracy a general condition for debt relief and aid is indefensible. Social reforms take time, and there is an acute need to come to the rescue of highly indebted poor countries. Postponement entails high social costs. It is particularly grotesque when rich countries seek to promote human rights by increasing people's misery, and to strengthen democracy by giving orders to African leaders.

At the beginning of the twenty-first century, sub-Saharan Africa mostly encountered closed doors. In a profound economic crisis with a strong demand for external finance, the main source available was development aid, and it was extremely limited. At the UN Millennium Assembly, the leaders of the world promised to give Africa special support. The question is, at the end of the day, what this will mean in practice. In my view, the rich countries should be generous and launch a new deal for Africa. They can afford it, and it would have positive consequences not only for Africa, but also for the rest of the world. Doors must be opened. The development agenda for Africa must be redefined with the active participation of African scholars and policy-makers, and unconventional ways must be found to provide effective assistance. As a minimum, debt levels should be reduced and resource flows increased, to alleviate poverty and contribute to sustainable development. Instead of external donors doing it, African leaders should fix the terms for an action for Africa themselves – as some have started to do.

Difficult, but not Impossible

Development assistance has been criticized, because it does not lead to development and does not benefit the poor. 'Development aid' is a very mixed bag. With numerous donor countries, a hundred recipients and thousands of specific activities in the course of several decades, this is to be expected. It is not possible to lump it all together. Much aid has been given to promote donor values, commercial interests, cultural ambitions, strategic and political objectives. This is particularly the case for the major powers. Bilateral resource flows go to a large extent to 'faithful allies', no matter what policies they pursue. Some projects may promote development, but other concerns are often dominant.

Even with the best intentions of promoting social and economic development, not all such projects have been successful. It is in the nature of things that development aid is first of all provided where conditions are difficult. It is not bank investment. Considerable funds are allocated to relieve acute distress. With regard to long-term development, many projects have led to minimal improvements or even to negative consequences. When things go wrong, the psychology of failure may be even more severe than the loss of a project. Often, the viability, appropriateness, relevance and sustainability of aid programmes have not been given full consideration. Good intentions are necessary, but not sufficient, to ensure effective aid. You have to know what you are doing. You must overcome your cultural myopia and adapt projects to local conditions. Conscious efforts must be made to counteract adverse effects of external intervention and resources. Too much money can be just as destructive as too little.

Much aid has nevertheless had a positive impact. But it has never worked in isolation. It has been one of many factors. It is generally acknowledged that aid contributed to a rapid development in many Asian countries over several decades. In African countries, important initiatives in health, education, water and agriculture would never have taken place without external finance. Aid made it possible to control river blindness in West Africa and to disseminate new types of rice, improve food security in the Sahel and spread information about family planning – to mention just a few examples. The progress that has been achieved in reducing mortality and increasing education must be seen in relation to the support that has been given.

Working with UNICEF, I saw that it was possible to provide meaningful assistance under precarious conditions, even if it was not without problems. UNICEF was characterized by vitality and dynamism, and recipient governments, as well as people at the grassroots, showed considerable trust in the organization. The dialogue with the authorities was generally frank and constructive. It was sometimes necessary to find compromises between different concerns in the choice of areas of intervention, but these were always in accordance with priority objectives. Interventions within health and education generally formed an integrated part of national strategies and aimed at poor segments of the population, even if they were not always the poorest. UNICEF systematically avoided prestige projects for the well-to-do. Activities that were supported, were clearly targeted, were implemented in close collaboration with other donors and local partners and had an impact – although at times it could have been greater. Many interventions aimed at solving acute crises or health problems. Revitalization of primary health care and education services focused on long-term building of capacities and institutions. Notable progress was achieved, although it remains to be seen how sustainable the services will be in the long run. Many factors may play a part. Regarding the rights of women and children, UNICEF took corrective action and supplemented government policies, besides supporting particularly vulnerable groups.

Had the access to resources been greater, more could be done. We are not talking about enormous amounts. It was often difficult to obtain modest donor contributions for high priority activities. In the course of the 1990s, allocations to the work supported by UNICEF in the areas of health and water in West and Central Africa were substantially reduced. At the same time, the funds for education and for groups in need of special protection increased. Before the end of the century, the polio campaigns started bringing in additional resources for health. Unpredictable donor contributions represented an insurmountable problem. Some countries in the region were not very popular and had great difficulties mobilizing resources even for basic health and education services. Others had goodwill, but found that contributions would come – or not come. It was not always possible to know why, and often the decisions did not take into account what impact this would have on the ground. Thus, important social initiatives were put on ice because financing did not materialize. Or they were suddenly interrupted, because donors changed their minds. There is good reason to consider more closely the criteria, stability and time perspectives of donor contributions, to obtain the expected results.

During recent years, the aid debate has become more intense and self-critical. The objective of poverty reduction has gained broader support. New forms of partnerships are being tried out. The planning, transparency and accountability of recipient governments are given more emphasis. At the same time, donors are requested not only to increase their assistance, but to accept coordination and integration of their aid into the national plans of recipient governments.

Accountability is a complicated issue. The donors do not live with the direct consequences of their assistance. Therefore, it is not sufficient that a donor government is accountable to the National Assembly and the population in the donor country for the allocation of development aid. It is not sufficient, either, that a recipient government is accountable to the donor for the utilization of resources. A further step should be to consider how a donor, as well as a recipient government, can be made accountable to the population in the recipient country that is affected by the programmes and projects. In other words, there should be a further democratization of aid.

No News from Africa

To be able to relate to developments in Africa in a sensible way, it is necessary to be informed. It was thought that modern media would make us all members of a common, global village. Instead, in Western countries like Norway we observe that most media display an alarming lack of coverage of people and events in sub-Saharan Africa. Generally, there is no news at all. When a news item appears, it is about a catastrophe or an accident. There are honourable exceptions. But it tells its own tale that one-third of Norwegians in the year 2000 held the view that the Norwegian media are too negative in their reporting about developing countries.

Knowledge is lacking about economic, political, social and cultural conditions in sub-Saharan Africa. At the same time, too little is being done to obtain more insight. Knowledge that is being produced often has weaknesses. The information is superficial, incomplete or unreliable. Many see what they want to see. Donors may focus on negative aspects to support claims for aid – or on positive aspects to show its benefits. Often developments are evaluated in relation to Western models that do not accord well with African realities. It is a basic problem that little information is produced by Africans themselves in African institutions, and that the voices of broad segments of the populations affected by development efforts are practically never heard.

With the complex challenges presented by the African continent, one would think that people who are involved in Africa's problems would maintain a certain humility regarding policies and strategies. However, many donors express themselves with noticeable self-confidence on a basis that must be extremely fragile. Paternalistic attitudes towards Africans and their behaviour are not uncommon. Even in a situation where basic rethinking is called for concerning economic and political development in most African countries, donor milieus do not stimulate much open and critical debate. Important institutions like the IMF and the World Bank have difficulties dealing with development approaches other than those based on Western market-oriented models. This is all the more worrying when one knows how differently African and Western societies function.

It is noteworthy how little emphasis aid organizations often give to acquiring knowledge. A little insight into local conditions is useful. But aid workers should not have too profound a knowledge about the countries where they are posted. It is feared that they might 'go native' and lose their 'objectivity' (read: Western perspective) in relation to local interests. Rotation arrangements make sure nobody stays too long in one place. Most aid workers also lead a protected life with limited contact with Africa and Africans. Pre-existing opinions and Western conceptions encounter few differing views. The thinking in Western capitals is more decisive for aid strategies than are local conditions in recipient countries. Thus, interventions become poorly targeted and have little positive effect.

People from other continents need not necessarily know everything about Africa in order to benefit from the insight that Africans have. But this happens far too rarely. Bilateral donors and international organizations have a regular dialogue with the authorities in recipient countries, and there is a certain contact with educated people in urban areas. But beyond this, there is little. The limited use of local expertise is also disquieting. After 40 years of development aid, nearly all the allocations for technical assistance are used for expatriates, instead of engaging people from the recipient countries themselves. There are in fact more expatriate advisers in Africa today than there were at the end of the colonial period. The number is estimated to be about 100,000. It is difficult to comprehend how the building of local capacity and national self-reliance is possible under such circumstances. At the same time, thousands of well-qualified Africans leave the continent every year. In this perspective, it is not surprising that Africans may perceive aid mostly as a way of giving Western experts a lucrative stay in exotic regions.

Basic reform is needed in relation to much aid. It is of special importance to acquire more knowledge of the human, social and cultural resources of Africa, so these can be utilized in a constructive way. A hidden, but promising area relates to women, and the last chapter will be about them.

EIGHTEEN

Hidden Hope: The World's Least-touched Resources

'The future of this planet depends on women.'
(UN Secretary General Kofi Annan, June 2000)

It has taken a long time to reach the understanding that women must play a central role, if African countries are to reduce poverty and social disparities and achieve democracy and human rights.

In 1945, the United Nations was created in a male-dominated world with widespread discrimination against women. There was just a handful of women at the founding conference. However, a Commission on the Status of Women was established to promote equality. The Commission worked steadily, but in obscurity, until a new feminist movement rose up in the USA around 1970. The spark led first to activism in Western countries, then in other parts of the world. The UN was mobilized. The International Women's Year was proclaimed in 1975 with the first World Conference of Women in Mexico. Other conferences followed in Copenhagen in 1980, Nairobi in 1985 and Beijing in 1995. All of them adopted declarations and worldwide plans of action for equality, development and peace. They became steadily more comprehensive and ambitious, demanding the elimination of discrimination and a strengthening of the rights of women in all areas of society. Women must participate in decision-making processes at all levels, so that the development meets their needs and interests.

After the women's conferences, the number of women professionals and leaders increased in the UN system. Focal points for women were created and strategies for women adopted. By the end of the century, there was a considerable number of women in the UN proper and in UN organizations working in the social sectors. However, organizations relating to economic life, industry, agriculture, business and trade, including the IMF and World Bank, were still very male-dominated.

Western countries have been strongly male-dominated. By mid-2002, only ten countries had more than 25 per cent women in their National Assemblies. Even fewer had such a representation in government. The

Nordic countries led the field, together with the Netherlands. Even if some countries gradually brought in gender perspectives in their aid policies, the efforts were rarely very dynamic and consistent.

When the African countries became independent, the ruling elites changed colour, but not gender. Both at national and international level, important decisions concerning development of the continent were made in male-dominated fora that favoured men. The needs of women and children were neglected or given low priority. The whole development process was hampered, because the resources of half of the population were not utilized in an effective way.

All states of the world endorsed the recommendations of the Women's Conferences. But how should one proceed? To begin with a Women in Development (WID) strategy was launched. Even if women contributed extensively to development, they benefited very little from the economic and social advances. The position of women should therefore be improved by special measures. Women-oriented projects were carried out. But they

---

Box 18.1 The Women's Conference in Beijing 1995

Main calls for concrete action in the Platform for Action:

- to protect and promote the human rights of women and the girl child as an integral part of universal human rights;
- to eradicate the persistent and increasing burden of poverty on women;
- to ensure equal access for girl children and women to education and training, health care and related services characterized by good quality and equality;
- to eliminate all forms of violence against women and the effects of armed conflict, including foreign occupation;
- to ensure equality in economic structures and policies, in all forms of productive activities and in access to resources;
- to remove the obstacles to women's full participation in public life and decision-making at all levels, also within the family;
- to establish mechanisms at all levels to promote the advancement of women;
- to ensure equal access to and participation in all communication systems, especially the media, and prevent stereotyping of women;
- to promote equality in the management of natural resources and in the safeguarding of the environment.

were few, small and isolated. After some years, the approach was changed. The context in which women were living and the interaction between women and men were emphasized. The focus was no longer on 'women', but 'gender'. The strategy for equality was now 'mainstreaming'. A gender perspective was to be applied to all programmes and projects. The effects on both women and men should be considered and the interests of both taken care of. By the end of the century, this had happened to a certain extent, but not at all consistently. In practice, 'integration' often meant that the objective of gender equality disappeared altogether. The fact that women are discriminated against and need to strengthen their position was disregarded. At the same time, women-specific measures were still few and limited.

World leaders cannot handle everything. But questions related to women rarely have high priority. The progress that has been achieved has been the result of the activism of individuals and groups, mostly women, but also some men. Gender roles and relationships touch on deep-rooted traditions and established power structures. Many men – as well as some women – feel that their position is threatened if the roles are changed and the status of women improved. In the last resort, the question is, who shall be given priority, receive resources, have power and influence? Regarding equality, it takes a very long time to move from rhetoric to realities.

On a global scale, there has been progress. It is accepted internationally – at least in theory – that equality is a prerequisite for development. Much information has been produced about the lives and conditions of women. Problems that previously were hidden have been brought into focus. Laws and regulations have been changed to strengthen the status of women. Some have obtained access to decision-making bodies. Measures have been implemented to improve the health and education of women and girls. Violence against women is illegal almost everywhere, and there has been worldwide mobilization against harmful traditional practices. But in the beginning of the twenty-first century, much still remains to be done. Women are a minority in governments and on executive boards. In economic terms, the gender divide is still widening. Women earn less, are more often unemployed and are generally poorer than men. Their reproductive roles are rarely recognized. They often lack the right to own land and other property. Girls and women form the majority of illiterate and out-of-school children. In spite of measures, violence against women is increasing both in the home and in armed conflict.

As in other parts of the world, action, consciousness-raising and education are needed to improve the status of women in Africa. It is a problem that the Western world has very stereotyped conceptions; African women are often perceived as powerless, weak and passive. Consequently, it does not pay to support them. Such a one-sided image is oppressing in itself. Most African women lack influence and have low productivity. But this is due to the conditions under which they live, not to their lack of intelligence or drive. Many women have an amazing capacity to manage, even if they have little to make do on. During my missions in West and Central Africa, I was impressed more than once by the way women organized, introduced innovations and implemented projects when the opportunities presented themselves. I will end by giving some concrete examples of the mobilization and efforts of women through small self-help groups, associations of market women and village cooperatives.

Mummy Mill and Mummy Gas

It is first of all in groups that women develop and expand their activities. Women collaborate locally in many places in West and Central Africa. The networks are more comprehensive, active and autonomous than Western women are used to. African women participate in traditional age and status groups. They work together performing productive tasks and caring for children. But the possibilities for self-help and improvement of conditions are limited, not least where poverty is widespread. There is considerable room for strengthening the activities of many groups and increasing the yield from their efforts. To have the expected impact, external assistance must be based an a realistic evaluation of openings and obstacles. Very many income-generating projects have failed because they were not founded on an adequate economic analysis. Women were taught to make products that could not be sold on the market. The result was increased efforts without increased income, in some cases even a loss, frustration and disappointment.

With training and modern technology – which need not be very ambitious and advanced, but must be adjusted to local conditions – women can increase their productivity and income, improve their level of learning and take on new roles. What is needed most in many rural areas is often literacy and numeracy, and simple equipment like a water pump or a grain mill. When a women's group in Togo was asked what they wanted, they answered with one voice: 'A mill! We lose so much time pounding the grains or going all the way to the mill.' They had saved some money, and UNICEF helped them borrow the rest. They were taught the necessary skills of how to run a mill, handle the machine and do accounts. The women had gained new self-confidence when they showed me the mill and explained how they used it. 'Maman moulin' (Mummy mill), 'Maman mesure' (measure) and 'Maman gas-oil' (petrol) were responsible for running the mill. These roles were completely new for rural women in Togo.

And they not only ground the grain of the women in the village. People came from neighbouring villages, so they obtained a nice surplus and could service their loan. The women in the group also saved time and energy, and started new activities like gardening and brewing.

Women's groups in Kélo in southern Chad went further. Traditionally, women are subordinate to men and attached to the home. In the course of 20 years of civil war, many men were killed or displaced. Others lost their livelihood. For the families to survive, women had to engage in income-generating activities such as selling agricultural products and foodstuffs, exchanging goods, etc. The women helped each other, established groups and 'tontines' (a voluntary savings system among the women) and got training. In 1995, 15 groups in Kélo with a total of 300 members created the 'Union of Kélo's Women's Groups'. They drew up statutes, elected a coordination committee and decided on a number of tasks. They wanted to strengthen the participation of women in agriculture, establish corn banks, organize income-generating activities, facilitate the processing of agricultural products, berries, mushrooms and plants, obtain credit, participate in health programmes, obtain municipal child care and orphanages, promote literacy for women, get girls to school and strengthen the solidarity among women. It was quite a list. They started by analysing what prevented them from having their wishes granted. Then, they suggested solutions and contacted institutions that could assist, first of all the local authorities and the church. The authorities approached UNICEF.

In the course of a little more than a year, four groups completed the first part of a literacy course. Ten hectares of soybeans were cultivated to improve nutrition and earn money. Courses were organized in family budgeting and hygiene. Children were immunized and salts distributed against diarrhoea. A campaign was prepared to get people in the district (in particular, teachers, fathers and other relatives) to support basic education for girls. As visitors, we had to admire a stove rebuilt for greater efficiency, taste soy juice and cookies (more healthy than tasty) and put on home-made *bassia* butter (used as a medicine or cosmetic). Songs were sung about immunization, and a young girl, Hapsita Ngariora, read 'Complaint from a young girl':

> I also want to go to school to learn to read and write and do maths. Mother wants to keep me at home to do the dishes. Father thinks I am a goldmine. No, please, I want to go to school. Papa, Mummy, the Society: help me succeed! The State, the Law and UNICEF: make sure the school suits me. It should help me get a good job. Without punishment I will prepare my future so Chad will advance. I too want to be indispensable. Economic and social progress demands that I contribute effectively. Parents, don't

complain any more. Protect me and give me money so that also *I* can go to school!

The authorities and UNICEF were ready in the autumn of 1996 to start the campaign for girls in school. There was only one problem: the 200 bicycles to transport the campaign groups out into the villages were still in the capital, N'djamena, 450 kilometres away. It was not possible to get them to Kélo before the rainy season, when the roads became impassable. The campaign had to be postponed a year.

Power over Markets

In Togo, women got involved in the wholesale business with textiles soon after independence. By the end of the century, several thousand women were engaged in the purchase, sales and sewing of locally produced as well as imported cloths. Africa is called the 'contact point for textiles'. There are extremely complicated networks of producers, agencies, wholesalers and retailers who deal with waxes, fancy (a cheaper print), batik and *kente* from the Netherlands, Great Britain and Japan, as well as from factories in West and Central Africa. The textiles are sold on both large and small markets. One of the biggest markets is the market for *tissu pagne* (textiles for traditional clothes) in Togo's capital Lomé, under the leadership of the famous 'Nanas Benz' and their daughters 'Les nanettes'. These are female wholesalers who do big business. They became known in the 1960s because of their luxurious cars, by preference Mercedes-Benz, therefore the nickname ('nana' means matron). The women are very enterprising and constitute the aristocracy of the textile trade. They know how to do business, have a feeling for fabrics and enjoy having scope for their abilities. A young, third-generation nanette who had just married expressed herself as follows: 'It would not occur to me to stop doing business. It is my job. It is my life. And what would they say in Lomé if I quit?' Profits vary according to the economic and political situation. But Togo is strategically placed for regional and international trade. During the 1990s, probably ten Nanas Benz or so had a turnover of more than US$250,000 per year.

Patience Sanvee is one of the most famous Nanas Benz. She has been focused on by the media because of her competence and charm. In 1999, she started reducing her workload, as she was 73 years old, but she looked lively and active with a braided Afro hairstyle and an undulating dress in red and blue wax. She has been trading since she was 20, as her grandmother, mother and aunts did before her. She was orphaned at six years old. Nevertheless, she went to school and became a midwife. She did not feel comfortable in this profession, and started selling cigarettes on the market instead. One day she started reselling textiles. 'To begin with, the customers gave me money in advance,' she remembers, 'and then I ordered the textiles from the wholesalers.' Gradually, she became very 'reliable', was good at bargaining and had a commercial eye for motifs. 'We get the Dutch to make waxes with African design,' Patience Sanvee explains:

> I had bestsellers where the design was 'My husband is competent', 'I run faster than my rival', 'If you go, I'll go' and particularly 'Billionaire'. [She shows me a photo where she is standing in front of a luxurious car with the billionaire cloth wrapped around both her and the car.] I organized wholesale trade at home once a month with 100 or 200 specially invited customers. Then, I traded in my shop right beside the market. The textiles were resold on the market in Lomé, in the rural areas and abroad.

She married a bank employee at the age of 22 and had five children, all sons, and two of them died. She hopes a cousin will continue her business.

The big market in Lomé is in a three-storey bunker, where textiles are sold on the second floor. Even if it is rather dark, visitors are bombarded by colours and designs: plants and animals, geometric forms, symbols from women's lives and, in the middle, a Pope and a Christ. More than five hundred female merchants are housed here. Between *pagne libraries*, where the piles of cloth are placed side by side like books on a shelf, the traders sit on their stools and stacks of cloth, eating *foufou* (mashed banana and cassava), chat and laugh. Around the market and in the countryside, thousands of women resell the textiles. Only in Lomé are there around 3,500 seamstresses making dresses, skirts, *boubous*, shirts and trousers.

The market women have organized themselves to regulate the trade and promote their interests. Both in Togo and Benin, they represent a political force of considerable importance. By the end of the century, the market women in Benin managed 54 markets totally with both male and female traders, although mostly female. The trade included everything from foodstuffs and kitchen equipment to textiles and cars. Four thousand women traders were organized in a joint association that monitored the activities of the individual traders. Justine A. T. Kakpo is responsible for the biggest market in the capital, Cotonou, and in addition is president of the National Association of Market Women. She has several assistants who go round the markets to maintain order and solve problems. If necessary, she contacts the authorities for support and help. In the autumn of 1999, the market women talked about going on strike and closing the markets to protest against the high duties on imported goods. 'Then the authorities get uneasy,' Justine Kakpo remarks, 'because they get large revenues from the market. But we discuss the matter with those who are responsible, before we take action. Usually, they take our demands into account.' However, the situation is difficult. There is less money about than before, and the authorities need taxes and duties.

Kakpo is 65 years old. She started with petty trade in the village. Now she is dealing with sophisticated textiles and has connections from Bangkok to the Netherlands and Paris. She married at the age of 30. Her daughters are also businesswomen. She has done well. Although she does not know French and can neither read nor write, she speaks five African languages. 'It is possible to be a capable businesswoman without going to school,' she assures me, and serves genuine French champagne to her collaborators and guests. 'But you have to be bright, and I know how to calculate.' In March 1999, she was elected a Member of Parliament in Benin, representing the non-formal trading groups. She hired an assistant who reads the documents for her and communicates her views to the others – and they listen to her. She explains further:

> We women are autonomous. We can earn money and do what we want with it. It is not like in the West. Here a man can have several wives. But we maintain our independence. We take care of the children and see that they get an education. We decide for ourselves. We can buy houses, start construction and engage in as many businesses as we want, as long as we pay taxes. We assist people who need a helping hand. We are influential.

Benin and Togo are not the only countries where the market women play an important role.

Women's Revolution in the Desert

We take a leap north-west to Mauritania, far up towards the Sahara.

> Our life is completely changed. Now we do things we never did before. We cultivate the land and breed livestock. We have cattle and dromedaries, sheep and goats. We produce cucumbers and tomatoes, beans and onions!

It is Baraketou speaking. We are sitting under a gigantic baldachin with geometrical zigzag patterns in intense colours. The ground is covered with thick woven carpets. We are half-sitting, half-lying on the soft pillows. Through the opening of the tent, there is a glimpse of the black starry night. It is completely quiet, except for the sad bleating of a goat. It is like the Arabian Nights. But this is Lemden, a small village near the border of the desert. We left the asphalt road and drove across the sand dunes, following twisted wheel tracks across hills and depressions, around bunches of straw and rumpled bushes. All of a sudden we were there. Small houses scattered in the sand and a swarm of people. Six hundred inhabitants, both big and small. In front, Baraketou Mint Cheikh Abdallahi, president of the Lemden cooperative, wrapped from top to toe in her dark veil.

> I would like to welcome you on behalf of the Women's Cooperative. We men and women of the desert are deeply moved when somebody makes the detour to come and see us. Our cooperative was founded in 1985. We have always tried to play a role as a pioneer and a model for the Brakna region. We have 135 women as members. We are busy with gardening and cattle breeding, handicraft and sewing. A well has been dug, and we have planted trees to stop desertification. Agriculture helps us ensure adequate nutrition for the children. We are an Islamic village. We have both a primary school and a 'mahadra' (Qur'anic school) with a library for the adults.

It is even more impressive than it sounds, because the background is dramatic. In Mauritania, the drought in the 1970s and 1980s destroyed most of the pastures and livestock. The majority of the nomads – who once amounted to more than 80 per cent of the population – had to give up their traditional livelihood and move to the city to survive. According to the statistics, only 10 per cent of the population was still nomadic in the 1990s. More than half of the country's inhabitants were living in the capital. In 30 years, Nouakchott grew from 5,000 to 700,000 inhabitants. It was first of all the able-bodied men who travelled to the town. Women, children and the elderly remained in the villages. Here, the situation was often very difficult. Baraketou explains:

> The marabout (the religious leader) contacted me while I was at the University of Nouakchott. He asked me to come home and take care of the village. It was on the verge of disintegrating completely. I moved back, and we organized the Women's Cooperative. To manage, we women had to take on tasks that Moor women traditionally did not have. It was incredibly tough and exciting. But we learnt a lot. And you can imagine how flexible we Mauritanian women are!

Towards the end of the century, there were no fewer than 334 women's cooperatives in the Brakna region. Actually, the women were keeping the region alive. The men commuted to the town and sent money home. Lemden managed to get assistance from international organizations like UNICEF for gardening equipment, a truck, school material and a small dispensary. UNICEF also supported a rural radio for the district. 'Brakna women's radio' conveys useful information and helps the women keep in touch. The majority are illiterate and listen a lot to the radio. A small savings and credit bank was established and a network for mutual support and training.

After a guided tour to see Lemden's garden and the schools, a feast is served according to Mauritanian tradition. A sumptuous feast – I never saw its like. First, dates with butter and then a lamb grilled whole and filled with boiled rice: *mechui*. Everybody sits on the ground and tears off big, succulent pieces with their hands. The rice is rolled between the fingers into small balls. Sweet tea is served in small glasses. The tea has to be poured out three times, so the guests will feel welcome. A servant goes around with a silver bowl, soap and pot of water, for people to wash their hands. Next come pancakes dipped in meat juice, dromedary liver and hump. Here, I have to pass. The hump consists of big yellow lumps of pure fat. Afterwards, comes home-made yogurt from dromedary milk, couscous of semolina with the pluck of the lamb (its heart, liver and lungs) and more of the sweet tea. Then, there is fruit. It is as if the stream of food will never end!

Under the tent canvas, men and women are seated separately. The men's group consists of representatives of the county and the municipality dressed in wide light-blue coats with yellow-white embroidery. As the guest of honour, the regional director sits with them as long as the meal lasts. Afterwards, I make the most of my status as a woman and join the women's group. Besides Baraketou, there are representatives from the local Women's Bureau, the Credit Bank and the Women's Cooperative – all wrapped in colourful veils over their long dresses. As the atmosphere becomes more relaxed, the women want to veil me. It is much better, they say. I will feel more comfortable. I am not sure, but all right. They wrap me up in the five-yard-long thin veil in accordance with tradition. Only my face and fingers stick out. Undeniably, it is easier to sit on the ground in a decent way when you can cover up with the veil. But the heat in the cocoon becomes quite intense.

The women made a great fuss of the veiling. They became very animated and started chatting about their everyday lives and relations with men. The lives of Mauritanian women are not as strictly regulated as in other Arab-Islamic countries, they note. They can travel alone, drink tea with men, participate in male-dominated conversations and breastfeed in public. Besides, they can relatively easily obtain a divorce and remarry. Some in the group are married. Others are divorced and single. Several marriages are not unusual. 'You can't always rely on the men,' the women confide to me:

> Many things may happen when they live alone in the capital. Some keep contact with the village and send money. Others don't. So we have to

manage on our own, earn money and provide for the children, even if it should be the responsibility of the men. Before, we women were more ladies of leisure. The men dealt with the livestock. We took care of the household. We dressed up according to nomadic tradition. Now conditions are much tougher. We have to do everything and work hard to survive. But we cope. We manage to do things we never thought we could – just look around. This village is the work of women!

The first time I visited Lemden was in 1996. Two years later I came back. The gardening activities had more than doubled. The number of animals had increased considerably. Children from other villages also came to the school. The Women's Bank was established with 126 co-operatives as members.

Nobody in Lemden spoke about a women's revolution. They had just done what they had to do to make life go ahead. Even if they had made a virtue of necessity, it was in fact a revolution. A new society was created. A large number of women changed their roles and tasks in a fundamental way. They acquired knowledge and skills they did not have before. They became more independent and developed more self-confidence. The catastrophe of the drought made it necessary to change. The traditional forms of life and family patterns were no longer possible. This was a disaster not only economically, but also socially and culturally. Families were broken up. Men lost the basis of their identity and income. Instead of being nomads in the desert, they had to settle in the barracks of the city and try to find new, urban occupations. The position of women was also difficult. But when things first went wrong, the situation offered new freedoms and new challenges for them, which they grasped and exploited. Others in the milieu supported them. So it was a revolution – in practice, if not formally.

The developments in Mauritania are special. But it is stimulating to see that women are capable of implementing extensive role changes in a society strongly influenced by tradition and with a consistent male dominance. It expands the scope of what can be regarded not only as theoretical, but also as practically possible to achieve.

Neither Beasts of Burden, nor Free and Equal

The above vignettes show how women can produce more, earn more and contribute more effectively to the development of society when circumstances provide the possibility for doing so. It is said that the women carry Africa. Under difficult conditions, they often do much more than is reasonable to keep hunger away, take care of their families and preserve social ties. But they reap few fruits from their hard work, because they lack rights, effective aids, knowledge and money. Like women in many parts of the world, they live in the paradox of being simultaneously overworked and underutilized. But the workload of African women is often exceptionally heavy and their resources painfully small.

To change the situation, women have to break out of the vicious circle of poverty and oppression. Nobody can do this for them. But circumstances can be arranged so that it is possible to reduce the workload, acquire more resources, improve conditions and exert greater influence. What is needed varies. Formal rules and arrangements, like the lack of economic rights and of access to credit, prevent some from utilizing their potential. Others lead such demanding lives that they must be given a helping hand to be able to advance. The contribution need not necessarily be great. Appropriate education and incentives, or a few resources, so that they can get something going, start a positive process and strengthen their position.

Given the weak status of women in many cases, it is essential that the external world plays a supportive role. But external donors must not only have a positive will to promote equality. They must know how to do it in a sensible way. Targeted measures are needed. At the same time, it must be clear that the intention is to strengthen the fundamental rights of women based on African realities, and not to automatically transfer approaches and roles from other cultures. The first step is a dialogue with those affected – men as well as women – to understand possibilities and limitations.

The woman writer from Ghana, Ama Ata Aidoo, who has also been minister of education, described the situation in a book published to coincide with the Women's Conference in Beijing in 1995:

> African women are some sort of riddle. We do not fit the accepted (Western) notion of us as mute beasts of burden. However, we are not as free and as equal as African men would have us believe. We have great problems. But we are struggling to be worthy heiresses to our past, to be planners today and builders of a better tomorrow. We need to intensify our struggle. Because in our hands lies, perhaps, the last possible hope for ourselves – and everyone else on the continent. After all, we are one of the world's least-touched resources.

Appendix

Data from UN organizations and the World Bank

Country	Population millions 2001	GNI per capita 2001 US$	Life expectancy 2001	U5MR 2001	% DPT3 2001	Births per woman 2001	MMR 1985–2001	Primary school		Adult literacy rate	
								% boys 1999	% girls 1999	men 2000	women 2000
Benin	6	360	54	158	76	5.8	500	x75	x50	52	24
Burkina Faso	12	210	47	197	41	6.8	480	40	28	33	13
Cameroon	15	570	50	155	43	4.8	430	x82	x71	82	69
Cape Verde	0.4	1,310	70	38	78	3.3	35	x100	x97	84	65
CAR	4	270	44	180	23	5.0	1,100	64	43	60	35
Chad	8	200	46	200	27	6.7	830	68	42	67	41
Congo	3	700	51	108	31	6.3	–	x99	x93	88	74
Dem Congo	53	x100	52	205	40	6.7	950	33	31	x83	x54
Eq Guinea	0.5	700	51	153	32	5.9	–	x89	x89	92	75
Gabon	1	3,160	53	90	38	5.4	520	x82	x83	80	62
Gambia	1	330	47	126	96	4.9	–	65	57	44	30
Ghana	20	290	57	100	80	4.3	x210	x75	x74	79	61
Guinea	8	400	48	169	43	6.0	530	54	37	55	27
Guinea Bissau	1	160	45	211	47	6.0	910	62	44	53	21
Ivory Coast	16	630	48	175	57	4.8	600	67	51	55	38
Liberia	3	x490	53	235	62	6.8	580	46	35	70	37
Mali	12	210	52	231	51	7.0	580	49	34	48	33
Mauritania	3	350	52	183	61	6.0	750	62	58	51	29
Niger	11	170	46	265	31	8.0	590	32	20	23	8
Nigeria	117	290	52	183	26	5.6	–	x38	x33	72	56
Senegal	10	480	54	138	52	5.2	560	64	54	47	28

Sierra Leone	5	140	40	316	44	6.5	1,800	60	55	51	23
Togo	5	270	52	141	64	5.5	480	99	78	72	43
Sum	314.9										
Sub-S. Africa	634	519	48	173	54	5.6	1,100	z66	z54	69	54
World	6,219	5,228	64	82	73	2.7	400	z87	z80	85	74

Notes: Population – millions (UN Population Division). GNI per capita – gross national income, previously gross national product per inhabitant in US dollars (World Bank). Life expectancy – life expectancy at birth (UN Population Division). U5MR – under-5 mortality rate, deaths per 1,000 live births (UNICEF). DPT3 – 1-year-old children fully immunized against diphtheria, pertussis (whooping cough) and tetanus. The numbers may vary considerably from year to year (UNICEF, WHO). Births per woman – the number of children that would be born per woman if she were to live to the end of her childbearing years and bear children according to prevailing fertility rates: the total fertility rate (UN Population Division). MMR – maternal mortality rate, deaths related to pregnancy per 100,000 live births. The data are not adjusted for underreporting and misclassification (WHO, UNICEF). Data refer to the most recent year available during the period specified in the column heading. Primary school enrolment ratio – the percentage of children enrolled in primary education who belong to the official primary school age group, net enrolment (UNESCO). 'z' refers to 1998. Literacy rate – percentage of persons aged 15 and over who can read and write (UNESCO). 'x' indicates data from years other than that specified in the column heading, or that refer only to a part of the country or differ from standard definitions.

Select Bibliography

Abondia, Josette D. (1993) *Kouassi Koko … ma mère*. Abidjan.

Achebe, Chinua (1958) *Things Fall Apart*. London.

— (1966) *A Man of the People*. London.

— (1987) *Anthills of the Savannah*. Oxford.

Adedeji, Adebayo (ed.) (1999) *Comprehending and Mastering African Conflicts. The Search for Sustainable Peace and Good Governance*. London/Ijebu-Ode.

Adedeji, Adebayo, Reginald Green and Abdou Janha (1995) *Pay, Productivity and Public Service: Priorities for Recovery in Sub-Saharan Africa. A Study for UNICEF and UNDP*. New York.

Aidoo, Ama Ata (1991) *Changes – A Love Story*. London.

— (1995) 'African Women: Then and Now' in *United Nations: Women: Looking Beyond 2000*. New York.

Alkali, Zaynab (1988) *The Stillborn*. Essex.

Allen, Judith van (1976) '"Aba Riots" or Igbo "Women's War"? Ideology, Stratification, and the Invisibility of Women', in Nancy J. Hafkin and Edna G. Bay (eds), *Women in Africa*, pp. 59–85. Stanford.

Amadiume, Ifi (1987) *Male Daughters and Female Husbands: Gender and Sex in an African Society*. London.

— (1997) *Reinventing Africa: Matriarchy, Religion and Culture*. London.

— (2000) *Daughters of the Goddess, Daughters of Imperialism: African Women Struggle for Culture, Power and Democracy*. London.

Amnesty International (2000) *Broken Bodies, Shattered Minds – Torture and Ill-treatment of Women*. London.

— (2000) *Hidden Scandal, Secret Shame – Torture and Ill-treatment of Children*. London.

Appiah, Kwame Anthony and Henry Louis Gates Jr (ed.) (1999) *The Encyclopedia of the African and African American Experience*. New York.

Awe, Bonlanle (1977) 'The Iyalode in the Traditional Yoruba Political System', in Alice Schlegel (ed.), *Sexual Stratification. A Cross-cultural View*. New York.

Ayittey, George B. N. (1998) *Africa in Chaos*. Hampshire.

Bâ, Amadou Hampâté (1991) *Amkoullel, l'enfant peul: mémoires*. Arles.

Bâ, Mariama (1979) *Une Si Longue Lettre*. Dakar/*So Long a Letter*. London.

Barley, Nigel (1994) *Smashing Pots, Works of Clay from Africa*. Washington DC.

Barry, Mariama (2000) *La Petite Peule*. France.

Bayart, Jean-François (1993) *The State in Africa: The Politics of the Belly*. New York.

Bayart, Jean-François, Stephen Ellis and Béatrice Hibou (1999) *The Criminalization of the State in Africa*. London.

Becker, Charles, Jean-Pierre Dozon, Christine Obbo and Moriba Touré (1999) *Vivre et penser le sida en Afrique / Experiencing and Understanding AIDS in Africa.* Dakar / Paris.

Beckwitz, Carol and Angela Fisher (1999) *African Ceremonies.* New York.

Benjaminsen, Tor A. and Gunnvor Berge (2000) *Timbuktu: myter, mennesker, miljø* (Timbuktu: Myths, People, Environment). Oslo.

Beyala, Calixthe (1987) *C'est le soleil qui m'a brûlée.* Paris.

Black, Maggie (1996) *Children First: The Story of UNICEF Past and Present.* New York.

Blom, Ida (ed.) (1993) 'Asia og Afrika. Tredje Verden (Asia and Africa. The Third World)', in *Kvinnehistorie* (Women's History), vol. 3. Oslo.

Boahen, A. Adu (1990) 'Colonialism in Africa: Its Impact and Significance', in *General History of Africa,* vol. VII, A. Adu Boahen (ed.), *Africa under Colonial Domination 1880–1935,* Abridged edition, pp. 327–39. Paris / London.

Brahimi, Denise and Anne Trevarthen (1998) *Les femmes dans la littérature africaine. Portraits.* Paris / Abidjan.

Brunet-Jailly, Joseph (1997) *Innover dans les systèmes de santé. Expériences d'Afrique de l'Ouest.* Paris.

Bruyas, Jean (2001) *Les sociétés traditionelles de l'Afrique noire.* Paris.

Busby, Margaret (ed.) (1992) *Daughters of Africa. An International Anthology of Words and Writings by Women of African Descent from the Ancient Egyptian to the Present.* London.

Bøås, Morten (2000) 'Borgerkrigen i Sierra Leone' (The Civil War in Sierra Leone), *Internasjonal Politikk* (International Politics), vol. 58 (4), pp. 559–82. Oslo.

Chabal, Patrick and Jean-Pascal Daloz (1999) *Africa Works. Disorder as Political Instrument.* London.

Chevrier, Jacques (ed.) (1988) 'La poésie', in Jacques Chevrier (ed.), *Anthologie africaine d'expression française,* vol. II. Paris.

Cohn, Ilene and Guy Goodwin (1994) *Child Soldiers.* Oxford.

Coles, Catherine and Beverly Mack (ed.) (1991) *Hausa Women in the Twentieth Century.* Madison.

Collective edition (2001) *Voice of African Children.* Dakar.

Commonwealth Expert Group on Women and Structural Adjustment (1989) *Engendering Adjustment for the 1990s.* London.

Condé, Maryse (1988) *Segu.* New York.

— (1990) *The Children of Segu.* New York.

Coquery-Vidrovitch, Catherine (1994) *Les Africaines: Histoire des femmes d'Afrique noire du XIX au XX siècle.* Paris / *African Women. A Modern History.* Colorado / Oxford.

Cornia, Giovanni Andrea, Richard Jolly and Frances Stewart (eds) (1987) *Adjustment with a Human Face.* Oxford.

Cornia, Giovanni Andrea, Rolf van der Hoeven and Thandika Mkandawire (eds) (1992) *Africa's Recovery in the 1990s: From Stagnation and Adjustment to Human Development.* Houndmills.

Cornia, Giovanni Andrea and Gerald K. Helleiner (eds) (1994) *From Adjustment to Development in Africa, Conflict, Controversy, Convergence, Consensus?* Chicago.

Dagan, Esther A. (1989) *Tradition en Transition: La mère et l'enfant dans la sculpture africaine – hier et aujourd'hui/Tradition in Transition: Mother and Child in African Sculpture – Past and Present.* Montreal.

— (1992) *The Spirit's Image, the African Masking Tradition – Evolving Continuity/L'Image de l'esprit, la tradition du masque africain – evolution et continuité.* Montreal.

Davidson, Basil (1969) *The African Genius. An Introduction to African Cultural and Social History.* Boston.

— (1991) *Africa in History.* New York.

— (1992) *The Black Man's Burden. Africa and the Curse of the Nation-state.* London.

— (1993) *A History of West Africa 1000–1800.* Essex.

— (1994) *Modern Africa. A Social and Political History.* London/New York.

Dei-Anang, Michael Francis (1946) *Wayward Lines from Africa. A Collection of Poems.* London.

Delarozière, Marie-Françoise (1994) *Perles d'Afrique.* Aix-en-Provence.

Delarozière, Marie-Françoise and Michel Massal (1999) *Jouets des enfants d'Afrique.* Aix-en-Provence.

Diabaté, Henriette and Leonard Kodjo (1991) *Notre Abidjan.* Abidjan.

Diop, David Mandessi (1973) *Hammer Blows and Other Writings.* Indiana.

Economic Commission for Africa (1994) *African Platform for Action.* Dakar.

Education for All (2000) *Assessment of Basic Education in Sub-Saharan Africa 1990–1999.* Harare.

Ellis, Stephen (1999) *The Mask of Anarchy. The Destruction of Liberia and the Religious Dimension of an African Civil War.* New York.

Emecheta, Buchi (1976) *The Bride Price.* New York.

— (1977) *The Slave Girl.* New York.

— (1979) *The Joys of Motherhood.* New York.

Eriksen, Tore Linné (1990) *Afrikas krise. Finnes det alternativer til Verdensbankens diagnose og medisin?* (Africa's crisis. Are There Alternatives to the World Bank Diagnosis and Medicine?) Oslo.

Fauque, Claude and Otto Wollenweber (1994) *Tissus d'Afrique.* Paris.

Fellesrådets Afrika-årbok (Yearbook of the Joint Council for Africa) (1995) *Demokrati i Afrika* (Democracy in Africa). Oslo.

— (1996/97) *Gjeld, strukturtilpasning og konflikt* (Debt, Structural Adjustment and Conflict). Oslo.

— (2000–2001) *Afrikanere om Afrika* (Africans about Africa). Oslo.

Femmes Africa Solidarité (2000) *Engendering the Peace Process in West Africa – The Mano River Women's Peace Network.* Geneva.

Fisher, Angela (1984) *Africa Adorned.* New York.

Government of Liberia, the Eminent Persons' Group on Advocacy for Children and UNICEF (2000) *Challenges and Opportunities for Fulfilling the Rights of Children in War-torn Liberia, a Situation Analysis, November 2000.* Monrovia.

Guttman, Cynthia (1995) *Breaking Through: TOSTAN's Non-formal Basic Education Programme in National Languages in Senegal.* Paris.

Hafkin, Nancy and Edna G. Bay (ed.) (1976) *Women in Africa: Studies in Social and Economic Change.* Stanford.

Hansen, Thorkild (1990) *Slavenes skip* (The Slave Ship). Oslo.

— (1990) *Slavenes øyer* (The Slave Islands). Oslo.

— (1997) *Slavenes kyst* (The Slave Coast). Oslo.

Haskins, Jim and Joann Biondi (1995) *From Afar to Zulu: A Dictionary of African Cultures*. New York.

Hermes, Niels and Robert Lensink (2001) *Changing the Conditions for Development Aid: A New Paradigm?* London.

Hoffer, Carol P. (1974) 'Madam Yoko: Ruler of the Kpa Mende Confederacy', in Michelle Zimbalist Rosaldo and Louise Lamphere (eds), *Woman, Culture and Society*, pp. 173–87. Stanford.

Holas, B. (1975) *The Image of the Mother in Ivory Coast Art*. Abidjan.

Ifeka-Moller, Caroline (1984) 'Female Militancy and Colonial Revolt: The Women's War of 1929, Eastern Nigeria', Shirley Ardener (ed.), *Perceiving Women*, 127–57. London/New York.

ILO (1998) *Child Labour in Africa, Targeting the Intolerable*. Geneva.

— (1999) *C182 Worst Forms of Child Labour Convention*. Geneva.

— (2002) *A Future without Child Labour*. Geneva.

IMF, OECD, UN and World Bank Group (2000) *2000, a Better World for All: Progress towards the International Development Goals*. Washington DC.

Institut Africain pour la Démocratie (1997) *Bonne Gouvernance et développement en Afrique*. Dakar.

Interagency Commission WCEFA (1990) *World Conference on Education for All: Meeting Basic Learning Needs, 5–9 March 1990, Jomtien, Thailand, Final Report*. New York.

Jolly, Richard (ed) (2002) *Jim Grant, UNICEF Visionary*. Florence.

Kabou, Axelle (1991) *Et si l'Afrique refusait le développement*. Paris.

Kaplan, Robert D. (1997) *The Ends of the Earth: A Journey to the Frontiers of Anarchy*. New York.

Kassindja, Fauziya (1998) *Do They Hear You When You Cry?* New York.

Kerchache, Jacques, Jean-Louis Paudrat and Lucien Stéphan (1993) *Art of Africa*. New York.

Kiros, Teodros (ed.) (2001) *Explorations in African Political Thought*. New York.

Ki-Zerbo, Joseph (1978) *Histoire de l'Afrique noire*. Paris.

Knappert, Jan (1989) *The A–Z of African Proverbs*. London.

Knippenberg, R., E. Alihonou, A. Soucat, J.-M. Ndiaye, J.-P. Lamarque and A. El Abassi (1997) 'Children in the Tropics, Eight Years of Bamako Initiative Implementation', *Bimonthly Periodical from the International Center for Childhood and the Family*, no. 229/230. Paris.

Knippenberg, Rudolf, William Reinke and Ian Hopwood (eds) (1997) 'Sustainability of Primary Health Care Including Immunization in Bamako Initiative Programs in West Africa: An Assessment of 5 Years' Field Experience in Benin and Guinea', in *The International Journal of Health Planning and Management*, vol. 12, supplement 1, June.

Kourouma, Ahmadou (2000) *Allah n'est pas obligé*. Paris.

Lange, Marie-France (1998) *L'École et les filles en Afrique, scolarisation sous conditions*. Paris.

Laye, Camara (1976) *L'Enfant noir.* Paris.

Machel, Graça (2001) *The Impact of War on Children.* London.

Magnier, Bernard (1995) *Poésie d'Afrique au Sud du Sahara 1945–1995.* Paris.

Maiga, Zakaria, Fatoumata Traoré Nafo and Abdelwahed El Abassi (1999) 'La Réforme du secteur santé au Mali, 1989–1996', in *Studies in Health Services Organization and Policy*, vol. 12.

Mehrotra, Santosh and Richard Jolly (1997) *Development with a Human Face: Experiences in Social Achievement and Economic Growth.* Oxford.

Mkandawire, Thandika and Charles C. Soludo (1999) *Our Continent Our Future. African Perspectives on Structural Adjustment.* Ottawa.

Monimart, Marie (1989) *Femmes du Sahel.* Paris.

Morton, James (1996) *The Poverty of Nations: The Aid Dilemma at the Heart of Africa.* London/New York.

Myer, Laure (1992) *Black Africa – Masks, Sculpture, Jewelry.* Paris.

— (1995) *Art and Craft in Africa – Everyday Life, Ritual, Court Art.* Paris.

Naemeka, Obioma (ed.) (1998) *Sisterhood, Feminisms and Power: From Africa to the Diaspora.* Trenton, NJ, and Asmara.

Naipaul, V. S. (1984) 'The Crocodiles of Yamoussoukro', in *Finding the Center*, pp. 75–17. New York.

Narayan, Deepa (2000) *Voices of the Poor – Can Anyone Hear Us?* New York.

Nathan, Tobie and Isabelle Stengers (1999) *Médecins et sorciers.* Paris.

Newell, Stephanie (ed.) (1997) *Writing African Women, Gender, Popular Culture and Literature in West Africa.* London.

Nwapa, Flora (1966) *Efuru.* Oxford.

— (1986) *Cassava Song and Rice Song.* Ogui-Enugu.

Oberlé, Philippe (1985) *Masques vivants de Côte d'Ivoire.* Colmar.

OECD (1985) *Twenty-five Years of Development Co-operation: A Review.* Paris.

— (2002) *The DAC Journal, Development Cooperation 2001 Report.* Paris.

Okonjo, Kamene (1976) 'The Dual-Sex Political System in Operation: Igbo Women and Community Politics in Midwestern Nigeria', in Nancy J. Hafkin and Edna G. Bay (eds), *Women in Africa*, pp. 45–58. Stanford.

Okri, Ben (1992) *The Famished Road.* London.

— (1997) *An African Elegy.* London.

— (1997) *A Way of Being Free.* London.

Olivier, Roland (1991) *The African Experience.* New York.

Oppong, Christine (1983) *Female and Male in West Africa.* London.

Organization of African Unity (1992) *Consensus of Dakar.* Dakar.

— (1990) *African Charter on the Rights and Welfare of the Child.* Addis Ababa.

Organization of African Unity and UNICEF (1992) *Africa's Children, Africa's Future, Human Investment Priorities for the 1990s* and *Background Sectoral Papers.* Dakar.

Ouane, Adama (ed.) (1995) *Vers une Culture multilingue de l'éducation.* Hamburg.

Philips, Tom (ed.) (1996) *Africa – the Art of a Continent.* Munich/New York.

Pirozzi, Giacomo (1999) *Children of Africa. A Collection of Photographs.* Johannesburg.

Ramonet, Ignacio, Philippe Leymarie, Christian de Brie and Anne-Cécile Robert

(2000) 'Afriques en Renaissance', *Le Monde diplomatique*, Manière de voir, 51, May–June.

Reno, William (1999) *Warlord Politics and African States*. London.

Roberts, Mary Nooter and Allen F. Roberts (1996) *Memory – Luba Art and the Making of History*. Munich/New York.

Rosaldo, Michelle Zimbalist and Louise Lamphere (ed.) (1974) *Woman, Culture and Society*. Stanford.

Sandbrook, Robert (2000) *Closing the Circle: Democratization and Development in Africa*. Toronto, London, New York.

Schlegel, Alice (ed.) (1977) *Sexual Stratification. A Cross-cultural View*. New York.

Schwartz-Bart, Simone and André Schwartz-Bart (2001) *In Praise of Black Women I: Ancient African Queens*. Madison, Wisconsin.

Segun, Mabel (1986) *Conflict and Other Poems*. Ibadan.

Senghor, Léopold Sédar (1990) *Oeuvre poétique*. Paris.

Sieber, Roy and Rosalyn Adele Walker (1988) *African Art in the Cycle of Life*. Washington DC.

Simensen, Jarle (1996) *Afrikas historie* (African History). Oslo.

Skard, Torild (1977) *Halve jorden – Innføring i kvinnepolitikk* (Half of the Earth – Introduction to Feminist Policies). Oslo.

Smyke, Patricia (1991) *Women and Health*. London and New Jersey.

South Commission (1990) *The Challenge to the South*. Oxford.

Soyinka, Wole (1962) 'The Lion and the Jewel', in *Collected Plays 2*. Oxford/New York.

— (1981) *Aké. The Years of Childhood*. New York.

Spiegelman, Judith M. and UNICEF (1986) *We are the Children. A Celebration of UNICEF's First 40 Years*. Boston/New York.

Stenseth, Nils Chr., Kjetil Paulsen and Rolf Karlsen (ed.) (1995) *Afrika – natur, samfunn og bistand* (Africa – Nature, Society, Aid). Oslo.

Stromquist, Nelly P. (1997) *Increasing Girls' and Women's Participation in Basic Education*. Paris.

Sundberg, Anne (1999) 'Class and Ethnicity in the Struggle for Power – the Failure of Democratization in the Congo-Brazzaville', in *Africa Development*, vol. XXIV, nos 1 and 2.

Sutherland, Efua (1958) 'New Life at Kyerefaso', in Margaret Busby (ed.), *Daughters of Africa*, pp. 314–18. London.

Sweetman, David (1984) *Women Leaders in African History*. Oxford.

Tadjo, Véronique (1983) *Latérite*. Paris.

Tandia, Alio Kissima (1999) *Poésie orale soninké et éducation traditionelle*. Dakar.

Tostensen, Arne, Inge Tvedten and Marikan Vaa (eds) (2001) *Associational Life in African Cities. Popular Responses to the Urban Crisis*. Stockholm.

Toubia, Nahid (1995) *Female Genital Mutilation. A Call for Global Action*. New York.

Toweh, Kelly David (1998) *The Disarmament, Demobilization and Reintegration of Child Soldiers in Liberia, 1994–(1997) The Process and Lessons Learned*. Monrovia/New York.

Townsend, Janet, Emma Zapata, Jo Rowlands, Pilar Alberti and Marta Mercado (1999) *Women and Power*. London.

Turshen, Meredeth and Clotilde Twagiramariya (ed.) (1998) *What Women Do in Wartime. Gender and Conflict in Africa.* London.

Tvedt, Terje (1990) *Bilder av 'de andre': om utviklingslandene i bistandsepoken* (Images of 'the Others': About the Developing Countries in the Aid Era). Oslo.

Umeh, Marie (ed.) (1998) *Emerging Perspectives on Flora Nwapa: Critical and Theoretical Essays.* Trenton, NJ/Asmara.

UNAIDS (2000) *Collaboration with Traditional Healers in HIV/AIDS Prevention and Care in Sub-Saharan Africa: A Literature Review.* Geneva.

— (2001) *HIV Prevention Needs and Successes: A Tale of Three Countries. An Update on HIV Prevention Success in Senegal, Thailand and Uganda.* Geneva.

— (2001) *Together We Can.* Geneva.

— (2002) *Report on the Global HIV/AIDS Epidemic 2002.* Geneva.

— (2002) *AIDS Epidemic Update,* December 2002. Geneva.

UNAIDS and Economic Commission for Africa (2000) *AIDS in Africa Country by Country.* Geneva.

UNCTAD (2000) *The Least Developed Countries 2000 Report.* Geneva.

UNDP (1991, 1992, 1993, 1994, 1995, 1996, 1997, 1998, 1999, 2000, 2001, 2002) *Human Development Report.* Oxford.

UNECA/UNICEF (1996) *Atlas of the African Child.* Nairobi.

UNESCO (1981–99) *General History of Africa,* 8 vols: vol. 1 Ki-Zerbo, J. (ed.) *Methodology and African Prehistory;* vol. 2, Mokhtar, G. (ed.): *Ancient Civilizations of Africa;* vol. 3, Fasi, M. El (ed.) and I. Hrbek (ass. ed.): *Africa from the Seventh to Eleventh Century;* vol. 4, Niane, D. T. (ed.): *Africa from the Twelfth to Sixteenth Century;* vol. 5, Ogot, B. A. (ed.): *Africa from the Sixteenth to Eighteenth Century;* vol. 6, Ajar, J. F .A. (ed.): *Africa in the Nineteenth Century until the 1880s;* vol. 7, Boahen, A. Adu (ed.): *Africa under Colonial Domination 1880–1935;* vol. 8, Mazrui, A. A. (ed.) and C. Wondji (ass. ed.): *Africa since 1935.* Paris/London/Berkeley.

— (1993, 1995, 1998, 2000) *World Education Report.* Paris.

— (2001) *Monitoring Report on Education for All.* Paris.

— (2002) *EFA Global Monitoring Report: Education for All, Is the World on Track?* Paris.

UNESCO Bureau Régional pour l'Education en Afrique (1999) *Rapport sur l'Etat de l'education en afrique, les progrès réalisés dans l'éducation des filles et des femmes.* Dakar.

UNESCO Institute for Statistics (2002) *Education Statistics 2001, Sub-Saharan Africa, Regional Report.* Nimes.

UNESCO Regional Office for Education in Africa (1997) *Report on the State of Education in Africa, Challenges and Reconstruction.* Dakar.

UNFPA (1990, 1991, 1992, 1993, 1994, 1995, 1996, 1997, 1998, 1999, 2000, 2001, 2002) *The State of the World Population.* New York.

UNICEF (1990) *First Call for Children. World Declaration and Plan of Action from the World Summit for Children. Convention on the Rights of the Child.* New York.

— (1990) *Children and AIDS: An Impending Calamity.* New York.

— (1993) *Girls and Women: A UNICEF Development Priority.* New York.

— (1993, 1994, 1995, 1996, 1997, 1998, 1999, 2000) *The Progress of Nations.* New York.

— (1990, 1991, 1992, 1993, 1994, 1995, 1996, 1997, 1998, 1999, 2000, 2001, 2002) *The State of the World's Children.* New York.

— (1997) *The Bamako Initiative in West and Central Africa – Origins, Operationalization and Challenges*. Abidjan.

— (1998) *Problématique du travail et du trafic des enfants domestiques en Afrique de l'Ouest et du Centre*. Abidjan.

— (2000) *Waterfront, a UNICEF Publication on Water, Environment, Sanitation and Hygiene*, no. 14, April. New York.

— (2001) *Progress since the World Summit for Children: A Statistical Review*. New York.

— (2002) *Child Trafficking in West Africa: Policy Responses*. Florence.

UNICEF Sénégal (2000) *Abandon de l'excision au Sénégal*. Dakar.

UNICEF, UNAIDS, WHO (2002) *Young People and HIV/AIDS, Opportunity in Crisis*. New York/Geneva.

UNICEF and UNIFEM (1995) *Convention on the Elimination of All Forms of Discrimination Against Women*. New York.

UNICEF, WHO, UNESCO, UNFPA (1993) *Facts for Life*. Oxfordshire.

United Nations (1995, 2000) *The World's Women: Trends and Statistics*. New York.

— (1995) *Women: Looking beyond 2000*. New York.

— (1996) *Impact of Armed Conflict on Children, Report of Graça Machel, Expert of the Secretary-General of the United Nations*. New York.

— (2001) *Beijing Declaration and Platform for Action with the Beijing +5 Political Declaration and Outcome Document*. New York.

United Nations Department of Public Information (2002) 'A Troubled Decade for Africa's Children', in *Africa Recovery*, reprint edition, May. New York.

United Nations Economic Commission for Africa (1989) *African Alternative Framework to Structural Adjustment Programmes for Socio-economic Recovery and Transformation (AAF-SAP)*. Addis Ababa.

— (1994) *African Platform for Action*. Dakar.

United Nations General Assembly (2000) *United Nations Millennium Declaration*, 55/2, 18 September. New York.

United Nations Secretary General (1998) *The Causes of Conflict and the Promotion of Durable Peace and Sustainable Development in Africa*, April. New York.

— (2000) *We the Peoples: The Role of the United Nations in the Twenty-first Century*, March. New York.

— (2001) *Special Session of the General Assembly on HIV/AIDS*, February. New York.

— (2001) *Children and Armed Conflict*, September. New York.

— (2001) *We the Children: Meeting the Promises of the World Summit for Children*, September. New York.

United Nations Special Session of the General Assembly (2002) *A World Fit for Children*. New York.

Vélis, Jean-Pierre (1995) *Blossoms in the Dust – Street Children in Africa*. Paris.

Vera, Yvonne (ed.) (1999) *Opening Spaces. An Anthology of Contemporary African Women's Writings*. Oxford.

Vylder, Stefan de (1998) *Socio-economic Causes and Consequences of HIV/AIDS*. Issue Paper, Health Division Document 1999: 3, SIDA. Stockholm.

Walle, Nicolas van de (2000) *The Impact of Multi-party Politics in Sub-Saharan Africa*. Michigan State University.

Witte, Hans A. (1995) 'Familiefællesskab og kosmiske magter – Religiøse grun-didéer i vestafrikanske religioner (Family Community and Cosmic Forces – Basic Religious Ideas in West African Religions)', in *De religiøse ideers historie* (The History of Religious Ideas), Mircea Eliade, vol. 4, chapter 45, pp. 189–216. Copenhagen.

World Bank (1988) *Education in Sub-Saharan Africa – Policies for Adjustment, Revitalization and Expansion*. Washington DC.

— (1990) *World Development Report: Poverty*. New York.

— (1991) *World Development Report: The Challenge of Development*. New York.

— (1993) *World Development Report: Investing in Health*. New York.

— (1994) *Enhancing Women's Participation in Economic Development*. Washington DC.

— (1994) *Better Health in Africa, Experience and Lessons Learned*. Washington DC.

— (1998) *Assessing Aid: What Works, What Doesn't, and Why*. New York.

— (1998/99) *World Development Report: Knowledge for Development*. New York.

— (2000) *Can Africa Claim the 21st Century?* Washington DC.

— (2000/2001) *World Development Report: Attacking Poverty*. New York.

— (2003) *World Development Report: Sustainable Development in a Dymaic World*. New York.

World Commission on Culture and Development (1996) *Our Creative Diversity*. Paris.

World Education Forum (2000) *Education for All 2000 Assessment: Global Synthesis, Statistical Document and the Dakar Framework for Action*. Paris.

World Health Organization (WHO) (1995, 1997, 1999, 2000, 2001, 2002) *The World Health Report*. Geneva.

— (1996) *Mother-Baby Package: Implementing Safe Motherhood in Countries*. Geneva.

— (1997) *Female Genital Mutilation: A Joint WHO/UNICEF/UNFPA Statement*. Geneva.

— (1997) *Polio – the Beginning of the End*. Geneva.

— (1998) *Female Genital Mutilation: An Overview*. Geneva.

— (1999) *Reduction of Maternal Mortality: A Joint WHO/UNFPA/UNICEF/World Bank Statement*. Geneva.

WHO/Government of Mali/UNICEF (1999) *Report on the Review of the Implementation of the Bamako Initiative in Africa/Rapport sur la Revue de la mise en oeuvre de l'initiative de Bamako en Afrique*. Bamako.

WHO/UNICEF (1996, 2002) *State of the World's Vaccines and Immunization*. Geneva.

Index